ATLAS OF THE INVISIBLE

ALSO BY
THE AUTHORS

LONDON:
THE INFORMATION
CAPITAL

◆

WHERE THE
ANIMALS GO

ATLAS OF THE INVISIBLE

MAPS & GRAPHICS THAT WILL CHANGE HOW YOU SEE THE WORLD

James Cheshire
Oliver Uberti

W. W. NORTON & COMPANY
Independent Publishers Since 1923

First published in Great Britain in 2021 by Particular Books, an imprint of
Penguin Books

Designed by Oliver Uberti

Printed in Italy

For information about permission to reproduce selections from this book,
write to Permissions, W. W. Norton & Company, Inc., 500 Fifth Avenue,
New York, NY 10110

For information about special discounts for bulk purchases, please contact
W. W. Norton Special Sales at specialsales@wwnorton.com or 800-233-4830

ISBN 978-0-393-65151-5

W. W. Norton & Company, Inc., 500 Fifth Avenue, New York, N.Y. 10110
www.wwnorton.com

W. W. Norton & Company Ltd., 15 Carlisle Street, London W1D 3BS

1 2 3 4 5 6 7 8 9 0

JAMES

for ISLA

OLIVER

for JUSTIN

CONTENTS

PREFACE & INTRODUCTION

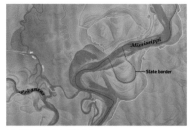

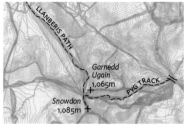

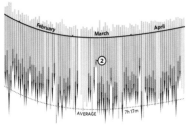

WHERE WE'VE BEEN

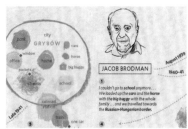

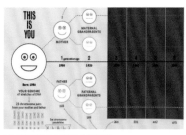

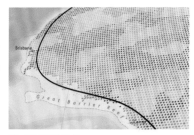

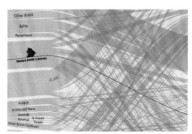

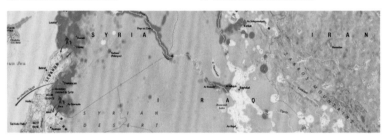

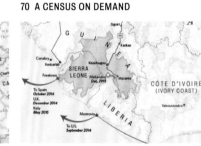

WHO WE ARE

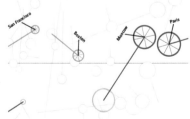

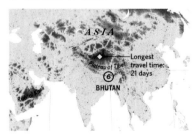

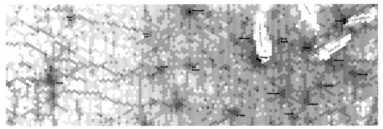

94 RIVERS OF CONNECTIVITY

98 OCTOPUS'S GARDEN

HOW WE'RE DOING

105 REDLINING RICHMOND

108 POWER FAILURE

110 STATES OF MIND

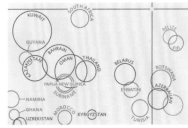

112 PASSPORT CHECK

114 CARBON OVERHEAD

118 IN EXHAUSTIVE DETAIL

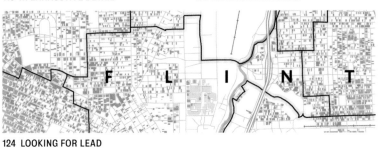

120 ELECTRIC CURRENTS

122 POLICING THE AIR

124 LOOKING FOR LEAD

128 UNTENABLE CONDITIONS

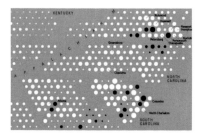

130 SOUTHERN INHOSPITALITY

132 UNEQUAL LOADS

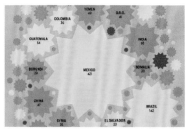

134 BURSTS OF COWARDICE

136 RAISING THEIR VOICES

138 A VISIBLE CRISIS

142 BOMBSHELL REPORTS

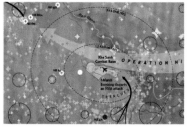

146 OPERATION NIAGARA

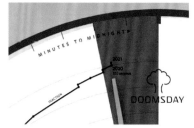

148 END TIMES

WHAT WE FACE

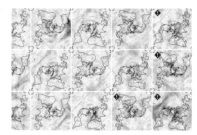

158 HEAT GRADIENT

160 TOO HOT TO HAJJ

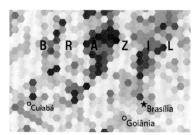

162 BURN SCARS

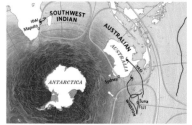

164 ONE STORMY SEA

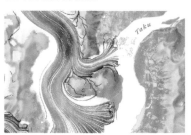

166 ICE FLOWS

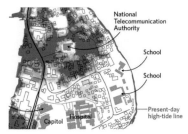

170 TREADING WATER

172 CAUGHT AT SEA

176 FASTEN YOUR SEATBELTS

178 ALL-SEEING EYES

180 MOVE FAST, BREAK MAPS

182 SALT IT WHERE THE SUN DON'T SHINE

184 HERE COMES THE SUN

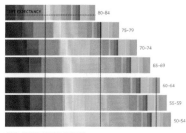

186 THE NEW AGES

EPILOGUE

191 PATTERNS OF BEHAVIOUR

*Lecturer at the UCL Department of Geography. Co-author
*ation Capital (@theinfocapital).", "entities": { "description
d_url": "http://spatial.ly", "indices": [0, 22], "url": "http:
sent": false, "followers_count": 9534, "following": false, "fri
e, "id": 105132431, "id_str": "105132431", "is_translation_
215, "LOCATION": "LONDON", "name": "James Cheshire", "noti]
ground_image_url": "http://abs.twimg.com/images/th
https://abs.twimg.com/images/themes/theme14/bg.gif",
//pbs.twimg.com/profile_banners/105132431/151155713
776001406838898638/a3C9FUfA_normal.jpg", "profile_
01406838898638/a3C9FUfA_normal.jpg" "profile_link_*

193 HIDDEN IN EVERY TWEET

194 PLAGUE IN OSAKA

196 TRACKING ICE

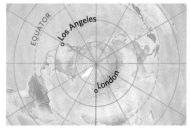

200 FLATTENING THE EARTH

PREFACE

Oliver had recently come to London to work on this book with me when the COVID-19 outbreak reached Europe. At the time experts were not yet ready to call it a pandemic, but the ubiquity of air travel made global spread seem inevitable. Jetlag kept Oliver up in the wee hours, scrolling headlines and refreshing dashboards. Each morning we discussed the latest news: the hospitals in Wuhan, the stranded cruise ships and how long each of us felt we had until the invisible appeared on our doorsteps.

I wanted to see more data before sounding an alarm, while Oliver expected the worst. The day he flew home to Los Angeles, I set my cartography class the task of mapping the growing case counts. I saw it as an opportunity for them to learn how to track a serious – but distant – situation, as it unfolded. I had not fully considered, I'll admit, how many of the hotspots that emerged on the maps were places where my students had family and friends.

The following week some students were absent as they rushed to return to their families before countries closed their borders. The UK locked down a few days later, on 23 March, and I found myself hauling hard drives home on the Tube and arranging a Zoom room. The danger remained abstract and invisible even as my wife's grandmother tested positive after being admitted to hospital. Her final days were spent in isolation, our goodbyes reduced to text messages. Without the communal rituals of closure, it was hard to believe she was gone.

It wasn't until late April, two months after Oliver's visit, that reality hit home. I was crunching data for our graphic on air pollution when I heard an ambulance pull up outside. From a window I watched the crew don their protective gear while leaning on our front wall, before entering the house next door. After a few hours they emerged, dejected. The arrival of undertakers confirmed our worst fears. This, I thought, is what it must've felt like to see plague doctors making their rounds, their faces hidden behind beaked masks. Our quiet lane was now marked like the streets of Soho on John Snow's infamous cholera map from 1854. What had been a historical example in my lectures was suddenly a cautionary tale for our own times.

For the first time I felt the presence of a killer in our midst. I felt the powerlessness, the grief. These emotions are missing from the data point that now haunts my neighbour's house. On official records her death is just another number to sum, another dot on a map of our street, our borough, our city, our

There were 20,000 deaths in the first six weeks of the UK outbreak. Each dot indicates a single death.

country, our world. It is crude, sanitized. It is also not the full story. For every confirmed case, there are those who got sick but never got tested. Were that column visible on the world's tally, by May 2020 it would have included marks for my wife and me. As I write, there are COVID-19 survivors suffering in obscurity from side effects still unknown to science. I later tested positive for antibodies; my wife's loss of smell still persists.

Oliver and I developed much of this book before COVID-19 existed. As the virus impacted nearly every facet of society, we could see with our own eyes, as Snow did, that our ability to survive a crisis is only as good as our knowledge of the assailant. In visualizing data, we transform it into information, which equips those in position to protect us. This holds true whether we're combating disease, inequality or the current climate emergency.

For centuries, atlases depicted what people could see: roads, rivers, mountains. Today, we need graphics to reveal the invisible patterns that shape our lives. *Atlas of the Invisible* is an ode to the unseen, to a world of information that cannot be conveyed through text or numbers alone. In the years to come, our hope is that the patterns we've made visible will inform how you view the choice between business as usual and rebuilding a better world.

James Cheshire, London, February 2021

COVID-19 deaths
1 March – 17 April 2020

Greater London

4,950

England & Wales

20,283

L O N D O N

0   10 km

Newcastle upon Tyne

Leeds

Liverpool   Manchester

W A L E S

Birmingham

E N G L A N D

Cardiff

Greater London

0   100 km

◆

We can draw conclusions about **THE INVISIBLE.**

We can postulate its existence with relative certainty. But all we can represent is an analogy, which stands for the invisible but is not it.

GERHARD RICHTER

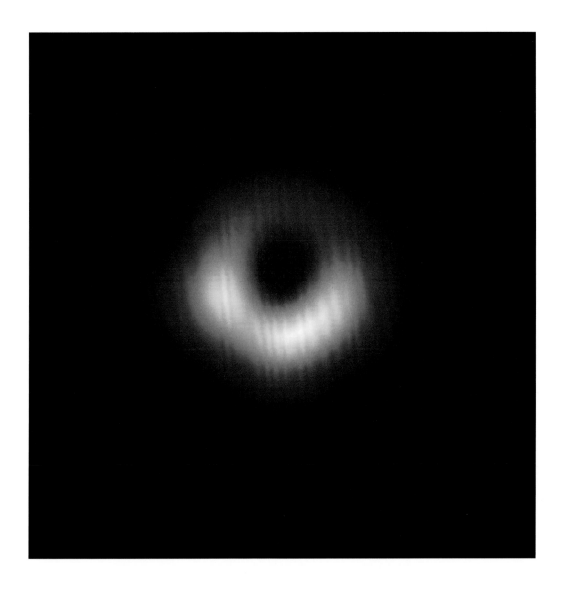

As a research student at MIT, Katie Bouman demonstrated the potential of imaging systems
'to observe things previously impossible to see'. Two years later, the Event Horizon Telescope Collaboration
translated petabytes of data from a stack of hard disks into the first-ever image of a black hole.

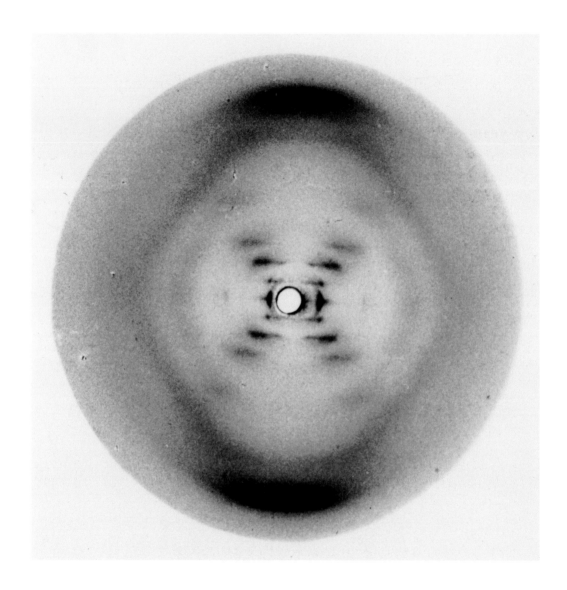

Rosalind Franklin and graduate student Ray Gosling bombarded a strand of DNA with X-rays
for more than sixty hours. When the rays bounced off the electrons in the molecule's atoms, they refracted
into this cruciform pattern, from which the double-helix structure of DNA was inferred.

BEHOLD, THE INVISIBLE

I magine the thrill of seeing what no one has ever seen before. The chemist Rosalind Franklin felt it in 1952 when her X-ray imaging experiments exposed the true structure of DNA. Seventy years later, Katie Bouman, a member of the Event Horizon Telescope Collaboration, clasped her hands in joy as imaging methods they developed brought a black hole into view for the first time.

To the untrained eye, both images are as undecipherable as glyphs from an alien language. But to Franklin the black smudges proved that our genetic code forms a double helix; to Bouman, the bright orange crescent revealed the energy from a black hole's photon ring. Both images owe their existence to years of research and technological developments, but it was the conceptual leaps of these scientists that allowed us to see the infinitesimally small and the incomprehensibly large.

It's not just size that renders something invisible. Sometimes we miss what we can't step back to see: cities grow around us, pollution blows over us, the earth warms underfoot. Sometimes the invisible only appears with the creep of time, as in the gentrification of neighbourhoods or the retreat of glaciers. Sometimes, in the case of historical events, the visible becomes invisible with the loss of a generation. The power of data lies in an ability to freeze time at a given moment. And in the same way that photo negatives must be processed before they can be viewed, the patterns hidden in a dataset only truly emerge through maps and graphics. These visualizations give us the power to zoom out, to compare, to remember.

How We Got Here

At the beginning of the nineteenth century, most scientific endeavours fell under the umbrella of 'natural philosophy'. In fact, the word 'scientist' was not in use until 1833. For those with the means, or access to wealthy benefactors, natural philosophy offered a way to understand the world at a time of rapid change. Against this backdrop, Alexander von Humboldt (1767–1835) emerged as one of the last great polymaths. He wanted to know everything about *everything*. In her acclaimed biography, *The Invention of Nature*, Andrea Wulf describes him as 'the lost hero of science' who fell out of favour as 'scientists crawled into their narrow areas of expertise'. Specialization caused many to lose sight of Humboldt's great vision for a scientific method 'that included art, history, poetry and politics alongside hard data'. Caring more for the 'natural' than the 'philosophy', Humboldt was most himself scaling a volcano, sampling seawater or measuring a cactus. He collected huge amounts of information on his travels and solicited as much from others. He would send out letters requesting data and insights, cut out key passages from their replies and place them in themed envelopes that amassed in boxes. Where others might see a hoarder's lair, he saw a world of interconnected systems. In the preface to his magnum opus, *Cosmos*, he wrote: 'Nature . . . is a unity in diversity of phenomena; a harmony blending together all created things, however dissimilar in form and attributes; one great whole animated by the breath of life.'

But Humboldt knew the eloquence of his writing was not enough. The 'one great whole' needed to be seen to be believed. So, he enlisted his friend Heinrich Berghaus to create an atlas to accompany *Cosmos*. The brief was expansive: '[M]aps for the world-wide distribution of plants and animals, for rivers and oceans, for the distribution of active volcanoes, for magnetic declination and inclination, intensity of magnetic energy, for the ebb and flow of ocean currents, air currents, the course of mountains, deserts and plains, for the distribution of human races, as well as for the representation of mountain heights, river lengths, etc.'

Berghaus, a professor of applied mathematics at Berlin Bauakademie, rose to the challenge. In 1838, the first part of *Physikalischer Atlas* was published. Further sections were released as Berghaus completed them. By the final instalment in 1848, he'd made seventy-five maps in all. The ever-modest Berghaus described his seminal work as 'a collection of maps of different formats, employing a variety of techniques'. In truth, he and Humboldt had redefined what an atlas could be. The bland outlines of places that filled atlas plates for centuries gave way to poetic views of nature's processes. *Physikalischer Atlas* stands apart as the first atlas to explore the world, not through questions of what was where or who owned what, but of how and why? How does climate influence the way people dress around the globe? Why does a region's climate depend more on its wind patterns than its latitude? Why does vegetation vary by altitude?

A Golden Age

Humboldt and Berghaus weren't alone. According to Michael Friendly, an eminent chronicler of data visualization, the nineteenth century was a 'perfect storm' of developments in statistics, data collection and technology that allowed for works 'of unparalleled beauty and scope'. Florence Nightingale invented 'coxcomb diagrams' to show seasonal patterns of mortality in the British Army, whilst John Snow was laying the foundation for modern disease mapping on the cholera-riddled streets of London (see p. 22). Towards the end of the century, Charles Booth organized door-to-door surveys to create household-level poverty maps (p. 22) that later inspired the maps of Florence Kelley in Chicago (p. 69) and W. E. B. Du Bois in Philadelphia.

By the end of the century, people were turning to statistical atlases for the latest data about their country's development. The French government created

Airborne lidar surveys offer a way to reveal the past. By timing how long it takes for lasers to bounce off the ground and return to a sensor aboard an aircraft, researchers can create precise maps of elevation. In this one, prior meanders of the Mississippi River emerge from millions of measurements.

SOURCE: USGS

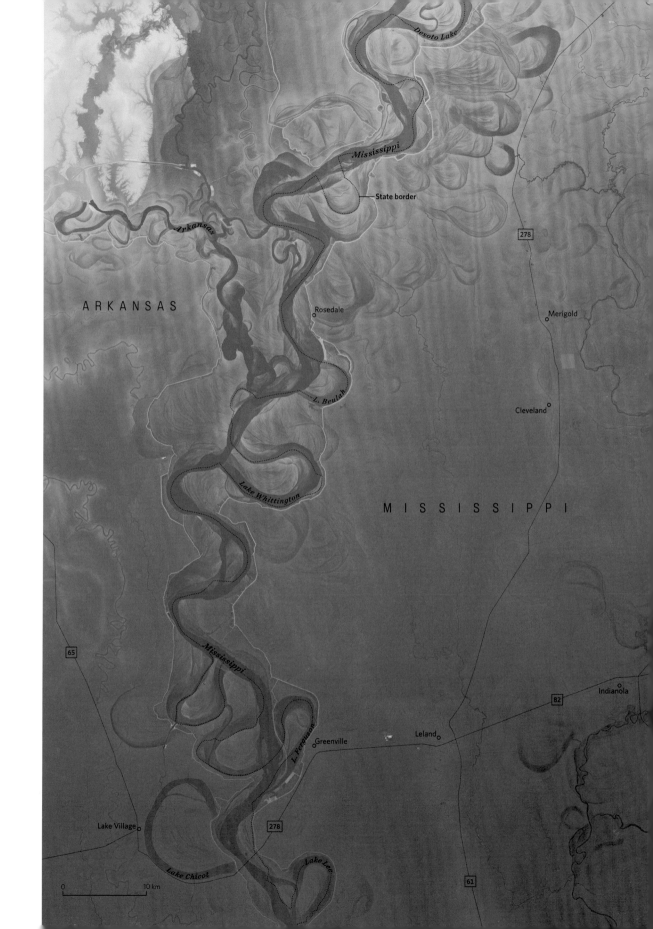

Desoto Lake

Mississippi

State border

Arkansas

ARKANSAS

Rosedale

278

Merigold

L. Beulah

Cleveland

Lake Whittington

MISSISSIPPI

65

Mississippi

82

Indianola

L. Ferguson

Greenville

Leland

278

Lake Village

61

Lake Chicot

Lake Lee

0   10 km

Heinrich Berghaus embellished this 1838 map of vegetation zones with botanical illustrations and diagrams of what grows at various altitudes.

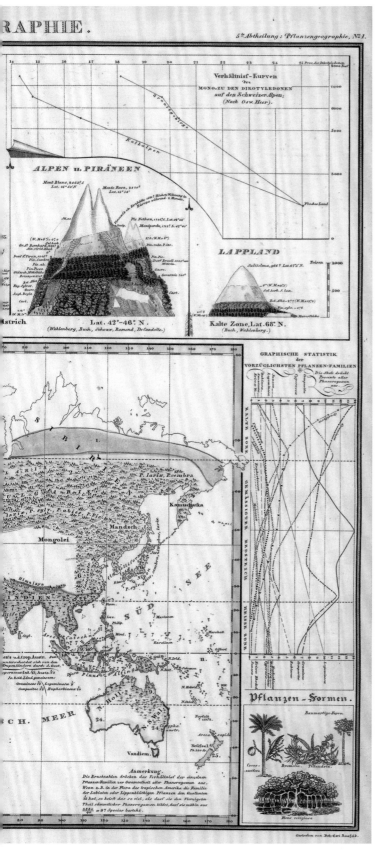

◆

Berghaus and
Humboldt had
redefined what an
ATLAS COULD BE.
The bland outlines
that filled atlas
plates for centuries
gave way to poetic
views of nature's
PROCESSES.

ATLAS OF THE INVISIBLE

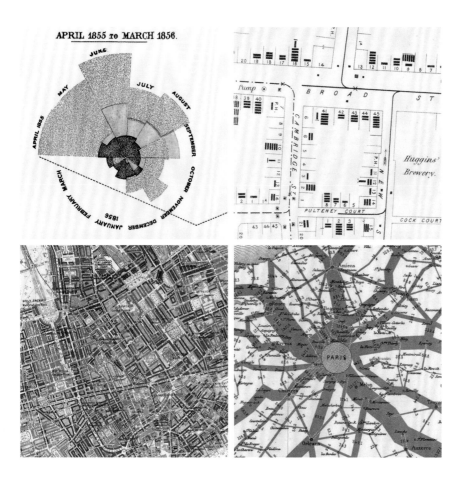

a Bureau of Statistical Graphics, whose *Album de Statistique Geographique* charted everything from public transport ridership (above) and the tonnage of freight on canals through to vineyard production and theatre attendance. The impacts of all these facets of life were now visible in unprecedented detail.

Both in terms of time and printing costs, large, multi-colour atlases were hugely expensive to produce. Eventually, publishers shortened the thematic sections of their atlases and standardized layouts. What's more, the novelty of seeing the world to understand it began to wear off. As Friendly notes, 'Pictures of data became considered, well, just pictures: pretty or evocative perhaps, but incapable of stating a "fact" to three or more decimals.' Statisticians were dissecting Humboldt's 'one great whole' into ever more precise parts.

Going Digital

The need for maps and graphics did not diminish completely in the first half of the twentieth century. They were crucial tools for newspapers and magazines to capture the turmoil of two World Wars, the advent of long-distance air travel

Clockwise from top left: Nightingale's coxcomb; the infamous Broad Street pump on Snow's cholera map; French railway ridership in 1890; poverty levels of London on Booth's hand-coloured chart.

SOURCES: DAVID RUMSEY HISTORICAL MAP COLLECTION (NIGHTINGALE); WELLCOME LIBRARY, LONDON (SNOW); LIBRARY OF THE LONDON SCHOOL OF ECONOMICS AND POLITICAL SCIENCE (BOOTH)

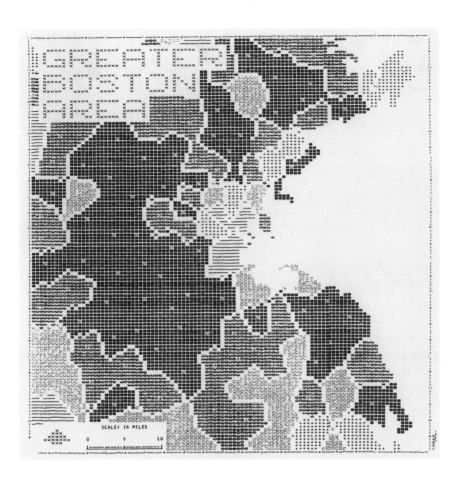

and an increasingly globalized economy. Eventually computing offered a
way for statistical analysis and printed maps to converge once more. In 1963,
Howard Fisher, a lecturer at Northwestern University, worked with a programmer, Betty Benson, to develop SYMAP, a system that could take data stored on
punch cards, perform calculations and then spit out a map (above). Previously,
city planners relied on large printed maps with transparent overlays to envis-
age different scenarios. For example, to plan a new road in a growing city,
you'd need maps of geology, land ownership, population growth and more.
Population projections alone might require five maps if you wanted estimates
every five years for twenty-five years. Each would be drafted by hand. If the
calculations had to change, you'd have to start over. SYMAP eliminated the
waste. To see estimates, say, every ten years, essentially all you had to do
was tweak the computer code and press 'Print'. In terms of their detail and
appearance, these early digital maps looked rudimentary against their hand-
made predecessors. But that wasn't their purpose. They offered proof that
mathematical functions could generate maps with the press of a button.

As with typewriter
art, SYMAP used a grid
of dashes, plus signs,
numerals and other
characters to form
images – in this case,
an elevation contour
map of Greater Boston.

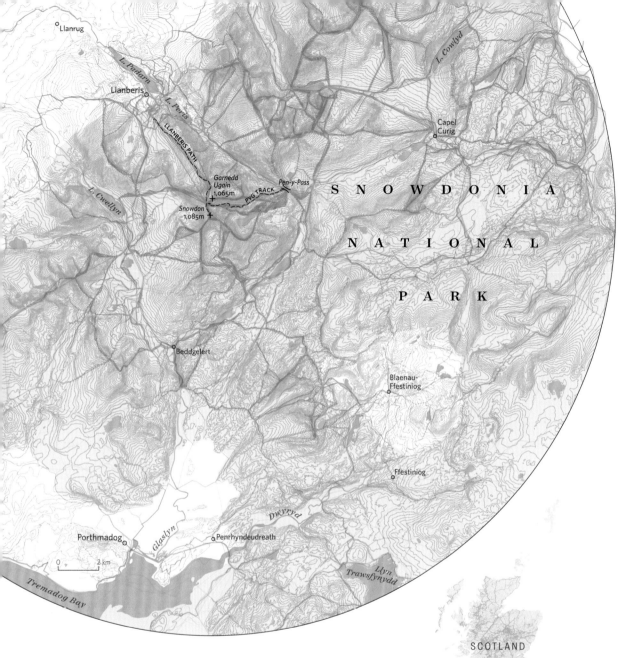

Llanrug

L. Padarn

Llanberis

L. Peris

LLANBERIS PATH

L. Cowlyd

Capel
Curig

L. Cwellyn

Garnedd
Ugain
1,065m
PYG TRACK
Pen-y-Pass

Snowdon
1,085m

S N O W D O N I A

N A T I O N A L

P A R K

Beddgelert

Blaenau-
Ffestiniog

Ffestiniog

Dwyryd

Porthmadog

Glaslyn

Penrhyndeudreath

0   2 km

Llyn
Trawsfynydd

Tremadog Bay

Trails of Data

Britain's national mapping agency has been creating adventure-planning apps.
In the 2010s, users recorded nearly eleven million tracks. To the right we show
some four hundred thousand of them. Charley Glynn, a cartographer who
helped develop the app, was surprised at how well walkers defined Britain's
coast. 'Though it's just a bunch of lines, it builds up a real, clear picture of a
place.' The data also reveals the country's most popular routes. Snowdonia
National Park in Wales has held the top spot for years. Hikers wind their way
to the 1,085-metre summit of Snowdon from all directions (above).

SCOTLAND

G R E A T   B R I T A I N

North
Sea

MAP AREA
Snowdonia Nat. Park

E N G L A N D

WALES

London

Celtic
Sea

Public routes, 2018

0   200 km

SOURCE: ORDNANCE SURVEY

These efforts matured into the Geographic Information Systems (GIS) that we used to make the maps in this book. In the same way that Humboldt stored data in envelopes and boxes, GIS allow cartographers to store data by theme, such as elevation, land cover and road networks. We can then combine these layers to calculate the accessibility of every place on Earth without making the journeys ourselves (pp. 92–3) or to help local governments determine which roads will be most in need of treatment for snow and ice (pp. 182–5).

We are the Map

Just as work was beginning on the first digital maps in the 1960s, the Ordnance Survey had just finished a thirty-year odyssey to create a more accurate map of Great Britain – by hand. Surveyors hauled scopes to the top of hills and placed them on concrete pillars they had installed called 'trig points'. These allowed a surveyor on one peak to accurately measure – or triangulate – its position in relation to pillars on neighbouring peaks. Though technologies such as GPS and lidar have rendered these analogue artifacts obsolete, six thousand five hundred of them still cover Britain. One such trig point – cracked and stripped of its paint by icy winds – clings to the top of Garnedd Ugain (pronounced *carneth e-gyn*), high in the Welsh mountains. On any given day, those walking beneath it en route to summit Snowdon, its slightly higher neighbour, are indirectly creating maps of their own. The Ordnance Survey app, which thousands use to navigate trails nationwide, allows hikers to record, plot and share their favourite routes, further establishing them as the ones to follow. These new maps may rely on the carefully laid paths of surveyors, but they have become dynamic in a way that only digital data can, allowing the wisdom of the crowds to decide where and where not to go.

The Ordnance Survey's online store offers a range of smartwatches and other 'wearables' to help hikers monitor how well they slept before a big climb, their heart rate as they puff up Pyg Track or their maximum speed as they coast down the Llanberis Path (left). Wearers can set sleep and exercise goals in order to help themselves lead healthier lives.

Obviously, health data can be highly personal. When we aren't always sure who can view it, some maps can become too revealing. In 2018, engineers for Strava, a popular fitness app, released a global map of where people exercise. From billions of data points, viewers could see bright patterns of activity along park paths and waterfronts. Nothing too surprising. A few months later, the keen eyes of

The exercise routes of Strava users delineated the perimeter of a US Air Force Base in Afghanistan.

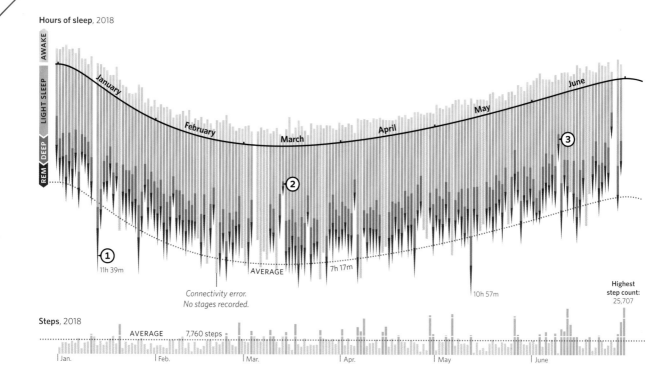

Hours of sleep, 2018

AWAKE
LIGHT SLEEP
DEEP
REM

January
February
March
April
May
June

① 11h 39m

② AVERAGE   7h 17m

③

*Connectivity error.
No stages recorded.*

10h 57m

**Highest
step count:
25,707**

Steps, 2018

AVERAGE   7,760 steps

Jan.   Feb.   Mar.   Apr.   May   June

Nathan Ruser, a researcher at the Australian Strategic Policy Institute, spotted pinpricks of colour in otherwise dark regions of the map. Zooming in revealed secret US military bases in parts of the Middle East and Africa (see previous page). Personnel who used Strava to record their daily workouts unknowingly shared their locations. Strava claims they had no idea their marketing effort disclosed classified information. Neither did the Pentagon. In effect, the most advanced military in the world had doxed themselves.

You don't have to own a wearable to leave a data trail. Digital threads unspool behind us now in nearly everything we do. Even if you fled to a deserted island and hurled your phone into the sea, a satellite would soon pass overhead and record the heat signature of your campfire (see pp. 162–3). Each passing second, the world's data gathers into a bigger tangle. For *Atlas of the Invisible*, we have pulled at the threads and mapped what we found. These graphics give tangible, visual form to a four-year search for stories that reveal what data can tell us about our past, who we are, how we're doing and what we face in the century ahead. It's been an eye-opening process. In researching the essays that begin each section, we uncovered the best and worst of humanity. We marvelled at the ingenuity of the early weather forecasters. We recoiled at the depravity of violent mobs in the Jim Crow South. In the end, we came away feeling hopeful about the moral arc of history and the promise of life in a world of data. We don't offer scientific breakthroughs about the building blocks of life or the mysteries of the universe, but we can share with you the joy of seeing the world anew.

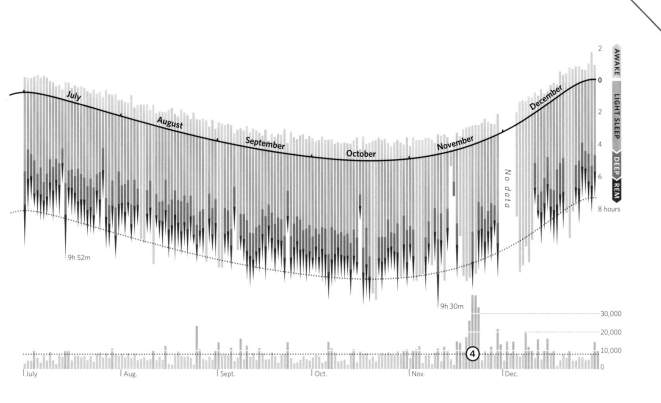

In 2018, Oliver's wife, Sophie, wore a Fitbit to track her sleep and steps. After a year with frequent travel for work, weddings and a honeymoon, she wasn't surprised to learn that she slept poorly on flights or soundly after a long hike. True insights were more personal: the data showed her waking briefly through the night, every night. Those mini disruptions added up (yellow bars). To get eight hours of sleep, she needed to be in bed for nine.

① January

A cross-country redeye on the night of 12 January left her zapped. Sophie logged her longest sleep of the year the following night.

② March

Preparations for an early-morning event at the UN kept her up the night before. She stole only three hours of sleep.

③ June

Below-average sleep in the run up to her wedding to Oliver was followed by hikes and long sleeps on a honeymoon in Yosemite.

④ November

The Fitbit mistook a five-day horse trek for a lot of walking. Subtracting those steps, her average daily step count was 7,757.

Using this Book

Like Humboldt and Berghaus nearly two centuries ago, our overall aim is to show you patterns not places. Among our many examples, we show how mobile phones reveal current migrations and how DNA can reveal ancient ones; we explore happiness and anxiety levels around the globe; and we illustrate how a warming planet affects everything from hurricanes to the hajj. Sometimes we take a bird's eye view; sometimes we zoom in to explore patterns on the ground. Sometimes you will encounter maps that present this spherical planet in unusual arrangements or from unfamiliar angles. The cartographically curious can find a full list of our map projections on page 200. Throughout, please remember that each graphic marks a point in time. We have sourced the most current data available as of late 2020. While some stats may have shifted since then, the overall trends should hold true.

WHERE WE'VE BEEN

'In striving to drain dry the waters of prejudice and oppression,
we must rely on measures of our own creation – upon the wisdom
of our laws and the decency of our institutions, upon our reasoning
minds and our feeling hearts. And as a constant spark to carry on,
upon our vivid memories of the evils we wish to banish from our world.
In our long struggle for a more just world, our memories are among
our most powerful resources.'

—JUSTICE RUTH BADER GINSBURG, *22 April 2004*

THE LIVES OF OTHERS

Two centuries ago, England was reeling from decades of war overseas. Tens of thousands of soldiers and sailors, newly unemployed and unhoused, were discharged onto the streets of London in the county of Middlesex. To remedy this, Parliament passed the Vagrancy Act of 1824, which still allows courts to prosecute anyone sleeping 'in the open air, or under a tent, or in any cart or waggon [sic], not having any visible means of subsistence and not giving a good account' of themselves.

Rather than addressing root causes, vagrancy laws render those without a home invisible. One such person was Lever Maxey, a 'rogue and vagabond' arrested in St Giles-in-the-Fields in 1784, locked in the Clerkenwell house of correction along with his wife and child and 'forthwith remove[d] and convey[ed]' by cart to a town sixty miles away. Maxey is visible once more thanks to the Vagrant Lives project, which digitized court records for 14,789 'vagrants' escorted out of Middlesex between 1777 and 1786. The dataset reveals a national network of removal (see inset) while a detailed log on the back of Maxey's removal order allowed us to trace an individual journey.

Revisiting his removal raises questions. Did Maxey actually do anything wrong? Most likely he and his family were simply homeless. To magistrates trying to manage in-migration from poorer parishes, that may have been enough. Prior to the 1824 Act, English vagrancy laws called for relocation, not punishment. Anyone caught living in a parish without documentation, who could not prove residency by birth, marriage, rent or employment, was returned to their parish of legal settlement as set forth in the Poor Relief Act of 1662. In Maxey's case, that was Wallingford. Upon receiving him, the parish had an obligation to help him secure a job and additional relief if necessary. History doesn't tell us whether Maxey welcomed the move. Was relocation, with the promise of employment, a net benefit for him and his family? Or was he subject to further hostility and pressured to move again? Perhaps Maxey had sought his fortune in the metropolis, only to be pushed out before he could make a start. Is life in London so different today?

Maxey's journey

Wallingford
21 Feb.

CHILTERNS

OXFORDSHIRE

Bix

Thames

Henley-on-Thames
20 Feb.

Maidenhead
19 Feb.

BERKSHIRE

Henry Adams, the vagrant contractor for Middlesex, delivered vagrants to constables of neighbouring counties via depots in the City or border towns such as Colnbrook. According to court records, ninety-two per cent were returned to parishes in England or Ireland. Few hailed from south or east of London because county officials could handle short transfers across the Lea or Thames without help from Adams.

SOURCES: VAGRANT LIVES PROJECT; ORDNANCE SURVEY

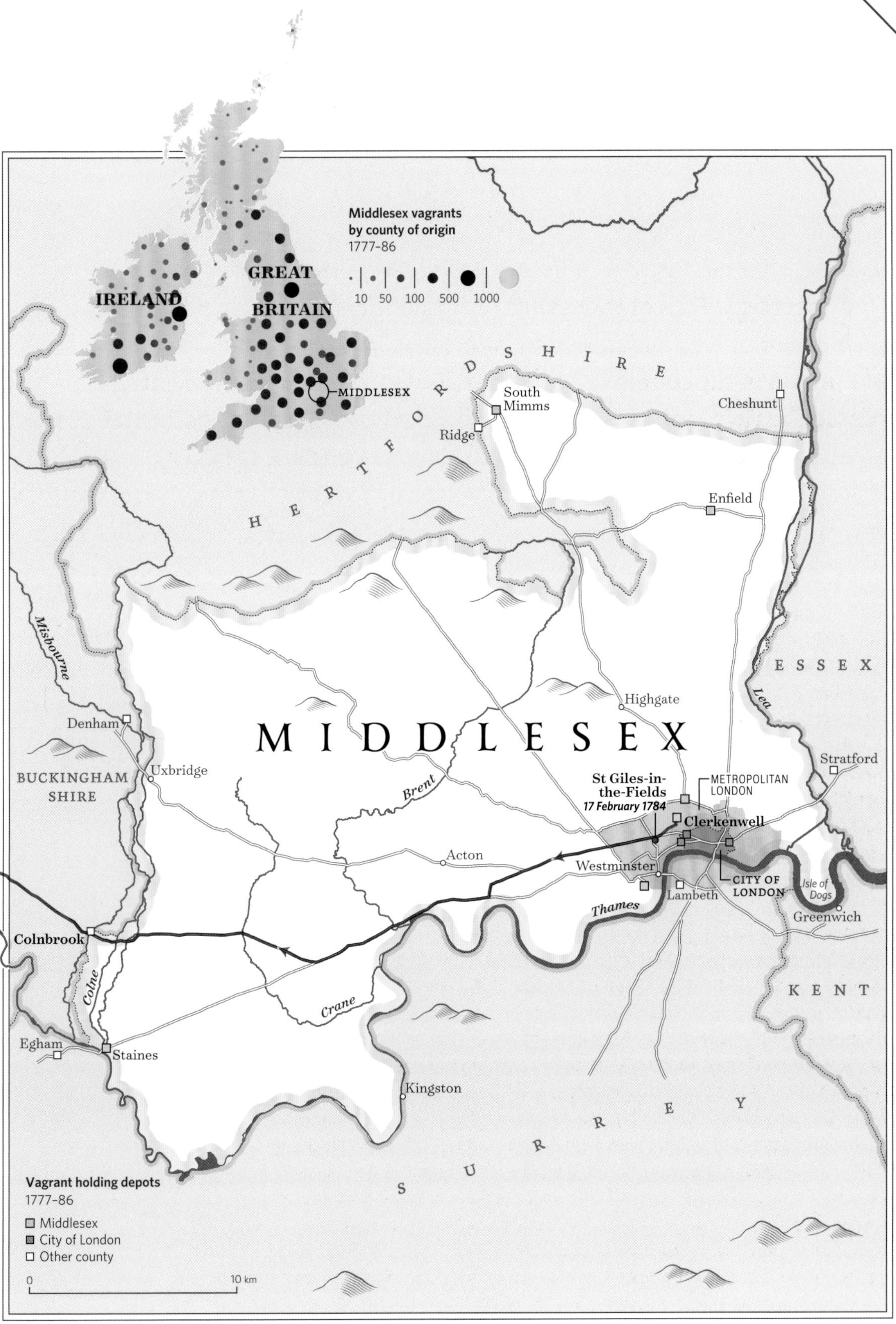

Middlesex vagrants
by county of origin
1777–86

· | · | ● | ● | ● | ⬤
10　50　100　500　1000

IRELAND

GREAT
BRITAIN

○—MIDDLESEX

H E R T F O R D S H I R E

South
Mimms

Cheshunt

Ridge

Enfield

E S S E X

Lea

Highgate

Stratford

M I D D L E S E X

Misbourne

Denham

Uxbridge

BUCKINGHAM
SHIRE

Brent

St Giles-in-
the-Fields
17 February 1784

METROPOLITAN
LONDON

Clerkenwell

Acton

Westminster

CITY OF
LONDON

Isle of
Dogs

Colne

Lambeth

Greenwich

Colnbrook

Thames

Crane

K E N T

Egham

Staines

Kingston

S U R R E Y

Vagrant holding depots
1777–86

⬚ Middlesex
◼ City of London
☐ Other county

0 　　　　　　　　10 km

A 2015 Freedom of Information request revealed that London's borough councils had moved some 17,000 households in temporary accommodations to another borough or another part of the country that year. In advance of the royal wedding in 2018, the leader of the Royal Borough of Windsor and Maidenhead cited the Vagrancy Act in an attempt to clear the streets lest they present 'a beautiful town in a sadly unfavourable light'. And in October 2020 the UK Home Office put forward plans to deport foreign rough sleepers.* In a recent survey of 458 rough sleepers in the UK, more than ninety per cent said police enforcement did not make them want to change their behaviour. Rather, it 'often left them feeling worse about themselves and more at risk of harm as many moved to more out-of-the-way places to sleep.' Have we learned nothing? Relocation doesn't end homelessness. It just ends sight of it. How can one expect to keep a job or get an education while constantly being uprooted?

Charities such as Crisis advocate for relief, not relocation or retribution. That means accommodation, food security, healthcare and job training. This approach has worked elsewhere. A 'housing first' initiative in the US state of Utah built permanent housing with on-site support services for hundreds of individuals, reducing chronic homelessness in the state by 71 per cent in ten years. In British Columbia, a study found that homeless residents secured housing faster after a one-time cash transfer of $7,500 than after a year of conventional social services. It cost the shelter system less too. By contrast, some 216,000 homes in England sat vacant in 2018 while 4,700 people slept out and another 83,700 took shelter in temporary accommodations. With the onset of COVID-19, the British government procured temporary housing for 14,500 people. Why not make the housing permanent?

For Adam Crymble, one of the historians behind the Vagrant Lives project, digging through Dickensian data reveals a constantly shifting definition of insiders and outsiders, of who can stay and who must go. 'The natural limits of our communities are not fixed,' he says, dismissing a post-Brexit notion that everyone who was born in Britain is 'us' and everyone who was not is not. 'Today, someone from Poland moving to London is considered an outsider. Go back two hundred years, and it was someone from Essex.'

VAGRANT LIVES is just one in a growing number of historical data digitization projects. In this chapter, we analyse and visualize a few datasets that challenge the stories we've been told about our past, especially regarding how humans moved – and were moved – across the planet. All the while, we recognize all that is lost to history. For example, court records don't tell us much about Lever Maxey the man, but at least they preserve his name. That basic humanity vanished for millions of enslaved Africans, whose lives were reduced to trans-actions at a scale that remains incomprehensible even when charted (pp. 50–53). We wish therefore to acknowledge the individuals summed in those flows. The African Names Database, which identifies 91,491 men, women and children liberated from slave ships in the final years of the trans-Atlantic trade, is an

◆

Have we learned
NOTHING?
Relocation doesn't
end homelessness.
It just ends
SIGHT OF IT.

*The UK government defines 'rough sleeping' as 'people sleeping or bedded down in the open air or in places not designed for habitation'. Not all homeless sleep outside.

excellent example of creating data in service of the people and narratives that can hide behind numbers. Preserving the memory of these individuals, even if all we record is their name, activates what the late Justice Ginsburg deemed 'our most powerful resources.'

She was speaking at a Days of Remembrance ceremony at the US Holocaust Memorial Museum, which sponsors exhibitions, leadership training and educational outreach in the hope of preventing such horrors from happening again. In 2007, the museum brought geographers and historians together for a weeklong workshop to explore how maps and data analysis might shed new light on one of history's darkest chapters. Of obvious interest to them were 'questions of *where* . . . where people were arrested, where they were sent, where they were murdered.' With access to the museum's extensive archive, the scholars set off mapping the growth of the SS camp system, the ghettoization of Budapest, the construction of Auschwitz and other ways in which the Holocaust 'transformed the meaning . . . of every place and space it touched.'

Still, for one of the attendees, historical geographer Anne Kelly Knowles, many of these maps left her deeply dissatisfied. The problem was twofold. First, she felt the apparent precision and 'god's-eye perspective' of mapping software reinforced the Nazis' dehumanizing view of the world. Then there was the nature of the historical records themselves, which, like Lever Maxey's removal order, were created by those in power, not those subjected to it. Knowles wanted to map the victims' points of view.

So she and her research assistants went back to the drawing board, literally. They listened to oral interviews with Holocaust survivors and then allowed themselves to respond in any way they saw fit – first with chalk and a black-board, then with string, cut paper and other media. It soon became clear that 'the most dramatic stories, those that carried the greatest emotional and personal significance, happened in . . . places too small to appear on any conventional map.' And because captives did not always know their whereabouts, the places they recalled often included relative locations (e.g. *between the barracks*) as well as objects imbued with meaning (a *window* framing a sibling's face).

One of her assistants, Levi Westerveld, began experimenting with a new kind of map. 'I had not yet taken a cartography class,' he recalls, 'so I was a bit limited.' That limitation turned out to be liberating. Free from the constraints of Cartesian coordinates, Westerveld explored ways to depict a survivor's experiences according to the associative geography of memory. In the lives of Jacob Brodman and Anna Patipa, he found two people whose narratives, originating on opposite sides of the Carpathian Mountains, would interweave. For each remembered place, he drew either a circle or a smudge, sizing it by its relative scale and adjusting the mark's opacity by how often the place was mentioned (i.e. its significance). To evoke uncertainty, he used pastels. In collaboration with Knowles and Westerveld, we've adapted the result of their exploration to fit on the following foldout. Preserved in this manner, memories of the Holocaust remain visible as long as we choose to look.

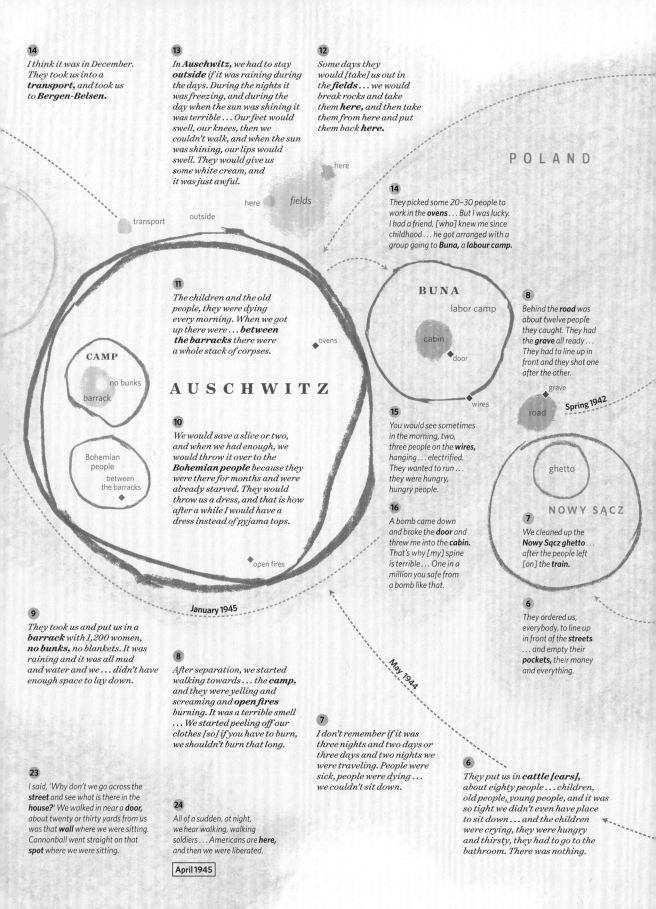

14 I think it was in December. They took us into a **transport,** and took us to **Bergen-Belsen.**

13 In **Auschwitz,** we had to stay **outside** if it was raining during the days. During the nights it was freezing, and during the day when the sun was shining it was terrible ... Our feet would swell, our knees, then we couldn't walk, and when the sun was shining, our lips would swell. They would give us some white cream, and it was just awful.

12 Some days they would [take] us out in the **fields** ... we would break rocks and take them **here,** and then take them from here and put them back **here.**

POLAND

here

here   *fields*

transport   outside

14 They picked some 20–30 people to work in the **ovens** ... But I was lucky. I had a friend, [who] knew me since childhood ... he got arranged with a group going to **Buna,** a **labour camp.**

11 The children and the old people, they were dying every morning. When we got up there were ... **between the barracks** there were a whole stack of corpses.

BUNA
labor camp

cabin

door

8 Behind the **road** was about twelve people they caught. They had the **grave** all ready ... They had to line up in front and they shot one after the other.

CAMP

no bunks

barrack

ovens

AUSCHWITZ

grave

road   **Spring 1942**

wires

10 We would save a slice or two, and when we had enough, we would throw it over to the **Bohemian people** because they were there for months and were already starved. They would throw us a dress, and that is how after a while I would have a dress instead of pyjama tops.

Bohemian people

between the barracks

15 You would see sometimes in the morning, two, three people on the **wires,** hanging ... electrified. They wanted to run ... they were hungry, hungry people.

ghetto

NOWY SĄCZ

7 We cleaned up the *Nowy Sącz ghetto* ... after the people left [on] the **train.**

16 A bomb came down and broke the **door** and threw me into the **cabin.** That's why [my] spine is terrible ... One in a million you safe from a bomb like that.

open fires

January 1945

6 They ordered us, everybody, to line up in front of the **streets** ... and empty their **pockets,** their money and everything.

9 They took us and put us in a **barrack** with 1,200 women, **no bunks,** no blankets. It was raining and it was all mud and water and we ... didn't have enough space to lay down.

8 After separation, we started walking towards ... the **camp,** and they were yelling and screaming and **open fires** burning. It was a terrible smell ... We started peeling off our clothes [so] if you have to burn, we shouldn't burn that long.

May 1944

7 I don't remember if it was three nights and two days or three days and two nights we were traveling. People were sick, people were dying ... we couldn't sit down.

23 I said, 'Why don't we go across the **street** and see what is there in the **house?'** We walked in near a **door,** about twenty or thirty yards from us was that **wall** where we were sitting. Cannonball went straight on that **spot** where we were sitting.

24 All of a sudden, at night, we hear walking, walking soldiers ... Americans are **here,** and then we were liberated.

April 1945

6 They put us in **cattle [cars],** about eighty people ... children, old people, young people, and it was so tight we didn't even have place to sit down ... and the children were crying, they were hungry and thirsty, they had to go to the bathroom. There was nothing.

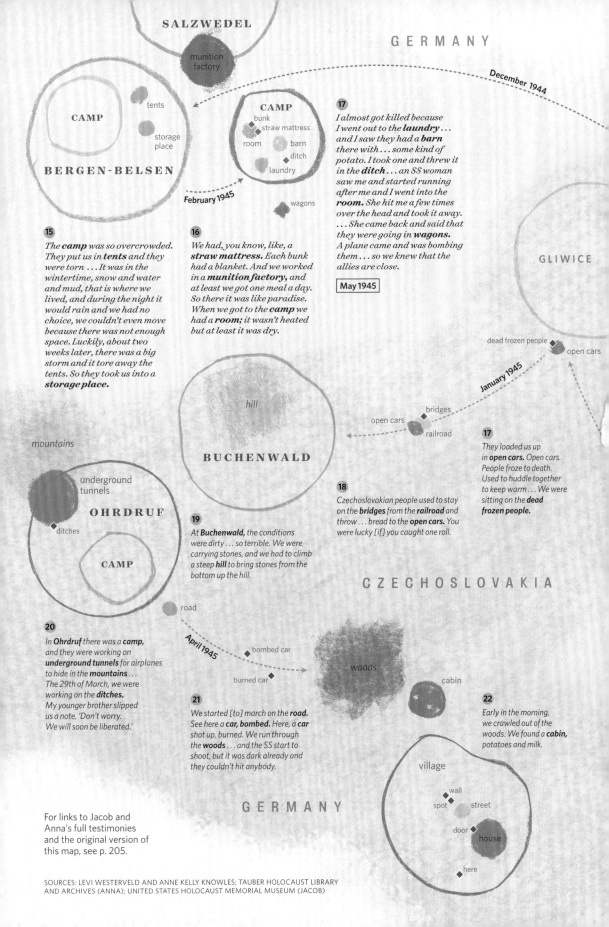

SALZWEDEL

GERMANY

munition factory

December 1944

CAMP

tents

storage place

CAMP

bunk
straw mattress

room
barn

ditch

laundry

wagons

CAMP

BERGEN-BELSEN

February 1945

17

*I almost got killed because I went out to the **laundry**... and I saw they had a **barn** there with ... some kind of potato. I took one and threw it in the **ditch**... an SS woman saw me and started running after me and I went into the **room.** She hit me a few times over the head and took it away. ... She came back and said that they were going in **wagons.** A plane came and was bombing them ... so we knew that the allies are close.*

May 1945

15

*The **camp** was so overcrowded. They put us in **tents** and they were torn ... It was in the wintertime, snow and water and mud, that is where we lived, and during the night it would rain and we had no choice, we couldn't even move because there was not enough space. Luckily, about two weeks later, there was a big storm and it tore away the tents. So they took us into a **storage place.***

16

*We had, you know, like, a **straw mattress.** Each bunk had a blanket. And we worked in a **munition factory,** and at least we got one meal a day. So there it was like paradise. When we got to the **camp** we had a **room;** it wasn't heated but at least it was dry.*

GLIWICE

dead frozen people

open cars

January 1945

hill

open cars

bridges

railroad

17

*They loaded us up in **open cars.** Open cars. People froze to death. Used to huddle together to keep warm ... We were sitting on the **dead frozen people.***

mountains

underground tunnels

BUCHENWALD

OHRDRUF

ditches

CAMP

19

*At **Buchenwald,** the conditions were dirty ... so terrible. We were carrying stones, and we had to climb a steep **hill** to bring stones from the bottom up the hill.*

18

*Czechoslovakian people used to stay on the **bridges** from the **railroad** and throw ... bread to the **open cars.** You were lucky [if] you caught one roll.*

CZECHOSLOVAKIA

road

April 1945

bombed car

burned car

woods

cabin

20

*In **Ohrdruf** there was a **camp,** and they were working on **underground tunnels** for airplanes to hide in the **mountains**... The 29th of March, we were working on the **ditches.** My younger brother slipped us a note, 'Don't worry. We will soon be liberated.'*

21

*We started [to] march on the **road.** See here a **car, bombed.** Here, a **car** shot up, burned. We run through the **woods** ... and the SS start to shoot, but it was dark already and they couldn't hit anybody.*

22

*Early in the morning, we crawled out of the woods. We found a **cabin,** potatoes and milk.*

village

wall

spot
street

door
house

here

GERMANY

For links to Jacob and Anna's full testimonies and the original version of this map, see p. 205.

SOURCES: LEVI WESTERVELD AND ANNE KELLY KNOWLES; TAUBER HOLOCAUST LIBRARY AND ARCHIVES (ANNA); UNITED STATES HOLOCAUST MEMORIAL MUSEUM (JACOB)

Large places in the testimonies of
Jacob Brodman and Anna Patipa, 1938–45

■ Main camp   ■ Subcamp   ⊠ Death camp

Present-day borders shown; SS camp network as of June 1943

Excerpted memories by year

Jacob — Grybów — Auschwitz

Anna — Perecín — Auschwitz

EYEWITNESS CARTOGRAPHY

In memories, meaning exists beyond geographic space.

From the map above, you could never imagine what Jacob Brodman or Anna
Patipa went through. You can see their displacement. You can see the extent of
the Nazi camp system around the time Jacob and Anna entered it. But would you
know what being torn from your home, separated from your family and marched
through a Polish winter *felt* like?

Adapted from *I Was There, Places of Experience in the Holocaust,* a cartographic
collaboration between geographers Anne Kelly Knowles and Levi Westerveld,
the graphic inside this foldout immerses you in the lived experiences of two
Holocaust survivors: Jacob Brodman (green) and Anna Patipa (gold). Starting
at the first numbered entry below their portraits, you can follow excerpts of
their testimonies through time and remembered space, from the day of their
deportation to the day of their eventual liberation.

Jacob and Anna are two of some 250,000 Jews estimated to have survived
the Nazi concentration camps. Six million did not. It's difficult to comprehend
numbers that large, so in the words and marks on this memory map, we hope
to engender a shared humanity instead.

SOURCES: LEVI WESTERVELD AND ANNE KELLY KNOWLES; TAUBER HOLOCAUST LIBRARY
AND ARCHIVES (ANNA); UNITED STATES HOLOCAUST MEMORIAL MUSEUM (JACOB)

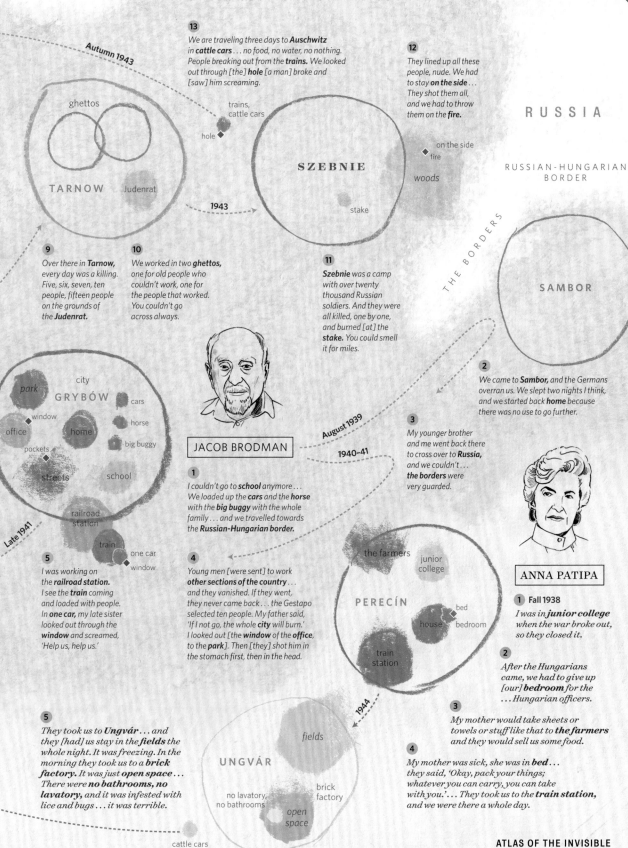

Autumn 1943

ghettos

13
We are traveling three days to **Auschwitz** in **cattle cars** . . . no food, no water, no nothing. People breaking out from the **trains.** We looked out through [the] **hole** [a man] broke and [saw] him screaming.

trains, cattle cars

hole

12
They lined up all these people, nude. We had to stay **on the side** . . . They shot them all, and we had to throw them on the **fire.**

RUSSIA

RUSSIAN-HUNGARIAN BORDER

on the side
fire

woods

TARNOW   Judenrat

SZEBNIE

stake

1943

THE BORDERS

SAMBOR

9
Over there in **Tarnow,** every day was a killing. Five, six, seven, ten people, fifteen people on the grounds of the **Judenrat.**

10
We worked in two **ghettos,** one for old people who couldn't work, one for the people that worked. You couldn't go across always.

11
Szebnie was a camp with over twenty thousand Russian soldiers. And they were all killed, one by one, and burned [at] the **stake.** You could smell it for miles.

2
We came to **Sambor,** and the Germans overran us. We slept two nights I think, and we started back **home** because there was no use to go further.

city
park   **GRYBÓW**
                                        cars
window
office   home   horse
pockets   big buggy
streets   school
railroad station
train   one car
                window

August 1939

3
My younger brother and me went back there to cross over to **Russia,** and we couldn't . . . **the borders** were very guarded.

JACOB BRODMAN

1940–41

1
I couldn't go to **school** anymore . . . We loaded up the **cars** and the **horse** with the **big buggy** with the whole family . . . and we travelled towards the **Russian-Hungarian border.**

Late 1941

5
I was working on the **railroad station.** I see the **train** coming and loaded with people. In **one car,** my late sister looked out through the **window** and screamed, 'Help us, help us.'

4
Young men [were sent] to work **other sections of the country** . . . and they vanished. If they went, they never came back . . . the Gestapo selected ten people. My father said, 'If I not go, the whole **city** will burn.' I looked out [the **window** of the **office,** to the **park**]. Then [they] shot him in the stomach first, then in the head.

the farmers
junior college

PERECÍN
                    bed
house   bedroom
train station

ANNA PATIPA

1 Fall 1938
I was in **junior college** when the war broke out, so they closed it.

2
After the Hungarians came, we had to give up [our] **bedroom** for the . . . Hungarian officers.

3
My mother would take sheets or towels or stuff like that to **the farmers** and they would sell us some food.

1944

fields

UNGVÁR

no lavatory, no bathrooms   brick factory
                    open space

5
They took us to **Ungvár** . . . and they [had] us stay in the **fields** the whole night. It was freezing. In the morning they took us to a **brick factory.** It was just **open space** . . . There were **no bathrooms, no lavatory,** and it was infested with lice and bugs . . . it was terrible.

4
My mother was sick, she was in **bed** . . . they said, 'Okay, pack your things; whatever you can carry, you can take with you.' . . . They took us to the **train station,** and we were there a whole day.

cattle cars

ATLAS OF THE INVISIBLE

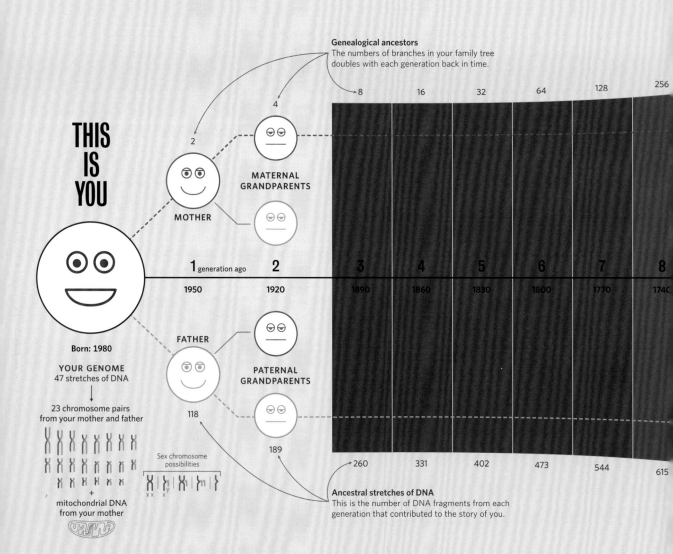

THIS
IS
YOU

Genealogical ancestors
The numbers of branches in your family tree doubles with each generation back in time.

8 16 32 64 128 256

4

2

MATERNAL
GRANDPARENTS

MOTHER

1 generation ago   2   3   4   5   6   7   8

1950   1920   1890   1860   1830   1800   1770   1740

Born: 1980

YOUR GENOME
47 stretches of DNA

↓

23 chromosome pairs
from your mother and father

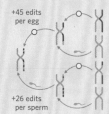

+
mitochondrial DNA
from your mother

Sex chromosome
possibilities

XX X

FATHER

PATERNAL
GRANDPARENTS

118

189

Ancestral stretches of DNA
This is the number of DNA fragments from each generation that contributed to the story of you.

260 331 402 473 544 615

You Are a Document . . .
Think of your genome as 47 volumes of genetic code. Each was compiled by tearing pages from earlier texts. On average, 71 pages are swapped out per generation. With each degree of separation, more of your origin story gets replaced.

+45 edits
per egg

+26 edits
per sperm

With Many Authors . . .
Meanwhile, the limbs of your family tree double with each prior generation (two parents, four grandparents, etc). Tracing it back three hundred years reveals over a thousand branches. At that point your genealogical ancestors begin to outnumber your genetic ones.

SOURCE: DAVID REICH, HARVARD UNIVERSITY

32,768

16,384

8,192

4,096

2,048

Number of genealogical ancestors surpasses the number of ancestral stretches of DNA that contributed to you

1,024

512

Mitochondrial DNA ancestor

9	10	11	12	13	14
1710	1680	1650	1620	1590	1560

686

757

828

899

970

1,041

1,112

Y chromosome ancestor

PARTIAL INHERITANCE

DNA kits do not tell the full story of you.

If you are thinking of joining the 30 million people who have purchased a DNA kit in search of their true ancestry, be careful which kit you choose. Many consumer kits trace only the maternal lineage of your mitochondrial DNA or the paternal path of your father's Y chromosome, indicated by dashed lines on this graphic. That's like reviewing a hundred-thousand-page book based on two random excerpts. Your genome – all twenty-three chromosome pairs and that bit of mitochondrial DNA – offers a far richer anthology of your family's past. And a revolution in genomics has helped researchers learn to read it.

Whole-genome studies now have the power to identify genetic risk factors for diseases, medications tailored to your genome's mutations and where on earth those mutations came from. What they don't do, however, no matter what anyone might claim, is prove you inherited traits from famous ancestors.

This is not to dismiss a sense of *cultural* inheritance. Cherishing an ancestor's cookbook or name (see p. 54) may foster an undeniable connection across the ages. Yet while such heirlooms can kindle a distant kinship, your genes most likely will not.

Of Waning Influence
By ten generations back, you will have 1,024 genealogical ancestors but only 757 genetic ancestors. By fourteen generations, that ratio is roughly 16 to 1, meaning many of the older branches on your family tree did not pass their DNA down to you.

Percentage of Yamnaya ancestry in select ancient DNA samples
c. 3300–1000 BCE

- Yamnaya
- Other ancestry

Forest — Steppe

→ Approximate migration route

0 — 800 km

Present-day shorelines shown

NORTH

EUROPE

Dnieper

~2700 BCE

CARPATHIAN MTS.

MODERN EUROPEAN CLINE

BRITISH ISLES

~2400 BCE

Danube

Black

Stonehenge

~2500 BCE

Within a few hundred years after Stonehenge's last Sarsen stone was hoisted into place around 2500 BCE, the genetic data of the hoisters was almost entirely overwritten.

ATLANTIC OCEAN

Mediterranean Sea

~2300 BCE

AFRICA

PURE MYTH

Ancient DNA shows nationalism is only a state of mind.

Over the past decade, geneticists in labs around the world have been extracting DNA from ancient human remains. Each sequenced strand adds to a map of genomic composition over time. In lieu of delineating national borders, its purpose is to connect dots and solve mysteries such as 'Who made Stonehenge?' Many in Britain may believe the monument was the work of their ancestors. DNA samples now prove that at the time the megalith builders broke ground on Salisbury Plain, the primary forebears of today's

SOURCES: DAVID REICH, HARVARD UNIVERSITY; NATURAL EARTH (TERRAIN)

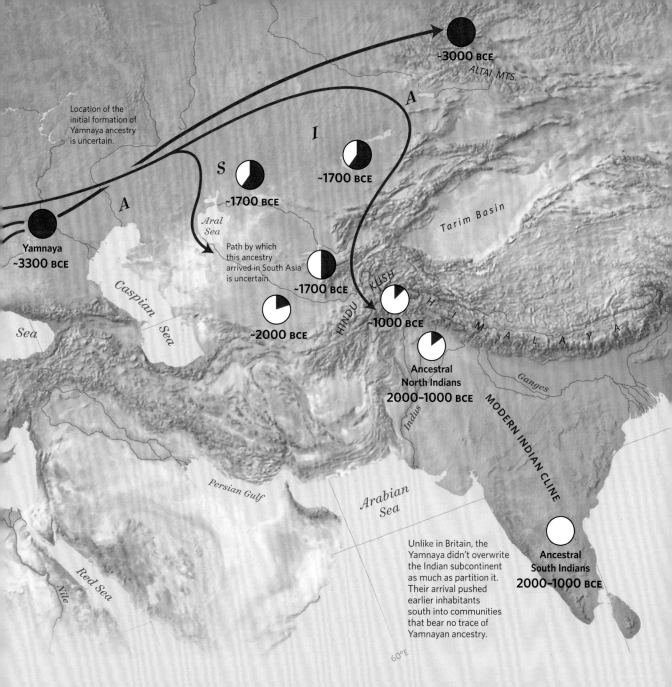

Location of the initial formation of Yamnaya ancestry is uncertain.

~3000 BCE
ALTAI MTS.

S I A

A

~1700 BCE

~1700 BCE

Yamnaya
~3300 BCE

Aral Sea

Path by which this ancestry arrived in South Asia is uncertain.

~1700 BCE

Caspian Sea

Sea

~2000 BCE

HINDU KUSH

HIMALAYA

Tarim Basin

~1000 BCE

Ancestral North Indians
2000-1000 BCE

Ganges

Indus

MODERN INDIAN CLINE

Persian Gulf

Arabian Sea

60°E

Red Sea

Nile

Unlike in Britain, the Yamnaya didn't overwrite the Indian subcontinent as much as partition it. Their arrival pushed earlier inhabitants south into communities that bear no trace of Yamnayan ancestry.

Ancestral South Indians
2000-1000 BCE

northern Europeans had not yet entered the picture. In fact, most Europeans owe a large percentage of their DNA to a group of people they have likely never heard of: the Yamnaya. Five thousand years ago, these nomadic herders flourished on the Steppe, a belt of harsh, dry grassland stretching between the Altai Mountains to the east and the Danube River to the west. The secret to their spread? The wheel.

The Yamnaya tamed horses, built wagons and followed the grasslands west, bringing their genes and language across Europe. Ancient DNA indicates that another contingent arced east and down through central Asia to the Indus Valley.

These genetic trails challenge notions of national purity. Before mixing with early Europeans and South Asians, the Yamnaya were themselves a mixture of earlier Steppe peoples and groups pushing north from the Caucasus Mountains. So it's no great cognitive leap to view human history as one continuous series of mixture from time immemorial to the present.

ANCESTRALIA

*The 'great southern land' was home to
millions before Europeans arrived.*

The first people to set foot on the shores of Australia
arrived about fifty thousand years ago, when sea
levels were 75 metres (246ft) lower. Back then, the Gulf
of Carpentaria and the Torres Strait were a savanna
that extended from Australia's northern coast to
New Guinea. DNA from hair samples shows that the
donors' ancestors took between one and five thousand
years to migrate both clockwise and counterclockwise
to the south coast of the continent we know today.
Individual communities soon emerged that included

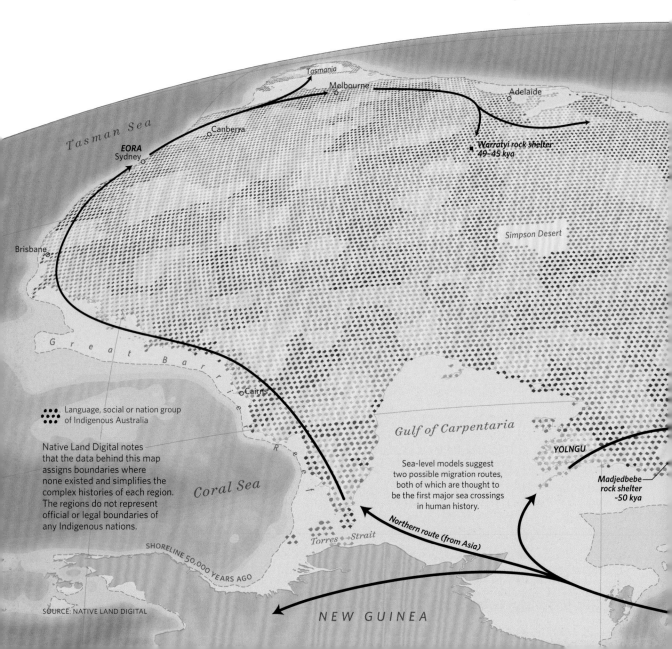

Tasman Sea

Tasmania

Melbourne

Canberra

Adelaide

*Warratyi rock shelter
49–45 kya*

EORA
Sydney

Simpson Desert

Brisbane

G r e a t   B a r r

Cairns

●●● Language, social or nation group
of Indigenous Australia

Native Land Digital notes
that the data behind this map
assigns boundaries where
none existed and simplifies the
complex histories of each region.
The regions do not represent
official or legal boundaries of
any Indigenous nations.

Gulf of Carpentaria

YOLNGU

*Madjedbebe
rock shelter
~50 kya*

R   e   e

Coral Sea

Sea-level models suggest
two possible migration routes,
both of which are thought to
be the first major sea crossings
in human history.

SHORELINE 50,000 YEARS AGO

Torres   Strait

Northern route (from Asia)

N E W   G U I N E A

the Pitjantjatjara who live beside Uluru, the sacred sandstone landmark, the Yolngu with their distinctive sign language and the Torres Strait Islanders famous for their ceremonial headdresses – cultures that existed for millennia before British settlers showed up near the end of the eighteenth century.

The establishment of Sydney in 1788, on the lands of the Eora, was but the first stroke in a two-century effort to whitewash the diversity on this map. The First Australians were subjected to European diseases, land appropriation and even a policy of child removal that continued to the 1970s.

Today, Native Land Digital, a Canadian nonprofit, hosts an online, interactive map of Australia's 392 Indigenous territories to inform discussions about land rights, language and local history. They've added Indigenous boundaries for other countries too, so readers in Japan, New Zealand (Aotearoa), Russia, Scandinavia and the Americas can acknowledge what ancestral land they inhabit.

Great Australian Bight

Nullarbor Plain

Devil's Lair cave
48 kya

Perth

PITJANTJATJARA
+ Uluru
(Ayers Rock)

SHORELINE 50,000 YEARS AGO

INDIAN OCEAN

Darwin

Southern route (from Asia)

Sea

Timor

TIMOR

Savu Sea

Laili Cave
46 kya

Liang Bua
46 kya

FLORES

NORTH

Scale varies in this perspective.

Straight-line distance from
Sydney to Perth is about 3,300 km.

Banda Sea

Flores Sea

ATLAS OF THE INVISIBLE

OCEANS OF DATA

*Origins of the global economy
reside in dusty logbooks.*

For the shipping industry, time has always
been money. In the 1840s Lieutenant M. F.
Maury of the US Navy realized sailors were
wasting both. Nautical charts didn't show
where the best winds and quickest routes
were, so many a vessel got stuck in the slow
lane. Maury encouraged mariners to record
and report weather observations along their
voyages. More than a thousand complied. In
return Maury used their data to create maps
of the ocean so detailed that a sailor could
set off on a voyage 'as though he himself
had already been that way a thousand times
before'. The results were startling. Maury's
maps cut the round trip between England
and Australia from 250 days to 160, saving
millions of dollars.

Steam and diesel have not taken the
wind out of the initiative's sails. In the 1980s,
the National Oceanic and Atmospheric
Administration began digitizing more
than three centuries' worth of observations
from ocean buoys and ship logs, including
Maury's. Scientists now use them to study
the climate and ocean currents, but the
records also capture the evolution of ever
faster shipping routes that now criss-cross
the globe. England to Australia and back
is now possible in 80 days.

These maps show ships in the database only,
not all shipping. It's also worth noting that locations
in logbooks were not always precise.

SOURCE: ICOADS

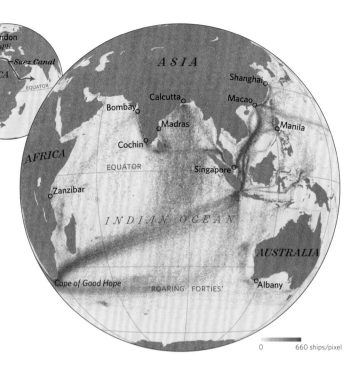

0   660 ships/pixel

AGE OF SAIL (1570–1860)
The discovery of the 'Roaring Forties' in 1611 by
Dutch explorer Hendrick Brouwer halved the sailing time
from Europe to the spice-rich islands of Southeast Asia.

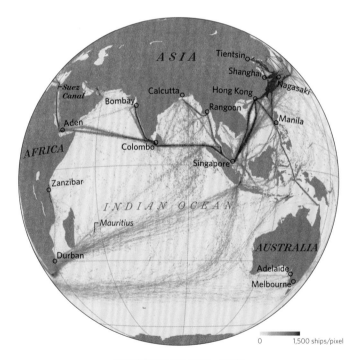

0   1,500 ships/pixel

AGE OF STEAM (1860–1920)
The Suez Canal opened in 1869, offering steamers
a straight run between Asia and Europe.

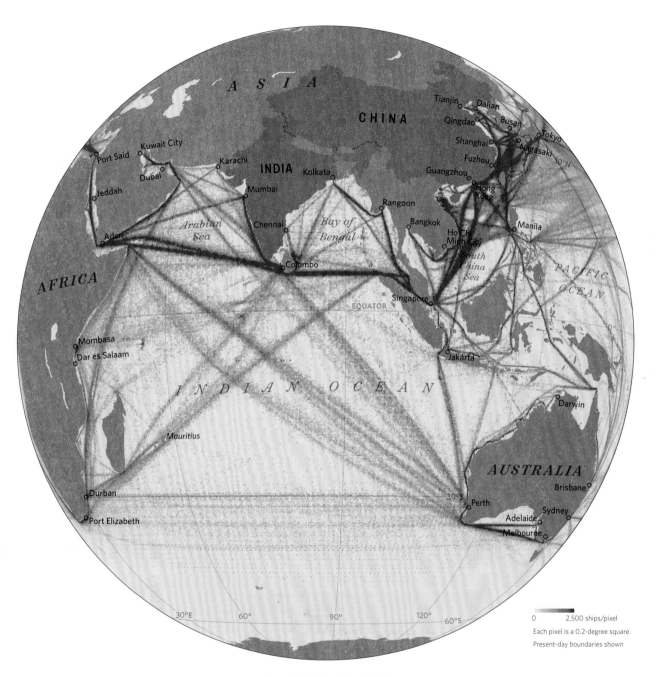

AGE OF DIESEL (1920–1970)

Cheap diesel has fuelled the tsunami of global shipping since the 1950s.
Our oceans are now striped with ships transporting clothes from India,
crude oil from the Middle East and soybeans to China.

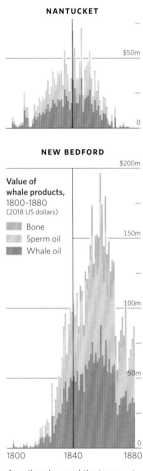

NANTUCKET

$50m

0

NEW BEDFORD

$200m

Value of whale products, 1800–1880
(2018 US dollars)

Bone
Sperm oil
Whale oil

150m

100m

50m

0

1800   1840   1880

As railroads eased the transport of goods, New Bedford surpassed Nantucket Island as America's whaling capital.

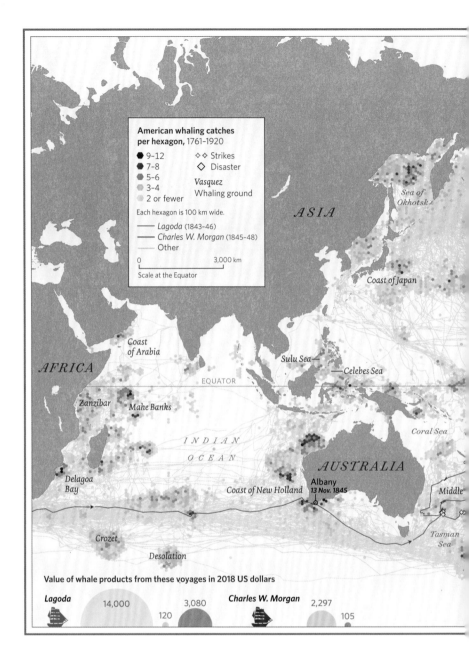

American whaling catches per hexagon, 1761–1920

● 9–12   ◇◇ Strikes
● 7–8   ◇ Disaster
● 5–6
● 3–4   *Vasquez*
● 2 or fewer   Whaling ground

Each hexagon is 100 km wide.

— *Lagoda* (1843–46)
— *Charles W. Morgan* (1845–48)
— Other

0   3,000 km

Scale at the Equator

ASIA

Sea of Okhotsk

Coast of Japan

Coast of Arabia

AFRICA

Sulu Sea

Celebes Sea

EQUATOR

Zanzibar   *Mahe Banks*

Coral Sea

INDIAN OCEAN

AUSTRALIA

Delagoa Bay

Albany
13 Nov. 1845

Coast of New Holland

Middle

Crozet

Tasman Sea

Desolation

Value of whale products from these voyages in 2018 US dollars

Lagoda   14,000   3,080   *Charles W. Morgan*   2,297

120   105

SEEING RED

The stains on this map pale before the bloodbath that followed.

Between 1761 and 1920 tens of thousands of whales were killed by the hand spears of American whalers. This map marks the death of 34,144 as recorded in and digitized from the logbooks of the ships responsible. For instance, the *Charles W. Morgan* (in purple) sought sperm oil from the South Pacific; the *Lagoda* (in blue) headed to the Gulf of Alaska in search of whalebone for umbrellas, corsets and hooped dresses.

By the time *Moby-Dick* came out in 1851, whaling towns such as Nantucket and New Bedford were the

SOURCES: WCS CANADA; AMERICAN OFFSHORE WHALING DATABASE; *WHALINGHISTORY.ORG*; KERRY GATHERS (PRODUCT DATA)

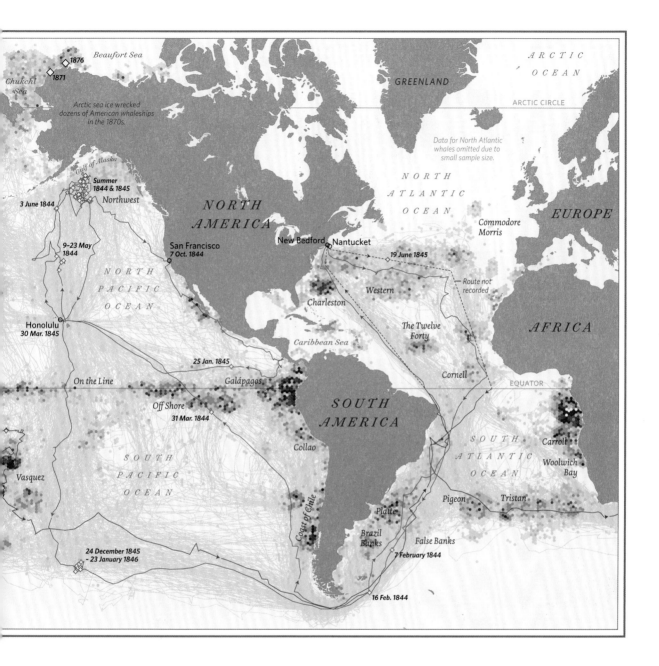

Map labels:

1876
1871
Beaufort Sea
Chukchi Sea
GREENLAND
ARCTIC OCEAN
ARCTIC CIRCLE

Arctic sea ice wrecked dozens of American whaleships in the 1870s.

Data for North Atlantic whales omitted due to small sample size.

Gulf of Alaska
Summer 1844 & 1845
Northwest
3 June 1844
9–23 May 1844
San Francisco
7 Oct. 1844
NORTH AMERICA
NORTH PACIFIC OCEAN
New Bedford Nantucket
19 June 1845
Commodore Morris
NORTH ATLANTIC OCEAN
EUROPE
Western
Route not recorded
Charleston
Honolulu 30 Mar. 1845
Caribbean Sea
The Twelve Forty
AFRICA
25 Jan. 1845
On the Line
Galápagos
Cornell
EQUATOR
Off Shore
31 Mar. 1844
SOUTH AMERICA
Collao
SOUTH ATLANTIC OCEAN
Carroll
Woolwich Bay
Vasquez
SOUTH PACIFIC OCEAN
Coast of Chile
Pigeon Tristan
Platte
24 December 1845 – 23 January 1846
Brazil Banks
False Banks
7 February 1844
16 Feb. 1844

wealthiest cities in the US. The New Bedford fleet alone employed ten thousand across 329 ships at its peak in 1857. But the boom was short-lived. Civil war, westward expansion, railroads and other industries diverted attention from the sea. To stay afloat, America's dwindling fleet intensified its hunt for oil-rich bowhead whales in the ice-choked Arctic. When two disasters in the 1870s resulted in millions of dollars in lost catch, gear and ships, investors began to question the risk since oil could now be found underground.

Norway seized this opportunity to develop means for industrial-scale slaughter. Steam and diesel power allowed fleets to catch faster species, while grenade harpoons ensured more strikes were kills. Researchers now estimate some 2.9 million whales were taken last century. In fact, more sperm whales were killed between 1962 and 1972 than in the 18th and 19th centuries combined. Understanding how many whales we lost tells us how many our oceans can support today – a key data point for measuring their recovery.

EQUATOR

Sulawesi

New Guinea

Arafura Sea

INDIAN OCEAN

Coral Sea

A U S T R A L I A

Perth

Albany
13 Nov. 1845

①

Coast of New Holland

Sydney

Tasmania

Charles W. Morgan

In the time and geographic extent of this spread, the *Charles W. Morgan* made 117 sightings, 73 of which led to strikes. Five months after leaving Nantucket, the ship reached Australia in November 1845. The crew spent nearly three years hunting sperm whales off the coasts of New Zealand, Tonga and Fiji before heading for home in August 1848. The Vasquez and French Rock grounds were most active in April and May. As the ocean cooled in the austral winter (June-Sept), the ship followed the whales north toward the Equator.

SOURCES: WCS CANADA; AMERICAN OFFSHORE WHALING DATABASE; *WHALINGHISTORY.ORG*

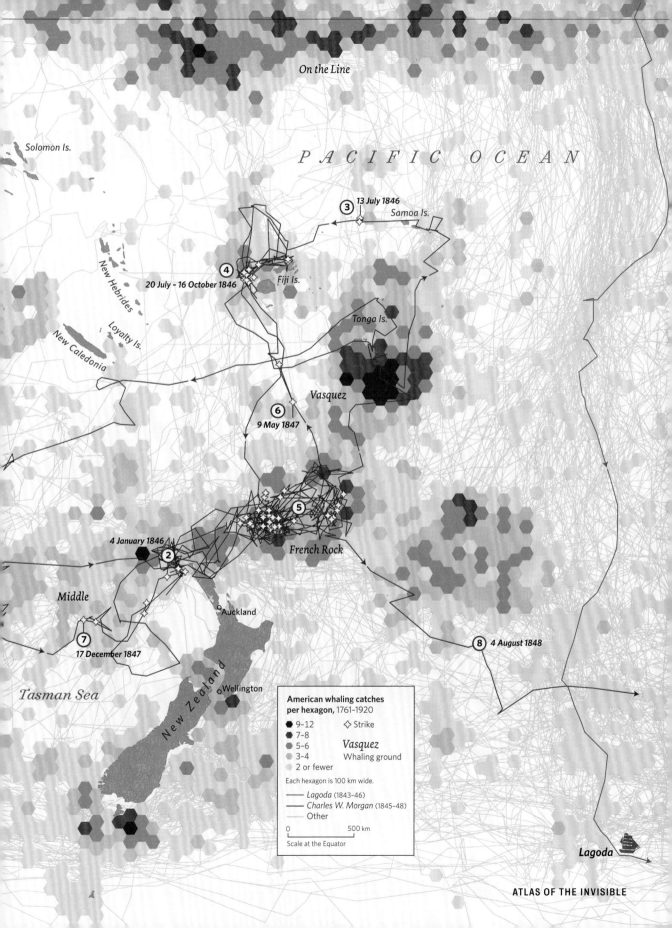

On the Line

Solomon Is.

P A C I F I C   O C E A N

③ 13 July 1846

Samoa Is.

④ 20 July – 16 October 1846

Fiji Is.

New Hebrides

Loyalty Is.

New Caledonia

Tonga Is.

Vasquez

⑥ 9 May 1847

⑤

French Rock

Middle

4 January 1846

②

○ Auckland

⑦ 17 December 1847

New Zealand

Tasman Sea

○ Wellington

⑧ 4 August 1848

American whaling catches
per hexagon, 1761–1920

- ● 9–12   ◇ Strike
- ● 7–8
- ● 5–6   *Vasquez*
- ● 3–4   Whaling ground
- 2 or fewer

Each hexagon is 100 km wide.

—— *Lagoda* (1843–46)
—— *Charles W. Morgan* (1845–48)
········ Other

0   500 km
Scale at the Equator

Lagoda

ATLAS OF THE INVISIBLE

MIDDLE

REGION OF EMBARKATION

WEST CENTRAL AFRICA
1

**Trans-Atlantic
Slave Trade
1514–1866**

AFRICA

Anomabu—

BIGHT OF BENIN
2

BIGHT OF BIAFRA
3

GOLD COAST
4

SENEGAMBIA
5

6 SOUTHEAST AFRICA
7 SIERRA LEONE
8 WINDWARD COAST

12.5 million

5,694,600 embarked

739,100 died en route

1,999,000

274,200

1,594,600

276,800

Venture Smith's journey

1,209,300

178,400

755,500

144,500

542,700

106,100

388,800

50,000

336,900

49,500

1,952,900
*West Central Africa
to Southeast Brazil*

693,200

666,900

355,100

730,000

296,600

301,600

231,500

INHUMANE FLOWS

*Decoupling slave voyage data from a map
reveals the true scale of complicity.*

Looking back on his life in 1798, a free Venture
Smith could still recall the day in Anomabu, sixty
years earlier, when his identity changed forever: 'I
was bought on board . . . for four gallons of rum, and
a piece of calico, and called Venture . . . Thus I came
by my name.' Venture (originally Broteer Furro) was
one of an estimated 12.5 million Africans captured,
shipped across the Atlantic and enslaved. He was also
one of the few captives known to have put memories
of the Middle Passage in writing.

To account for the millions whose stories we'll
never hear, researchers on four continents have

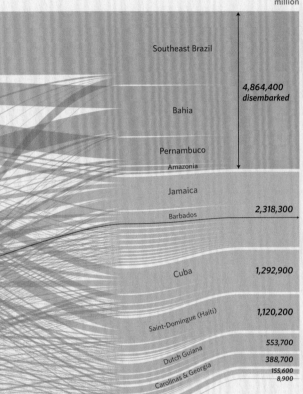

10.7 million

REGION OF DISEMBARKATION

Southeast Brazil

4,864,400 disembarked

Bahia

Pernambuco

Amazonia

Jamaica

Barbados — 2,318,300

Cuba — 1,292,900

Saint-Domingue (Haiti) — 1,120,200

Dutch Guiana — 553,700

388,700

Carolinas & Georgia

155,600

8,900

BRAZIL. ❶

BRITISH CARIBBEAN. ❷

SPANISH AMERICAS. ❸

FRENCH CARIBBEAN. ❹

DUTCH CARIBBEAN ❺

UNITED STATES ❻

AFRICA & OFFSHORE ATLANTIC EUROPE

NORTH AMERICA

SOUTH AMERICA

'*After an ordinary passage, except great mortality by the small pox, which broke out on board, we arrived at the island of Barbadoes.*' —VENTURE SMITH

teamed up to compile a searchable online database of 36,000 trans-Atlantic voyage records. Gathered from logs and ledgers, the details on ships, itineraries and crews as well as the age, gender and mortality rate of the enslaved offer a window into the past that had previously been sealed shut.

On this spread, we have sorted crossings by regions of embarkation and disembarkation. Initially we drew these flows with arrows on a traditional map, but the tiny islands of the British Caribbean appeared insignificant when, in fact, they were the second largest trading group. Proportional flows make no

mistake as to the worst offenders. Brazil, whose role in the slave trade had long been obscured by its own leaders, is now appallingly clear. Of the 10.7 million Africans thought to have survived the Middle Passage, nearly half disembarked in the Portuguese colony.

For Venture and some four hundred thousand other souls, the first port of call was not their last. In 2019, another set of researchers added 11,400 previously overlooked voyages that began and ended in the Americas. On the next spread, you'll see how slavery's tangled web of exploitation stretched not only across an ocean but also throughout the New World.

REGION OF EMBARKATION

JAMAICA
BRAZIL
BARBADOS
DUTCH CARIBBEAN
BRITISH CARIBBEAN
DOMINICA
DANISH WEST INDIES
UNITED STATES
PUERTO RICO
OTHER AMERICAS
FRENCH CARIBBEAN
SPANISH AMERICAS
OTHER CARIBBEAN
ST. BARTHÉLEMY
DUTCH GUIANAS
WRECKED, SOLD OR TAKEN AT SEA

Intra-American Slave Trade
1550–1840

As disease ravaged the Amerindian population in the early 1500s, the Spanish Crown began contracting other nations to import labour for them. The Spanish flag may not have flown over many ships from Africa, but it certainly did over the ports where 260,000 captives on intra-American voyages ultimately disembarked.

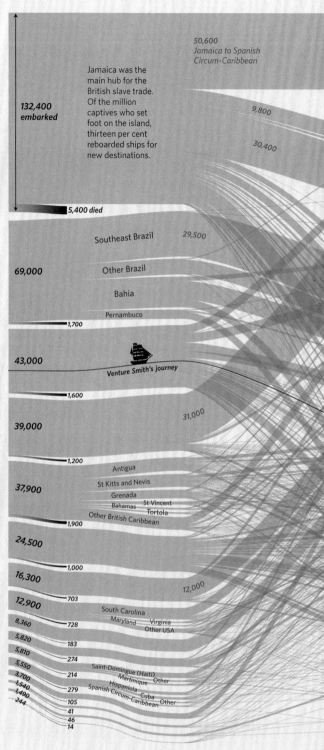

132,400 embarked

Jamaica was the main hub for the British slave trade. Of the million captives who set foot on the island, thirteen per cent reboarded ships for new destinations.

50,600
Jamaica to Spanish Circum-Caribbean

9,800

30,400

5,400 died

Southeast Brazil   29,500

69,000   Other Brazil

Bahia

Pernambuco

1,700

43,000   Venture Smith's journey

1,600

31,000

39,000

1,200   Antigua
St Kitts and Nevis
Grenada
Bahamas   St Vincent
Other British Caribbean   Tortola

37,900

1,900

24,500

1,000

16,300

12,000

703
South Carolina
Maryland   Virginia
Other USA

12,900

8,360   728

5,820   183

5,810   274

5,550   214   Saint-Domingue (Haiti)
Martinique   Other

3,700   279   Hispaniola
Spanish Circum-Caribbean   Cuba   Other

1,540   105

1,480   41

244   46

14

SOURCE: INTRA-AMERICAN SLAVE TRADE DATABASE, *SLAVEVOYAGES.ORG*

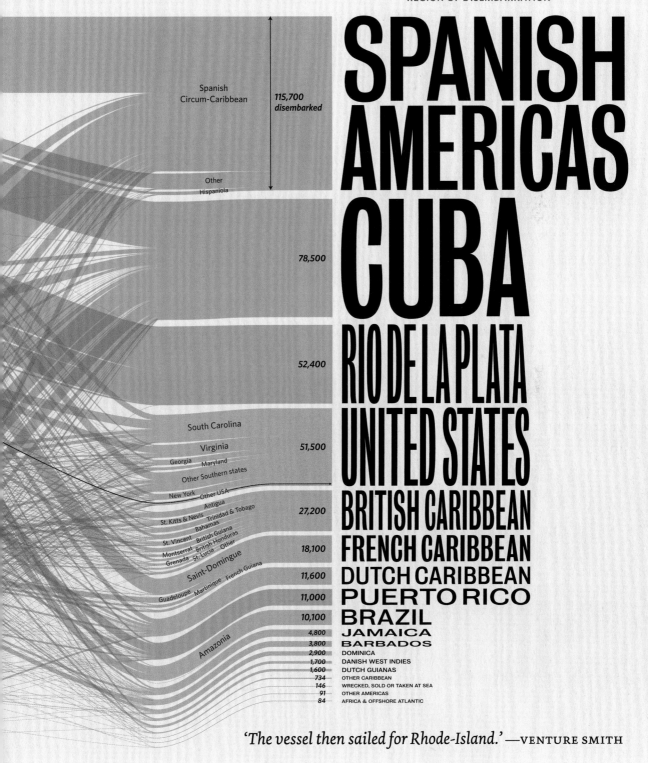

SPANISH AMERICAS
CUBA
RIO DE LA PLATA
UNITED STATES
BRITISH CARIBBEAN
FRENCH CARIBBEAN
DUTCH CARIBBEAN
PUERTO RICO
BRAZIL
JAMAICA
BARBADOS

Spanish Circum-Caribbean — 115,700 disembarked

Other Hispaniola

78,500

52,400

South Carolina
Virginia
Georgia Maryland
Other Southern states
New York Other USA
Antigua
St. Kitts & Nevis Trinidad & Tobago
Bahamas
St. Vincent British Guiana
Montserrat British Honduras
Grenada St. Lucia Other

51,500

27,200

18,100

Saint-Domingue

11,600

Guadeloupe Martinique French Guiana

11,000

10,100

Amazonia

4,800
3,800
2,900 DOMINICA
1,700 DANISH WEST INDIES
1,600 DUTCH GUIANAS
734 OTHER CARIBBEAN
146 WRECKED, SOLD OR TAKEN AT SEA
91 OTHER AMERICAS
84 AFRICA & OFFSHORE ATLANTIC

'The vessel then sailed for Rhode-Island.' —VENTURE SMITH

JONSSON

MURPHY

SMITH

HANSEN JOHANSSON KORHONEN

JENSEN

UNITED KINGDOM

IVANOV
TAMM
BERZINS
DEJONG JANKAUSKIENE
PEETERS NOWAK KOCHETKOV
MARTIN DASILVA KOVAC MELNYK
MULLER GRUBER RUSU
NOVAK HORVAT POPA
SIMIC JOVANOVIC IVANOV
POPOVIC
GASI
HOXHA PAPADOPOULOS

GARCIA
SILVA

BORG

TOTH

YILMAZ

COHEN

Europe

Professions and family ties are important in European naming. Mullers and Melnyks were once millers; Popovics were priests. Patronyms point to a father's name: Jonsson (son of Jon), Johansson (son of Johan) and so on.

Top surname per country, 2020

M M M M
100,000 50,000 10,000 3,000
Names sized by frequency per million

HAMDI
MOHAMED BRAHIMI MOHAMMED MOHAMED
BA TRAORE ABDOU MAHAMAT MOHAMED
JALLOW NDIAYE OUEDRAOGO CHE MAHAMAT DENG ABEBE MOHAMED
MUHAMAD ILUNGA AKELLO MWANGI
DIALLO KOUASSI MENGUE MANUEL ISHIMWE JUMA
DOSSOU AKAKPO NDAYISHIMIYE
MENSAH PHIRI BANDA COSSA RAKOTONIRINA
KAMARA JOHANNES MOYO
MODISE DLAMINI
NAIDOO

NOMENCULTURE

What we're named reveals where we're from.

Names are a statement of identity that can be passed down for generations. You may have a surname you can trace back to an 11th-century Norman baron or you might have just acquired one from your spouse. Either way it likely derives from the language you speak, your culture, your family's origins or historic events. For example, the spread of Islam brought variants of Mohamed to the fore in northeast Africa,

ROLLE

RODRIGUEZ

BROWN JOSEPH PEREZ

UNITED
STATES

SMITH
SMITH

HERNANDEZ

YOUNG

LOPEZ HERNANDEZ

HERNANDEZ

LOPEZ

RODRIGUEZ

GONZALEZ GONZALEZ

RODRIGUEZ PERSAUD

ZAMBRANO SILVA PINAS

FLORES MAMANI

GONZALEZ

GONZALEZ RODRIGUEZ

GONZALEZ

WILLIAMS

JOSEPH

JOSEPH

WILLIAMS

CHARLES

MOHAMMED

MARSTERS

The Americas
The prevalence of
European names and
patronyms (e.g. Gonzalez,
Hernandez and Perez)
is yet another legacy
of colonization and
the slave trade.

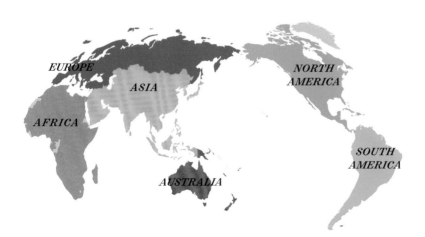

EUROPE

ASIA

NORTH
AMERICA

AFRICA

SOUTH
AMERICA

AUSTRALIA

Top forename per country, 2020

| 100,000 | 50,000 | 10,000 | 3,000 |

Names sized by frequency per million

Forenames

Whilst our surnames say something about where we're from, our forenames reveal who our parents want us to be. For millions of us, that's just like everyone else judging by how many of us are given variants of the religious names John, Mohammed, Joseph and Mary.

Frequency of four popular forenames or their variants in the top ten for each country, 2014

■ John   ■ Mohammed   ■ Joseph   ■ Mary

Six of Croati... variants of M...

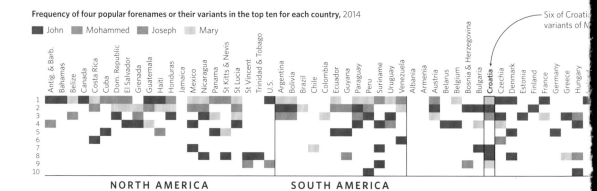

NORTH AMERICA   SOUTH AMERICA

SOURCE: UCL WORLDNAMES DATABASE

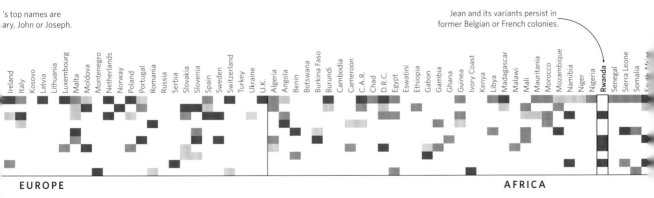

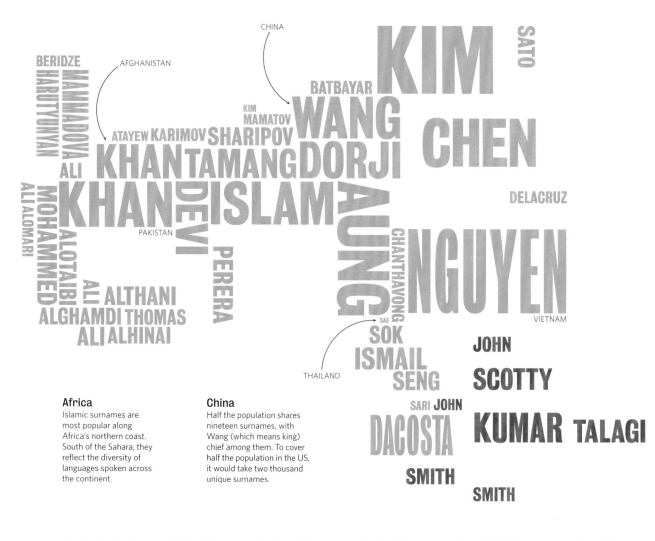

Africa
Islamic surnames are most popular along Africa's northern coast. South of the Sahara, they reflect the diversity of languages spoken across the continent.

China
Half the population shares nineteen surnames, with Wang (which means king) chief among them. To cover half the population in the US, it would take two thousand unique surnames.

whilst the influence of the Khans persists in Pakistan and Afghanistan. On these maps, each country's most popular name is sized by its frequency.

Between countries there can be big differences. In Thailand, the top surname, Sae, is actually quite rare because the law requires each family name to be unique. Next door in Vietnam, many share the surname, Nguyen, because it's both the name of the nation's last dynasty and a derivation of 'Ruan', a name Chinese officials assigned for tax purposes when they ruled the region two millennia ago.

As for forenames, flip this foldout over and you'll see that in Thailand, where people more often go by nicknames than their official forenames, even the top forename, Siriporn, is not ubiquitous like Maria is in Catholic Portugal.

Just as the history of naming varies by country, so do public records. The dataset we used was compiled from sources such as telephone directories and voting registers. These can be biased towards certain groups, such as male 'heads of household'. So if you think names are missing from the map, that might be why.

GIORGI
SEVINC
TIGRAN
SERDAR ULUGBEK
HIROSHI
MOHAMMAD
HAJI
AIGERIM
AZAMAT
RUSTAM
GANBOLD JI-U
WEI
MUHAMMAD
R A M
SONAM
YUTING
MOHAMMAD
ALI MOHAMMAD
MOHAMMAD
MOHAMMED
ABDUL
ABDUL
MOHAMMED
MOHAMED
SOUKSAVANH
MARY
AUNG
HUNG
SIRIPORN SOPHEAK
MOHAMMED
MOHAMED
MOHD
JUNIOR
MOHAMMED
AHMED ALI
TAN
JOHN
JOHN
SITI
MUNI NOOROA
JORDAN
JOHN JOSE
DAVID JOHN

THAILAND

Jordan's top ten includes Mohammad, Mohammed, Mahmoud and Yousef.

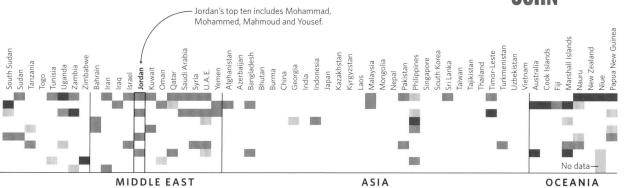

MIDDLE EAST   ASIA   OCEANIA

No data

80 years old   70   60   50   40   30   20

EGON SCHIELE — SEMI-NUDE GIRL, RECLINING
JEAN-MICHEL BASQUIAT — BOY AND DOG IN A JOHNNYPUMP
MARCEL DUCHAMP — NUDE DESCENDING A STAIRCASE
TOMASSO MASACCIO — THE TRIBUTE MONEY
PABLO PICASSO — LES DESMOISELLES D'AVIGNON
GIORGIO de CHIRICO — MYSTERY AND MELANCHOLY OF A STREET
GEORGES SEURAT — A SUNDAY AFTERNOON ON THE ISLAND OF LA GRANDE JATTE
GEORGE BELLOWS — STAG AT SHARKEY'S
SALVADOR DALÍ — THE PERSISTENCE OF MEMORY
RAPHAEL — THE SCHOOL OF ATHENS
THÉODORE GÉRICAULT — THE RAFT OF THE MEDUSA
CLAUDE MONET — ON THE BANK OF THE SEINE
JASPER JOHNS — THREE FLAGS
GUSTAVE COURBET — THE STONE BREAKERS
EDVARD MUNCH — THE SCREAM
CARAVAGGIO — THE CALLING OF ST. MATTHEW
UMBERTO BOCCIONI — DYNAMISM OF A CYCLIST
HENRI de TOULOUSE-LAUTREC — AT THE MOULIN ROUGE
EUGÈNE DELACROIX — LIBERTY LEADING THE PEOPLE
GEORGES BRAQUE — NEWSPAPER, BOTTLE, PACKET OF TOBACCO
PETER PAUL RUBENS — THE RAISING OF THE CROSS
AMEDEO MODIGLIANI — JEANNE HEBUTERNE WITH HAT AND NECKLACE
FRIDA KAHLO — SELF-PORTRAIT WITH HAT AND NECKLACE
JAN VERMEER — THE LETTER
ROMARE BEARDEN — GOLGOTHA
ANDY WARHOL — CAMPBELL'S SOUP CANS
SANDRO BOTTICELLI — THE BIRTH OF VENUS
REMBRANDT van RIJN — THE NIGHT WATCH
JEAN-FRANÇOIS MILLET — THE SOWER
FREDERIC EDWIN CHURCH — COTOPAXI
WINSLOW HOMER — SNAP THE WHIP
VINCENT van GOGH — WHEAT FIELD AND CYPRESS TREES
MICHELANGELO — SISTINE CHAPEL
JAMES MCNEILL WHISTLER — WHISTLER'S MOTHER
HENRI MATISSE — THE JOY OF LIFE
JEFF KOONS — PUPPY
JACKSON POLLOCK — AUTUMN RHYTHM
KAZIMIR MALEVICH — SUPREMATIST COMPOSITION
JOHN CONSTABLE — WIVENHOE PARK
FERNAND LÉGER — THE CITY
GIOTTO di BONDONE — ARENA CHAPEL PADUA
GEORGIA O'KEEFE — BLACK IRIS III
PIERO della FRANCESCA — TRUE CROSS
PIETER BRUEGEL the ELDER — PEASANT WEDDING

GRACED BY GENIUS

Even for masters, the age of inspiration varies.

It's tempting to view genius as the province of youth.
After all, Picasso revolutionized painting at the age of 26.
But what if, while exceptional, he was also an exception? The sunburst above depicts the lives of 88 artists from the thirteenth century to today in order of the age at which they completed a notable work. Two-thirds of these works were completed by artists in their thirties and forties: Delacroix raised the flag for Romanticism at 32, Michelangelo finished the Sistine ceiling at 37 and Kehinde Wiley unveiled his portrait of President Obama at age 41. If you're feeling washed-up, take heart: Yayoi Kusama was building Infinity Mirror Rooms at 91.

Psychologists who study age and achievement talk of the countless hours needed to master a discipline; preternatural talents, they claim, reach mastery fastest. Still, youth may be overrated. In 1933, the art critic Roger Fry hypothesized two types of artists: firebrands like Picasso for whom 'the exaltation and passion of youth transmits itself directly into everything they touch' and tinkerers like Cézanne who toiled largely in private for decades. Both can be canonical, and in our limited sample there are certainly more of the latter. In this light, perhaps it's time to paint over traditional portraits of precocity.

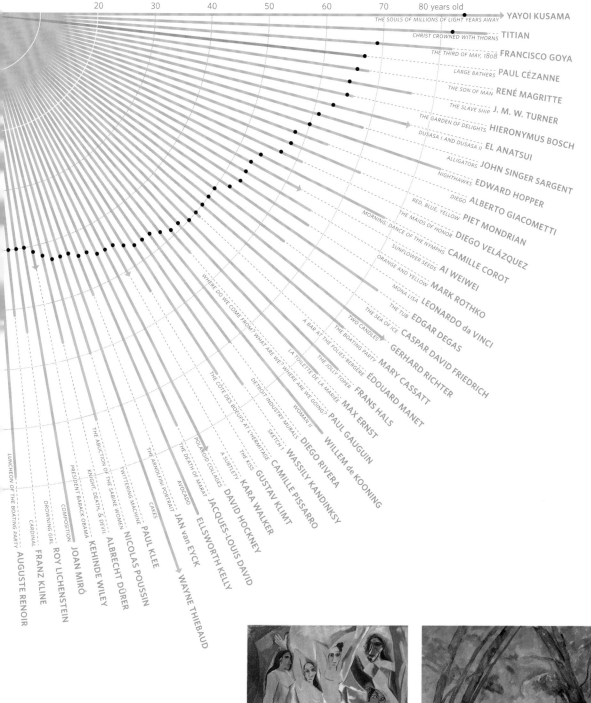

20 30 40 50 60 70 80 years old

THE SOULS OF MILLIONS OF LIGHT YEARS AWAY **YAYOI KUSAMA**
CHRIST CROWNED WITH THORNS **TITIAN**
THE THIRD OF MAY, 1808 **FRANCISCO GOYA**
LARGE BATHERS **PAUL CÉZANNE**
THE SON OF MAN **RENÉ MAGRITTE**
THE SLAVE SHIP **J. M. W. TURNER**
THE GARDEN OF DELIGHTS **HIERONYMUS BOSCH**
DUSASA I AND DUSASA II **EL ANATSUI**
ALLIGATORS **JOHN SINGER SARGENT**
NIGHTHAWKS **EDWARD HOPPER**
DIEGO **ALBERTO GIACOMETTI**
RED, BLUE, YELLOW **PIET MONDRIAN**
THE MAIDS OF HONOR **DIEGO VELÁZQUEZ**
MORNING: DANCE OF THE NYMPHS **CAMILLE COROT**
SUNFLOWER SEEDS **AI WEIWEI**
ORANGE AND YELLOW **MARK ROTHKO**
MONA LISA **LEONARDO da VINCI**
THE TUB **EDGAR DEGAS**
THE SEA OF ICE **CASPAR DAVID FRIEDRICH**
TWO CANDLES **GERHARD RICHTER**
THE BOATING PARTY **MARY CASSATT**
A BAR AT THE FOLIES-BERGÈRE **ÉDOUARD MANET**
THE JOLLY TOPER **FRANS HALS**
LA TOILETTE DE LA MARIÉE **MAX ERNST**
WHERE DO WE COME FROM? WHAT ARE WE? WHERE ARE WE GOING? **PAUL GAUGUIN**
WOMAN II **WILLEM de KOONING**
DETROIT INDUSTRY MURALS **DIEGO RIVERA**
SKETCH 1 **WASSILY KANDINSKY**
THE CÔTE DES BŒUFS AT L'HERMITAGE **CAMILLE PISSARRO**
THE KISS **GUSTAV KLIMT**
POLAROID COLLAGES **KARA WALKER**
A SUBTLETY **DAVID HOCKNEY**
THE DEATH OF MARAT **JACQUES-LOUIS DAVID**
THE ARNOLFINI PORTRAIT **ELLSWORTH KELLY**
AVOCADO **JAN van EYCK**
CAKES **WAYNE THIEBAUD**
THE ABDUCTION OF THE SABINE WOMEN **PAUL KLEE**
TWITTERING MACHINE **NICOLAS POUSSIN**
KNIGHT, DEATH, & DEVIL **ALBRECHT DÜRER**
PRESIDENT BARACK OBAMA **KEHINDE WILEY**
COMPOSITION **JOAN MIRÓ**
DROWNING GIRL **ROY LICHENSTEIN**
CARDINAL **FRANZ KLINE**
LUNCHEON OF THE BOATING PARTY **AUGUSTE RENOIR**

Eminent artists

— Lifespan
(as of February 2021)

• Age when the listed
artwork was completed

If you're wondering
how we determined
who and what to chart,
it's simple: we chose
works we admire.

In 1907, a young Pablo Picasso distorted the art world with *Les Desmoiselles d'Avignon*. The tenets of the Cubism movement – flatness and multiple viewpoints – stemmed from the life's work of Paul Cézanne, who was still revising his *Large Bathers* when he died in 1906 at the age of 67.

WHO WE ARE

'A Bill for taking a census has passed the House of Representatives, and is with the Senate. It contained a schedule for ascertaining the [occupations] of the Society, a kind of information extremely requisite to the Legislator . . . It was thrown out by the Senate as a waste of trouble and supplying materials for idle people to make a book.'

—JAMES MADISON, *in a letter to Thomas Jefferson, 14 February 1790*

DRAWING LINES

T wenty miles from where the US Constitution was signed, Oliver's grade school, like most American public schools, began each day with a pledge of allegiance to a flag that ended with the portentous phrase 'with liberty and justice for all'. In classrooms he learned about the revolution, inalienable rights and representative democracy. He heard about freedom and bravery and all the things that made the American experiment possible. He did not hear much about the Census. This strikes us now as absurd.

Liberty and equality were revolutionary *words*. A population count in order to apportion seats in government? That was a revolutionary *idea*. Historically, censuses had been a tool for taxation or conscription. America's founders wanted to try something new. And so on 2 August 1790, with Congress having approved six census questions – not including Madison's one about occupations – sixteen US marshals and some 650 assistants set out on horseback to begin enumerating free white males, free white females and all other free and taxable persons. (In a compromise that betrayed the racism of the time, the slaveholding Southern states and the less populous Northern states agreed that only three-fifths of the enslaved population would count toward a state's representation.)

Once Census takers finished tallying their designated areas, they were each instructed to post a 'correct copy' in public 'for the inspection of all concerned.' The stakes were high. The First Census cost more than any other public project in the young, indebted nation's budget, and there was great pressure to prove – in the words of President Washington – 'our present growing importance' to doubters overseas. He predicted a population of five million.

As the results trickled in, Washington was forced to admit 'it appears that we shall hardly reach four millions.' Still, he understood that 'the *real* number will greatly exceed the *official* return; because, from religeous [sic] scruples, some would not give in their lists; from an apprehension that it was intended as the foundation of a tax, others concealed or diminished theirs; and from indolence of the mass, & want of activity in many of the deputy Enumerators, numbers are omitted.'

By 1792, the final results were in: 3.9 million people across fourteen states and two territories (3.6 million after excluding two-fifths of the enslaved). Congress now had to decide how many seats there should be in total and how to divvy them up. Unfortunately, the Constitution provided little guidance. *Article I, § 2* just says the total number cannot exceed one representative for every thirty thousand

APPORTIONMENT of US REPRESENTATIVES

1789		1792
3	NH	4
8	MA	14
–	VT	2
1	RI	2
5	CT	7
6	NY	10
4	NJ	5
8	PA	13
1	DE	1
6	MD	8
10	VA	19
–	KY	2
5	NC	10
5	SC	6
3	GA	2
65		105

The Constitution listed an initial number of seats per state (left). After the First Census and the addition of Vermont and Kentucky, only Georgia lost one (right).

people and each state gets at least one congressperson (see table). You only have to consider the original wording for a minute to see the problem: congressional seats cannot be divided equally by a common ratio. Take Maryland, which reported 319,728 persons. A divisor of 30,000 creates 10.66 representatives. What do you do with the fractions? Alexander Hamilton recognized this dilemma, as did Thomas Jefferson. Hamilton argued for a variable ratio based on the national population divided by a set number of 120 House seats. Jefferson favoured keeping a uniform divisor, ditching the fractions and letting the House size vary.

Hamilton initially prevailed, but he did not have Washington on his side. In the first-ever presidential veto, Washington shot Hamilton down because his bill benefited the northern states unfairly. Congress reconvened and approved Jefferson's method. Since then, Congress has tried four different formulas for converting the decennial count into congressional seats, which goes to show that even the noblest endeavours can be manipulated.

IT'S NOT JUST THE NUMBER OF SEATS that matters; it's also the size and shape of their constituencies. If you are in power, you can redraw the electoral map to your advantage – a process called gerrymandering. Named after Governor Eldridge Gerry, who in 1812 created an election district as serpentine as a salamander, gerrymandering remains a simple idea: 'pack' supportive neighbourhoods into a single district to ensure your own victory there; then 'crack' neighbourhoods that prefer the opposition to splinter their influence across multiple districts. In the US, urban areas with more diverse populations tend to favour Democrats while their less diverse rural counterparts lean Republican. When redrawing the lines after a new census, Republicans aim to crack urban districts and pack rural areas; Democrats try the opposite. The result is an extremely convoluted electoral map that, unless both parties can agree on a 'sweetheart gerrymander' to protect incumbents, guarantees legal disputes.

A master of this process was the late Thomas Hofeller, a Republican political strategist. At a redistricting training session in 2011, he showed a slide that said, 'Don't bring out the maps until the END of a meeting. Once they see maps, all other forms of communication WILL cease.' Consciousness of guilt? Check. Remorse? Far from it. Hofeller wanted to go further. In 2015, Hofeller and Republican leaders hatched a plan to add a question about citizenship status to the 2020 Census. That may seem innocent enough until you remember that what made the US Census revolutionary was its central purpose: to determine where representatives are allotted. Hofeller's strategy was to discourage respondents in an opponent's strongholds, thus thinning their ranks in Congress.

US Censuses have asked about citizenship many times before and as recently as 1950. But in 2020's political climate, the US Census Bureau feared the addition of a citizenship question would deter responses from Hispanics and immigrants. For Hofeller, this was the point. If large cities, which tend to vote for Democrats, are undercounted, they lose seats in Congress. Cities can also lose seats if other parts of the country eat into their portion of the pie. Take New York. Between the

Notably gerrymandered US Congressional Districts after the 2010 Census

Alabama's 1st

California's 3rd

Connecticut's 1st

Illinois's 4th

New York's 8th

Ohio's 4th

Ohio's 8th

Tennessee's 4th

Texas's 15th

Texas's 35th

2000 and 2010 Censuses, its population increased (2.1%) but far less than the nation overall (9.7%). So when it came time to reallocate representatives, the state lost two. This wasn't the first time either. Since 1940, New York has lost more congressional seats – 18 – than any other state, which is why, as the 2020 Census approached, it led a lawsuit to prohibit the citizenship question. To keep pace with burgeoning states like Texas and Florida, New York needed to count everyone it could.

Dept of Commerce vs. New York eventually reached the Supreme Court. In his majority opinion, Chief Justice Roberts noted that while it's not unlawful to ask demographic questions, the Trump administration's motives for asking this particular question were 'arbitrary and capricious'. To those who claimed undercount concerns were overblown, Roberts said historical response rates proved that government action could have a 'predictable effect' on the behaviour of respondents. In effect, the Court upheld the census's core mission: to count all persons. Soon after, New York City began a concerted effort to win back the hearts and minds of anyone who had become or was already suspicious of the census (see right).

ULTIMATELY, A SUCCESSFUL CENSUS is a matter of trust. Sometimes the most accurate counts come from within a community. For example, we can look to Chicago in the 1880s, a time of industrialization and social upheaval when thousands were moving to the city in search of the American Dream. Florence Kelley, a recent graduate of the University of Zurich (and Cornell before that), the definitive translator of Engels' 1845 *The Condition of the Working Class in England* and an authority on child labour in the United States, had just left her abusive husband and found refuge at Hull House, the first of many settlement houses opening around the nation. Settlement houses sought to reform poor communities by recruiting educated volunteers like Kelley to teach, aid and live among less fortunate neighbours.

With three young children to support, Kelley also needed a paying job. She soon secured a position collecting data for the Illinois Bureau of Labor Statistics and the US Bureau of Labor in Washington. In 1893 the Bureau tasked her and four 'schedulemen' (questionnaires were called schedules back then) with a detailed survey of the neighbourhood around Hull House. The schedulemen lived at Hull House that summer, and every evening fellow residents transcribed their findings before submitting them to a broader study of slum conditions across Chicago, New York, Baltimore and Philadelphia.

As the weeks wore on and data accrued, Kelley and Jane Addams (a founder of Hull House) saw a new way to advocate for social change. Inspired by Charles Booth's contemporaneous, hand-coloured maps of London poverty, they took their data on the ethnic origins, wages and employment history of households in the neighbourhood and created a series of meticulous maps (see p. 69). The resulting publication, *Hull-House Maps and Papers*, has a particular authenticity because the map makers were from the community in question. Some of those recorded on the maps helped make them.

In a 'Prefatory Note', Addams wrote, '[We] offer these maps and papers . . . not as exhaustive treatises, but as recorded observations which may possibly be of

◆

Ultimately,
a successful census
is a matter of
TRUST.
Sometimes the most
accurate counts
come from within a
COMMUNITY.

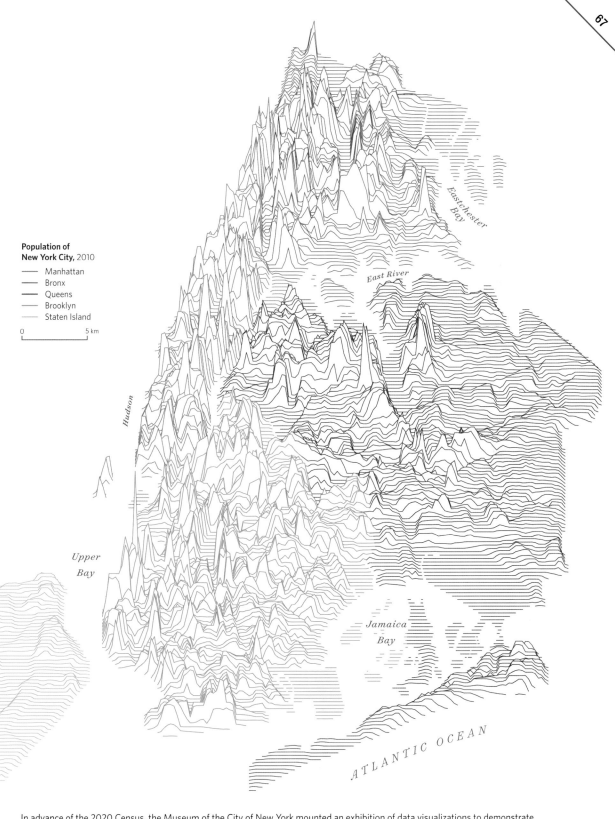

**Population of
New York City,** 2010

—— Manhattan
—— Bronx
—— Queens
—— Brooklyn
—— Staten Island

0   5 km

*Eastchester
Bay*

East River

Hudson

*Upper
Bay*

*Jamaica
Bay*

ATLANTIC OCEAN

In advance of the 2020 Census, the Museum of the City of New York mounted an exhibition of data visualizations to demonstrate the value of the decennial count. Our contribution mapped the city as a landscape of population peaks and valleys. More people live in the mountains of Brooklyn (2.5 million) than in every other city in the rest of the state combined (2.2 million).

value, because they are immediate, and the result of long acquaintance.' Her value for rich social data echoed Madison's. How could you begin to address a growing list of societal ills without first gathering facts? In the case of Hull House, such fact-finding was, to paraphrase Chief Justice Roberts, neither 'arbitrary' nor 'capricious'. The residents never lost sight of the sensitivity of the questions they were asking. In the notes to accompany their maps, they wrote:

> Insistent probing into the lives of the poor would come with bad grace even from government officials . . . and sensational throbs of curious interest are ineffectual as well as unjustifiable. The painful nature of minute investigation, and the personal impertinence of many of the questions asked, would be unendurable and unpardonable were it not for the conviction that the public conscience when roused must demand better surroundings for the most inert and long-suffering citizens.

Three decades before women won the right to vote in the US, the women of Hull House had created what Florence Kelley's biographer, Kathryn Kish Sklar, described as 'the single most important work by American women social scientists before 1900'. And the revolution didn't stop there. Kelley campaigned for fair working hours and minimum wage laws for women, federal funds for infant and maternal healthcare and was a member of the first board of directors of the National Association of the Advancement of Colored People,* whilst Jane Addams, in an effort to end World War I, founded the Women's International League for Peace and Freedom and became the first American woman to win the Nobel Peace Prize.

ALAS, THE LONG-PROVEN SUCCESS of door-to-door mapping within a community has not been enough to slow the move away from this approach. Paying thousands of enumerators to knock on doors is still expensive; the 2020 count was estimated to cost $15.6 billion. Understandably, some governments will look for alternatives, particularly if the findings are expected to favour groups who do not support the governing party. The challenge remains the same as it was for Madison in 1790: how do we gather invisible and 'extremely requisite' data without putting a thumb on the scale? How do we form a more perfect census?

In the past decade, humanity has generated more data about itself than it did in the previous century. Mobile phones, satellites and computer models offer patterns that can inform who we are as individuals and societies. They don't offer the authenticity of the Hull-House maps or the detail of a census, but the expanse and frequency of the data collected are revolutionary too. In this chapter we show you how mobile phones can facilitate head counts seasonally or in the wake of a disaster; we examine how our patterns of movement across borders could aid regional policies or a pandemic response; we use data from satellites to observe the effects of war, trade and urbanization; and we assess levels of access to essential services around the world. These examples are only a sample of what's possible, but they feature enough information 'for idle people to make a book.'

◆

In the past **DECADE,** humanity has generated more data about itself than it did in the previous **CENTURY.**

*W. E. B. Du Bois was the NAACP's Director of Publicity and Research. In his 1932 eulogy to Kelley he reflected that 'for all Florence Kelley's sins against convention, none – not even her socialism and pacifism, her championing of sex equality and religious freedom, her fight for children and democracy – none cost her more fair-weather friends than her demand for the rights of twelve million Americans who are black.'

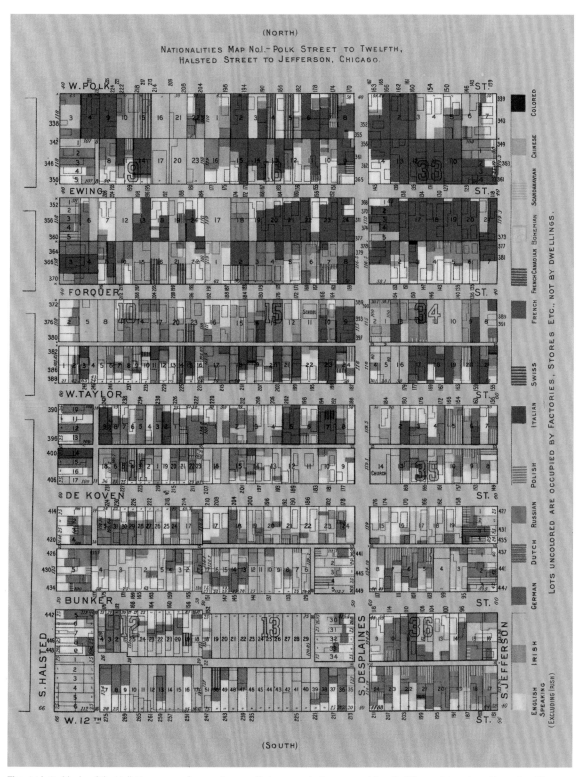

The vivid city blocks of the Hull-House maps form cartograms that pursue clarity over precision. On this one, lots coloured by nationality highlight settlement patterns such as an Italian (blue) enclave on Polk and Ewing Streets. Swatch size indicates the ratio of each group per lot.

UNITED KINGDOM

English Channel

BELGIUM

Lille

HAUTS-DE-FRANCE

GERMANY

LUX.

NORMANDIE

Paris
ÎLE-DE-FRANCE
MAP AREA

GRAND EST

Strasbourg

BRETAGNE

Rennes

PAYS DE
LA LOIRE

CENTRE-VAL
DE LOIRE

Nantes

BOURGOGNE-
FRANCHE-COMTE

F R A N C E

SWITZERLAND

Bay of
Biscay

NOUVELLE-AQUITAINE

AUVERGNE-RHONE-ALPES

Lyon

ITALY

Bordeaux

**Population change
per square kilometre**
May–August 2007

INCREASE
More than 1,000
501–1,000
101–500
51–100
11–50
+/- 10 people
11–50
51–100
101–500
501–5,000
More than 5,000
DECREASE

0   100 km

OCCITANIE

PROVENCE-ALPES-
COTE D'AZUR

Toulouse

Montpellier

MONACO
Nice

S
P
A
I
N

ANDORRA

Marseille

Mediterranean Sea

CORSICA
(FRANCE)

A CENSUS ON DEMAND

With mobile phone data, populations can be estimated anytime, anywhere.

When a nation conducts a census, typically every ten years, forms are planned, mailed, completed, returned, tabulated and analysed. The whole process takes years—and money. The 2011 UK Census cost £482 million to administer. Some nations cannot afford such expense. Even if they can, decennial counts are freeze-frames. By asking for our place of residence, a traditional census yields a map of where we sleep, not where we work or travel during the day. Nor does it show seasonal changes or how a sudden disaster, conflict or epidemic impacts a nation.

In 2014, researchers at the University of Southampton demonstrated that mobile phone records could fill in the gaps. Using census figures as a guide, they refined a method to convert anonymized phone data densities into reliable population densities. As a proof of concept, the team mapped the flows from French cities to beaches in the summer months. Now they're developing fast, cheap and near real-time tools for countries without a recent census. For example, when an earthquake struck Nepal in 2015, they were able to detect and direct aid to the displaced population. This is not to say a traditional census is obsolete. We still need to fill out those forms to capture extra details, such as age, gender and ethnicity, that tell us not just how many of us are in the room, but who's here.

SOURCES: WORLDPOP; DEVILLE ET AL. (2014)

Persan

Parc Astérix

L'Isle-Adam

FORÊT DE
L'ISLE-ADAM

Oise

Pontoise

Charles
de Gaulle
Airport

Seine

Le Bourget
Airport

Canal de l'Ourcq

FORÊT DE
SAINT-GERMAIN

Sartrouville

Chambourcy

Villemomble

Château de
Saint-Germain-
en-Laye

P A R I S

Marne

Eiffel
Tower

Cathédrale
Notre-Dame
de Paris

*Domaine national
de Saint-Cloud*

Château de
Versailles

Fort d'Ivry

Vélodrome de
Saint-Quentin-
en-Yvelines

Orly
Airport

Yerres

Palaiseau

Vigneux-
sur-Seine

The French flock to
airports and rail stations
to escape summers in
'the Hexagon'. Destinations
abroad include Martinique,
Seychelles and Morocco.
Closer to home, parks,
forests and riverbanks help
Parisians beat the heat.

FORÊT DE SÉNART

Champrosay

Arpajon

Essonne

Seine

Railway

0   8 km

AN AMERICAN EXODUS

Our phones record our movements. In a crisis, that's a good thing.

When Hurricane Maria struck Puerto Rico in September 2017, aid workers scrambled to identify areas of greatest need. With downed trees and washed-out roads limiting access, they had to rely on remote sensing to understand the storm's impact. Light-detecting satellites revealed where the island lost power while a novel use of mobile phone data revealed where the island lost people.

By matching anonymized users to their nearest cell towers, a company called Teralytics was able to take a coarse measure of population change in Maria's wake. Users who spent most of their time near towers in Puerto Rico before the hurricane were considered residents. If those residents started connecting to towers in the mainland United States after the storm, Teralytics assumed they had fled the island. While this approach did not capture everyone, it offered a fair proxy. In the first four months, more than 300,000 of Puerto Rico's 3.3 million residents were detected in new locations. As the red emigration arcs on this spread reveal, Florida alone received nearly half the influx with many landing in Miami and Orlando. Not until January 2018 were Puerto Ricans more often recorded connecting to cell towers back home.

Changes in mobile phone locations
for Puerto Rican residents
September 2017 – January 2018

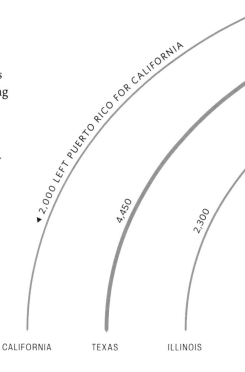

2,000 LEFT PUERTO RICO FOR CALIFORNIA

4,450

2,300

CALIFORNIA   TEXAS   ILLINOIS

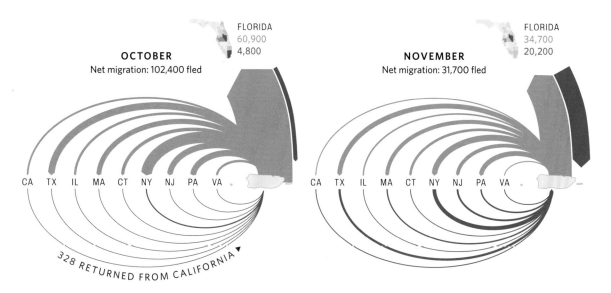

OCTOBER
Net migration: 102,400 fled

FLORIDA
60,900
4,800

CA   TX   IL   MA   CT   NY   NJ   PA   VA

328 RETURNED FROM CALIFORNIA ▶

NOVEMBER
Net migration: 31,700 fled

FLORIDA
34,700
20,200

CA   TX   IL   MA   CT   NY   NJ   PA   VA

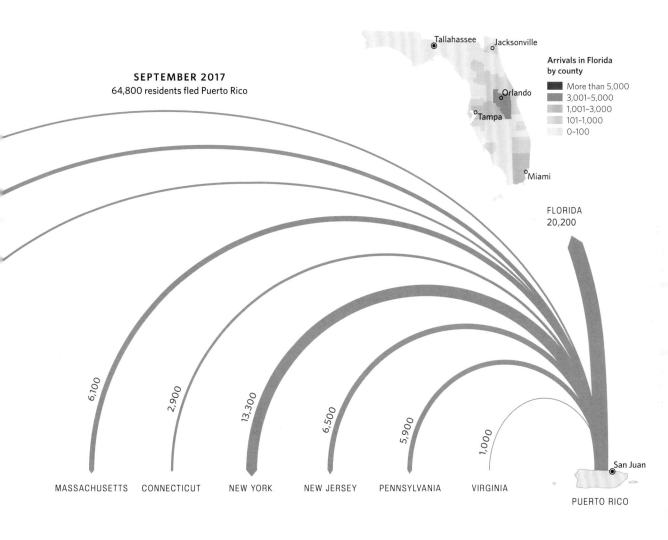

SEPTEMBER 2017
64,800 residents fled Puerto Rico

Arrivals in Florida
by county
- More than 5,000
- 3,001–5,000
- 1,001–3,000
- 101–1,000
- 0–100

Tallahassee
Jacksonville
Orlando
Tampa
Miami

FLORIDA
20,200

6,100
2,900
13,300
6,500
5,900
1,000

MASSACHUSETTS   CONNECTICUT   NEW YORK   NEW JERSEY   PENNSYLVANIA   VIRGINIA

San Juan

PUERTO RICO

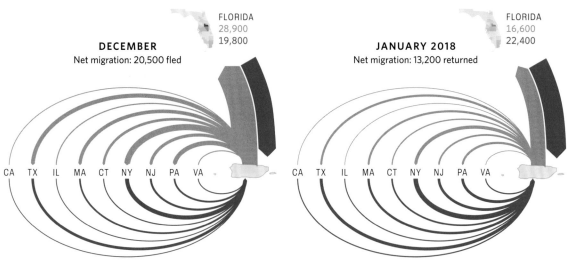

DECEMBER
Net migration: 20,500 fled

FLORIDA
28,900
19,800

CA   TX   IL   MA   CT   NY   NJ   PA   VA

JANUARY 2018
Net migration: 13,200 returned

FLORIDA
16,600
22,400

CA   TX   IL   MA   CT   NY   NJ   PA   VA

ATLAS OF THE INVISIBLE

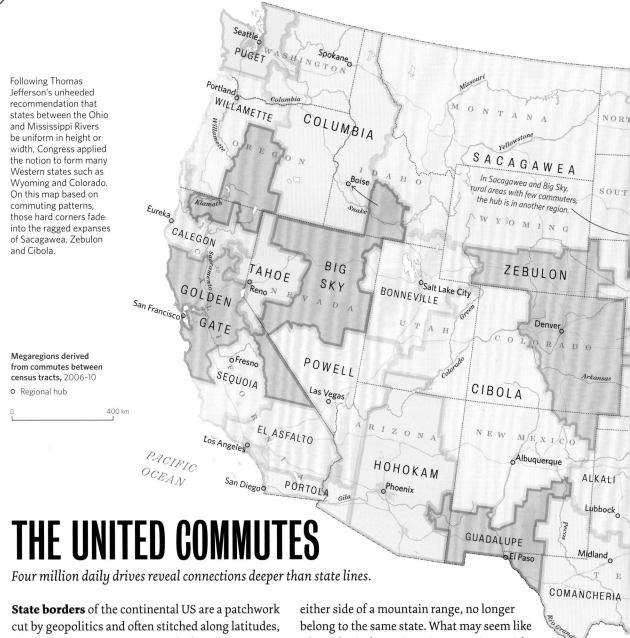

Following Thomas Jefferson's unheeded recommendation that states between the Ohio and Mississippi Rivers be uniform in height or width, Congress applied the notion to form many Western states such as Wyoming and Colorado. On this map based on commuting patterns, those hard corners fade into the ragged expanses of Sacagawea, Zebulon and Cibola.

In Sacagawea and Big Sky, rural areas with few commuters, the hub is in another region.

Megaregions derived from commutes between census tracts, 2006–10

○ Regional hub

0   400 km

THE UNITED COMMUTES

Four million daily drives reveal connections deeper than state lines.

State borders of the continental US are a patchwork cut by geopolitics and often stitched along latitudes, rivers and mountain ranges. Each shape has a story behind it. However, such histories rarely reflect the present needs of a state's residents. If we were to redraw the boundaries today, how might we do it?

In 2016, geographers Garrett Nelson and Alasdair Rae proposed an answer. By connecting the home and work locations of four million Americans, they produced an array of commuting hubs. They then ran these through a community-detection algorithm, which grouped highly connected hubs together. As a result, Philadelphia and Pittsburgh, two cities on

either side of a mountain range, no longer belong to the same state. What may seem like a hypothetical exercise raises questions with real-world implications. Currently, if Ohio takes better care of its roads than Michigan, the potholes between Toledo and Detroit will be felt every day of a commuter's life. Whereas if borders were redrawn as shown, that entire commute would be governed by the Entrelacs Department of Transportation.

Boundaries based on where people actually spend their lives would allow leaders to plan regional transit, power grids and housing with their eyes on the road ahead rather than in the rear-view mirror.

SOURCES: NELSON AND RAE (2016); AMERICAN COMMUNITY SURVEY

DAKOTA

LAURENTIDE

MINNESOTA

DAKOTA

Minneapolis

Sioux Falls

Missouri

PLATTE

NEBRASKA

Omaha

Platte

IOWA

Des Moines

QUIVIRA

KANSAS

Kansas City

St. Louis

MISSOURI

TWAIN

GUTHRIE

OKLAHOMA

Oklahoma City

Canadian

ARKANSAS

Memphis

OUACHITA

Red

WHITEROCK

Dallas

Sabine

YANAGUANA

Austin

AKOKISA

Houston

RIO GRANDE

Corpus Christi

TERREBONNE

LOUISIANA

New Orleans

MISSISSIPPI

ALABAMA

Birmingham

KING

Gulf of Mexico

Lake Superior

Marquette

GICHI GAMI

M

WISCONSIN

WINNEBAGO

Milwaukee

Lake Michigan

ENTRELACS

Detroit

Lake Huron

Chicago

SANDBURG

CORNTASSEL

Illinois

INDIANA

TECUMSEH

Indianapolis

ILLINOIS

TOLEDO STRIP

CUYAHOGA

Cleveland

L. Erie

OHIO

Columbus

Ohio

CHILLICOTHE

WEST VIRGINIA

Louisville

PENNYROYAL

KENTUCKY

BLUE RIDGE

Nashville

Knoxville

CUMBERLAND

TENNESSEE

Tennessee

VIRGINIA

Roanoke

ROANOKE

Raleigh

NORTH CAROLINA

Charlotte

CATALPA

SOUTH CAROLINA

Pee Dee

Savannah

PEACHTREE

Atlanta

GEORGIA

Chattahoochee

LOWCOUNTRY

Charleston

Alabama

FLORIDA

St. Johns

SUNLAND

Orlando

COSTA DE PALMAS

Miami

ATLANTIC OCEAN

MAINE

MAYFLOWER

CHAMPLAIN

VT.

N.H.

Connecticut

Boston

NEW YORK

HAUDENOSAUNEE

Buffalo

Albany

MASS.

Hartford

CONN. R.I.

QUINETUCKET

Hudson

MANAHATTA

New York

NEW JERSEY

PENNSYLVANIA

ALLEGHENY

Pittsburgh

FRANKLIN

Philadelphia

DEL.

Delaware

Susquehanna

MARYLAND

CHESAPEAKE

Potomac

Washington

MONTICELLO

Richmond

When Texas and California sought to join the US in the 1840s, both had enough political or economic sway to keep their vast claims. Today, commuters subdivide the two giant states each into seven micro-geographies.

Michigan's Upper Peninsula, once an arm of the Wisconsin Territory, was a concession to Michigan for ceding the Toledo Strip to Ohio in 1836. Here, the Upper Peninsula becomes autonomous whilst the Lower Peninsula gets Toledo back.

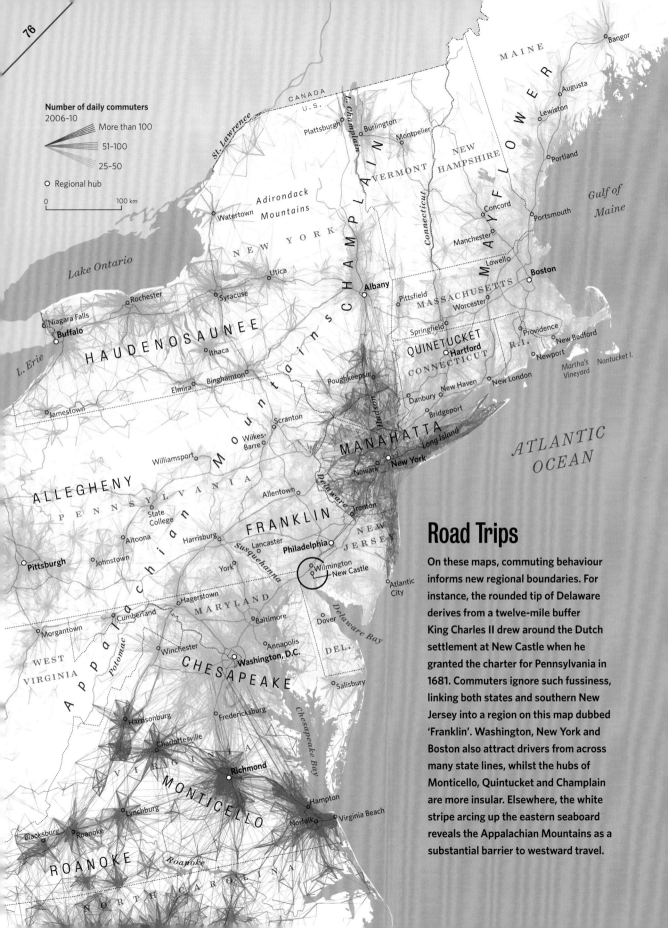

Number of daily commuters
2006–10

More than 100

51–100

25–50

○ Regional hub

0   100 km

Road Trips

On these maps, commuting behaviour informs new regional boundaries. For instance, the rounded tip of Delaware derives from a twelve-mile buffer King Charles II drew around the Dutch settlement at New Castle when he granted the charter for Pennsylvania in 1681. Commuters ignore such fussiness, linking both states and southern New Jersey into a region on this map dubbed 'Franklin'. Washington, New York and Boston also attract drivers from across many state lines, whilst the hubs of Monticello, Quintucket and Champlain are more insular. Elsewhere, the white stripe arcing up the eastern seaboard reveals the Appalachian Mountains as a substantial barrier to westward travel.

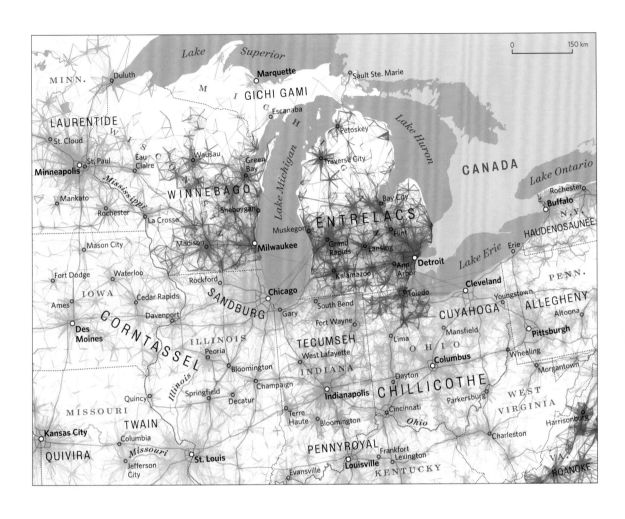

Lake Superior

MINN.
Duluth
Marquette
Sault Ste. Marie
M
I GICHI GAMI
C Escanaba
H
LAURENTIDE
St. Cloud
Petoskey
Lake Huron
CANADA
Lake Ontario
Rochester
Buffalo
N.Y.
Wausau
St. Paul
Eau
Claire
Green
Bay
Traverse City
Bay City
Minneapolis
WISCON
Mankato
Mississippi
WINNEBAGO
Sheboygan
ENTRELACS
Flint
HAUDENOSAUNEE
Rochester
La Crosse
Muskegon
Lansing
Erie
Lake Erie
Mason City
Madison
Milwaukee
Grand
Rapids
Ann
Detroit
PENN.
Fort Dodge
Waterloo
IOWA
Rockford
Chicago
Kalamazoo
Arbor
Cleveland
Youngstown
ALLEGHENY
Altoona
Cedar Rapids
SANDBURG
Gary
South Bend
Toledo
CUYAHOGA
Ames
Davenport
Fort Wayne
Lima
Mansfield
Pittsburgh
Des
Moines
CORNTASSEL
ILLINOIS
Peoria
TECUMSEH
West Lafayette
OHIO
Columbus
Wheeling
Morgantown
Bloomington
INDIANA
Dayton
WEST
Quincy
Springfield
Champaign
Indianapolis
CHILLICOTHE
Parkersburg
VIRGINIA
Harrisonburg
MISSOURI
Decatur
Terre
Haute
Bloomington
Cincinnati
Ohio
Kansas City
TWAIN
Columbia
St. Louis
PENNYROYAL
Frankfort
Lexington
Charleston
VA.
QUIVIRA
Missouri
Jefferson
City
Evansville
Louisville
KENTUCKY
ROANOKE

OKLA.
OUACHITA
Pine Bluff
Birmingham
ARKANSAS
Columbus
Tuscaloosa
Starksville
KING
Texarkana
El Dorado
MISSISSIPPI
ALABAMA
WHITEROCK
Longview
Monroe
Meridian
Montgomery
Tyler
Shreveport
Vicksburg
Jackson
Alabama
LOUISIANA
Natchez
Lufkin
Mississippi
Hattiesburg
FLA.
Alexandria
TERREBONNE
TEXAS
Baton
Rouge
Mobile
Pensacola
AKOKISA
Biloxi
Beaumont
Lake
Charles
Lafayette
Slidell
Houston
Port
Arthur
New Orleans
Houma
Galveston
Gulf of Mexico
0   150 km

Commuters in the
Midwest cross existing
state boundaries
daily to create highly
connected regions
such as Corntassel
and Chillicothe. By
contrast, residents of
Louisiana and southern
Mississippi stay true to
their home state.

ATLANTIC
OCEAN

MAURITANIA

Nouakchott

SENEGAL

Kayes
Oct. 2014

Mali
After attending a
funeral in Guinea, a girl
and her grandmother
travelled home by bus
along the N6 motorway
to Mali, bringing Ebola
back with them.

M A L I

Dakar
August 2014

Bamako

Senegal
Rapid response limited
Senegal's outbreak to
one patient, a Guinean
student who traveled
overland to Dakar while
on summer break from
Conakry University. The
young man contracted
Ebola from his brother,
who had recently visited
Sierra Leone.

THE
GAMBIA   Banjul

GUINEA-BISSAU

Bissau

Kourémalé

Siguiri

G   N6

Kankan

U

I

Conakry

Forécariah

Kissidougou

**Spread of Ebola across
road network clusters**
2014–16

    Road network cluster

    Cluster where outbreak began

    Patient zero

    Transmission route

SIERRA
LEONE

Meliandou
Dec. 2013

Macenta

N
E
A

CÔTE D'IVOIRE
(IVORY COAST)

Freetown

To Spain
October 2014
U.K.
December 2014
Italy
May 2015

Yamoussoukro

0   300 km

L   I   B   E   R   I   A

Monrovia

To U.S.
September 2014

ROADS TO RECOVERY

In commerce and contagion, the connections between places matter most.

In December 2013, a toddler in the village of Meliandou in southern Guinea developed a fever. He died four days later. Epidemiologists now consider this boy, Emile Ouamouno, 'patient zero' in the 2014–16 West African Ebola epidemic. Within a month of his death, Emile's mother, sister and grandmother were dead too. A woman who attended his grandmother's funeral fell ill and passed the disease to a healthcare worker who passed it to her doctor in Macenta who passed it to his brothers in Kissidougou. By the time enough testing,

training, contact tracing and community education were in place to suppress the virus, more than 11,000 people had died in Guinea, Liberia and Sierra Leone.

If the outbreak had begun on an island, containment would have been relatively straightforward: screen anyone who leaves. But in the tight-knit geography of West Africa, screening every inland border crossing is impractical. One possible solution: identify a region's most likely transmission routes in advance. With the aid of an algorithm,

SOURCES: STRANO ET AL. (2018); CDC (CHART)

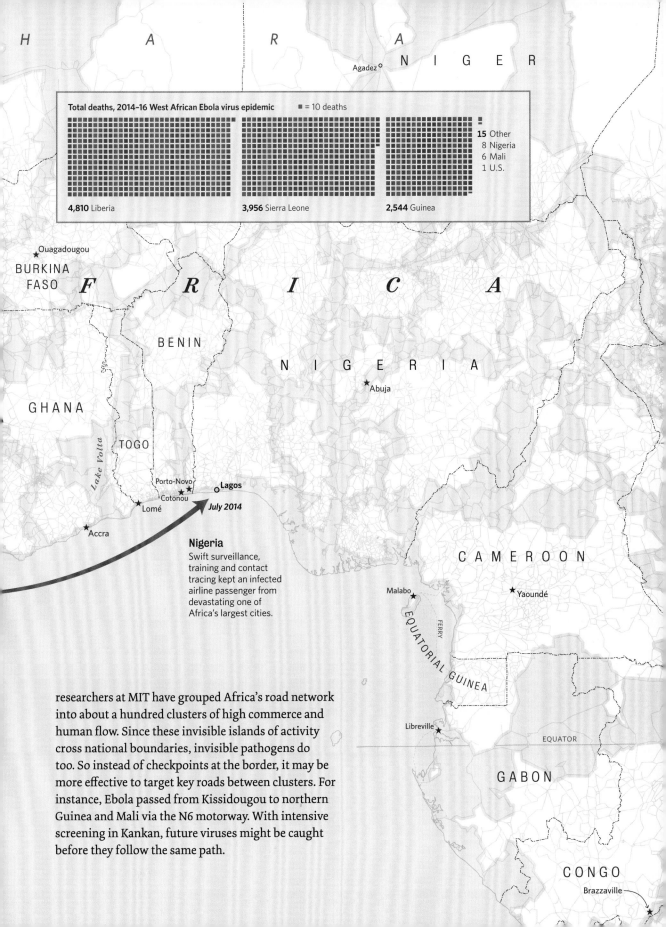

H A R A N
Agadez ○
N I G E R

Total deaths, 2014–16 West African Ebola virus epidemic   ■ = 10 deaths

4,810 Liberia	**3,956** Sierra Leone	**2,544** Guinea

15 Other
8 Nigeria
6 Mali
1 U.S.

Ouagadougou ★
BURKINA
FASO
F R I C A

BENIN

GHANA
TOGO
NIGERIA
★ Abuja

Lake Volta

Porto-Novo
★ ★ ○ Lagos
Cotonou
★ *July 2014*
Lomé

★ Accra

Nigeria
Swift surveillance,
training and contact
tracing kept an infected
airline passenger from
devastating one of
Africa's largest cities.

CAMEROON

Malabo ★
★ Yaoundé

EQUATORIAL GUINEA

FERRY

Libreville ★
EQUATOR

GABON

researchers at MIT have grouped Africa's road network
into about a hundred clusters of high commerce and
human flow. Since these invisible islands of activity
cross national boundaries, invisible pathogens do
too. So instead of checkpoints at the border, it may be
more effective to target key roads between clusters. For
instance, Ebola passed from Kissidougou to northern
Guinea and Mali via the N6 motorway. With intensive
screening in Kankan, future viruses might be caught
before they follow the same path.

CONGO
Brazzaville →

Edinburgh

DENMARK

Copenhagen

Moscow

UNITED
KINGDOM

Dublin

IRELAND

London

Berlin

Minsk

GERMANY

POLAND

Warsaw

BELARUS

Brussels

Rhine

BELG.

Kyiv

Paris

E U R O P E

UKRAINE

ATLANTIC
OCEAN

FRANCE

Vistula

Milan

ROMANIA

Belgrade

Bucharest

SERBIA

Danube

Black Sea

Rome

Madrid

ITALY

Istanbul

PORTUGAL

SPAIN

Ankara

GREECE

T U R K E Y

Lisbon

Athens

M e d i t e r r a n e a n S e a

Algiers

Tunis

SYRIA

Casablanca

TUNISIA

Tripoli

IRAQ

MOROCCO

Alexandria

Cairo

AREA ENLARGED

ALGERIA

LIBYA

Nile

SAUDI
ARABIA

EGYPT

Medina

Aswan

S A H A R A

Jeddah

Mecca

Red Sea

A F R I C A

Niger

NIGER

CHAD

SUDAN

Khartoum

Niamey

N'Djamena

NIGERIA

Addis Ababa

GHANA

Lagos

ETHIOPIA

Accra

Port Harcourt

TURKEY

Konya

TAURUS MOUNTAINS

Ceyhan

Adana

Sanliurfa

Gaziantep

Al Hasakah

Hatay

Aleppo

Ar Raqqah

Euphrates

Latakia

SYRIA

Dayr az Zawr

NORTHERN
CYPRUS

Nicosia

CYPRUS

Dhekelia
(U.K. Base)

Hamah

Akrotiri
(U.K. Base)

Homs

Mediterranean Sea

Tadmur
(Palmyra)

Beirut

LEBANON

Change in light emissions
2012–16

Damascus

*Boundary
claimed by Syria*

Darker   Lighter

Syrian refugees, 2016

◆ Refugee camp

→ Border crossing

GOLAN
HEIGHTS

As Suwayda

Dara

Air travel to Egypt

Haifa

Irbid

S Y R I A N

0   100 km

SOURCES: NASA-NOAA
SUOMI-NPP VIIRS; UNHCR
(REFUGEE CAMPS)

Tel Aviv-Yafo

WEST
BANK

Jordan

Amman

D E S E R T

Jerusalem ★

GAZA
STRIP

*Dead
Sea*

ISRAEL   JORDAN

Port Said

Al Qurayyat

EGYPT

Sakaka

Suez

S I N A I

Al Aqabah

Gulf of Suez

Gulf of Aqaba

SAUDI ARABIA

Tabuk

RUSSIA

URAL LINE

Kazan

Yekaterinburg

TRANS-SIBERIAN RAILWAY

Omsk

Novosibirsk

Irkutsk

Volga

Nur-Sultan

K A Z A K H S T A N

A S I A

MONGO

Urumqi

UZBEKISTAN

Bishkek

Tashkent

KYRGYZSTAN

Tarim Basin

AZERB.

Baku

Caspian Sea

TURKMENISTAN

TAJIKISTAN

Dushanbe

Ashgabat

Plateau of Tibet

C

Tehran

Kabul

H

I

M

A

L

Lhasa

IRAN

AFGHANISTAN

Islamabad

Brahmaputra

Lahore

Indus

Delhi

NEPAL

Kathmandu

A

Y

A

PAKISTAN

Jaipur

Kanpur

Patna

BANGLADESH

Ganges

Dhaka

Karachi

Kolkata

MYANMA
(BURMA)

Ad Dammam

Dubai

INDIA

Raipur

Doha

Muscat

QATAR

U.A.E.

O
M
A
N

Mumbai

Arabian Sea

Hyderabad

Bay of Bengal

Rangoon

India

When Prime Minister Modi was elected in 2014 he promised electricity to all of India, a country where many were off the grid. Since then more than 25 million households have received a free or heavily subsidized link to the national grid as part of the plan, which in 2017 he named Saubhagya, Hindi for 'good fortune'.

Bengaluru

Chennai

Salem

7

INDIAN OCEAN

Me

Lake
Baikal

Chita

Khabarovsk

Ulaanbaatar

TRANS-MONGOLIAN LINE

Sapporo

Vladivostok

Shenyang

NORTH
KOREA

JAPAN

Yellow

Beijing

Tianjin

Pyongyang

CHINA

Seoul

Tokyo

SOUTH
KOREA

Osaka

Chengdu

Yangtze

Shanghai

Chongqing

Change in light emissions
2012–16

Darker   Lighter

0   500 km

SOURCE: NASA-NOAA
SUOMI-NPP VIIRS

PACIFIC
OCEAN

Guangzhou

Shenzhen

Hong Kong

Hanoi

North Korea

On average, North Koreans
consume just 602 kilowatt
hours a year, seventeen
times less than South
Koreans. The regime's
official newspaper *Rodong
Sinmun* puts a positive spin
on it: '[Detractors] clap
their hands and get loud
over a satellite picture of
our city with not much light,
but the essence of society
is not on flashy lights.'

South
China
Sea

VIETNAM

Mekong

THAILAND

Manila

Bangkok

PHILIPPINES

China

The number of long-
distance migrants
increased from 163 million
in 2012 to 169 million in
2016. As a result, rural
areas are dimming as cities
light up (pp. 86–7).

Ho Chi Minh City

MALAYSIA

Kuala Lumpur

ATLAS OF THE INVISIBLE

LIGHT LEVELS

A new satellite illuminates humans in the dark.

En route to the moon on December 7, 1972, astronauts aboard Apollo 17 saw
the Earth receding into the blackness of space and took a photograph that
forever changed how we view our planet. The iconic image came to be known as
'The Blue Marble.' Forty years later, scientists at NASA unveiled the 'Black Marble'
– a mosaic of nighttime images that jolts our perspective once more.

In recent years, a revolutionary light sensor and the advent of algorithms to
remove moonlight and other natural variables have allowed satellite imagery
to be comparable from night to night and year to year. On this foldout, we've
combined light emissions data from 2012 and 2016 to reveal places where lights
have switched on (yellow), where they have dimmed (blue) and where they have
remained the same (grey). From these patterns, it's possible to see the effects
of war, economic development, urbanization and increases in energy efficiency
as well as sudden changes in human activity. For example, NASA has supplied
images of outages to aid first responders in the wake of hurricanes and to reveal
the extent of a blackout that enshrouded Venezuela for days (p. 108). Turn the
page to see how conflict has darkened the Middle East.

**Change in light emissions
2012–16**

Darker   Lighter

Western Europe

While energy use may
still be rising in Europe,
down-facing street lamps,
LED bulbs, smart sensors
and other measures have
reduced light pollution in
many cities.

Nigeria

Lagos has grown by more
than thirty per cent since
2010. With more than 14
million inhabitants, it is now
the second-largest urban area
in Africa (Cairo: 21 million).

Saharan States

It is estimated that
80 million people live in
Niger, Chad and Sudan, yet
few lights appear outside
their capitals. Because
access to electricity is
limited, people use solid
fuel for heating and light,
which renders them
invisible to NASA's
light-seeking satellites.

Russia

Development along the
Trans-Siberian Railway
forms a constellation from
Moscow to Lake Baikal,
then on to Mongolia, China
and Vladivostok.

Saudi Arabia

The government has been
investing billions to boost
tourism. In 2017, they
announced plans for a
mega-city along the Red Sea,
which at forty times the
size of Mumbai, will flood
the coast with light.

Syria

The destruction of Aleppo
during the Syrian civil war
has, for many reasons,
made it one of the darkest
spots on the map. Egypt,
Iraq, Jordan, Lebanon
and Turkey have taken in
millions of refugees. Camps
create pools of light near
the Syrian border and in
northern Iraq, where nightlife has begun to switch
back on after the Iraq war.

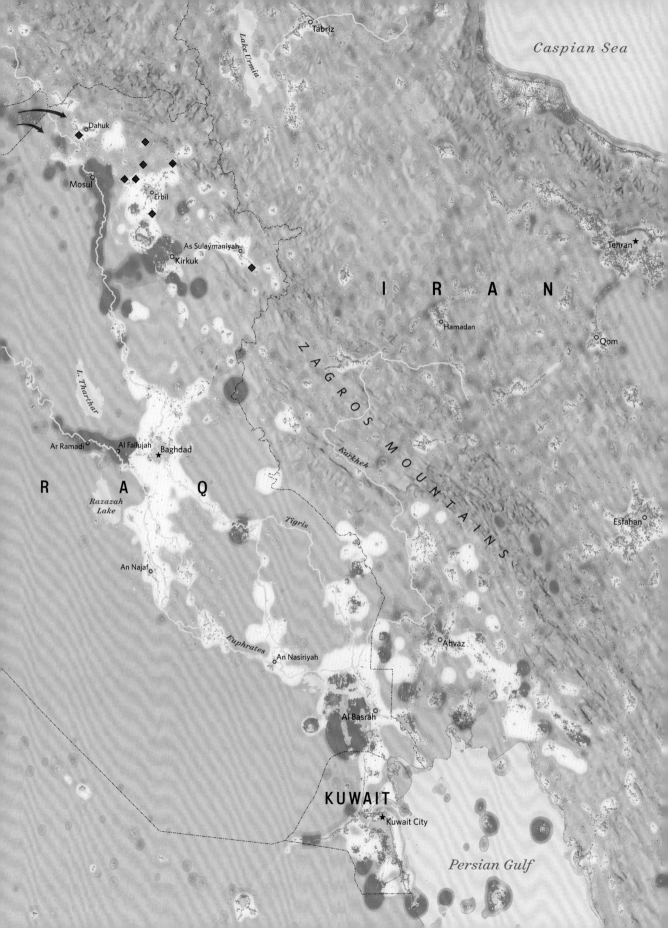

Caspian Sea

Tabriz

Lake Urmia

Dahuk

Mosul

Erbil

As Sulaymaniyah

Kirkuk

IRAN

Tehran

Hamadan

Qom

ZAGROS MOUNTAINS

L. Tharthar

Karkheh

Ar Ramadi

Al Fallujah

Baghdad

I R A Q

Razazah Lake

Esfahan

Tigris

An Najaf

Ahvaz

Euphrates

An Nasiriyah

Al Basrah

KUWAIT

Kuwait City

Persian Gulf

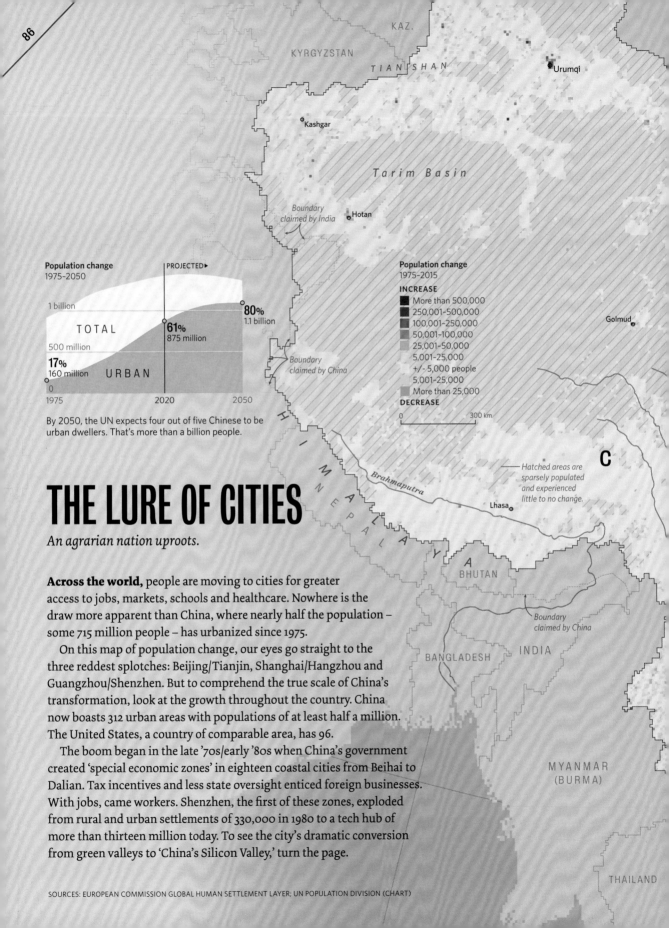

KAZ.

KYRGYZSTAN

TIAN SHAN

Urumqi

Kashgar

Tarim Basin

Boundary claimed by India

Hotan

Golmud

Population change
1975–2050

PROJECTED ▶

1 billion

TOTAL

61%
875 million

500 million

80%
1.1 billion

17%
160 million

URBAN

0

1975   2020   2050

By 2050, the UN expects four out of five Chinese to be
urban dwellers. That's more than a billion people.

Population change
1975–2015

INCREASE

■ More than 500,000
■ 250,001–500,000
■ 100,001–250,000
■ 50,001–100,000
■ 25,001–50,000
■ 5,001–25,000
■ +/– 5,000 people
■ 5,001–25,000
■ More than 25,000

DECREASE

0   300 km

Boundary claimed by China

H
I
M
A
L
A
Y
A

Brahmaputra

Lhasa

C

— *Hatched areas are sparsely populated and experienced little to no change.*

A

BHUTAN

Boundary claimed by China

BANGLADESH   INDIA

MYANMAR
(BURMA)

THAILAND

THE LURE OF CITIES

An agrarian nation uproots.

Across the world, people are moving to cities for greater
access to jobs, markets, schools and healthcare. Nowhere is the
draw more apparent than China, where nearly half the population –
some 715 million people – has urbanized since 1975.

On this map of population change, our eyes go straight to the
three reddest splotches: Beijing/Tianjin, Shanghai/Hangzhou and
Guangzhou/Shenzhen. But to comprehend the true scale of China's
transformation, look at the growth throughout the country. China
now boasts 312 urban areas with populations of at least half a million.
The United States, a country of comparable area, has 96.

The boom began in the late '70s/early '80s when China's government
created 'special economic zones' in eighteen coastal cities from Beihai to
Dalian. Tax incentives and less state oversight enticed foreign businesses.
With jobs, came workers. Shenzhen, the first of these zones, exploded
from rural and urban settlements of 330,000 in 1980 to a tech hub of
more than thirteen million today. To see the city's dramatic conversion
from green valleys to 'China's Silicon Valley,' turn the page.

SOURCES: EUROPEAN COMMISSION GLOBAL HUMAN SETTLEMENT LAYER; UN POPULATION DIVISION (CHART)

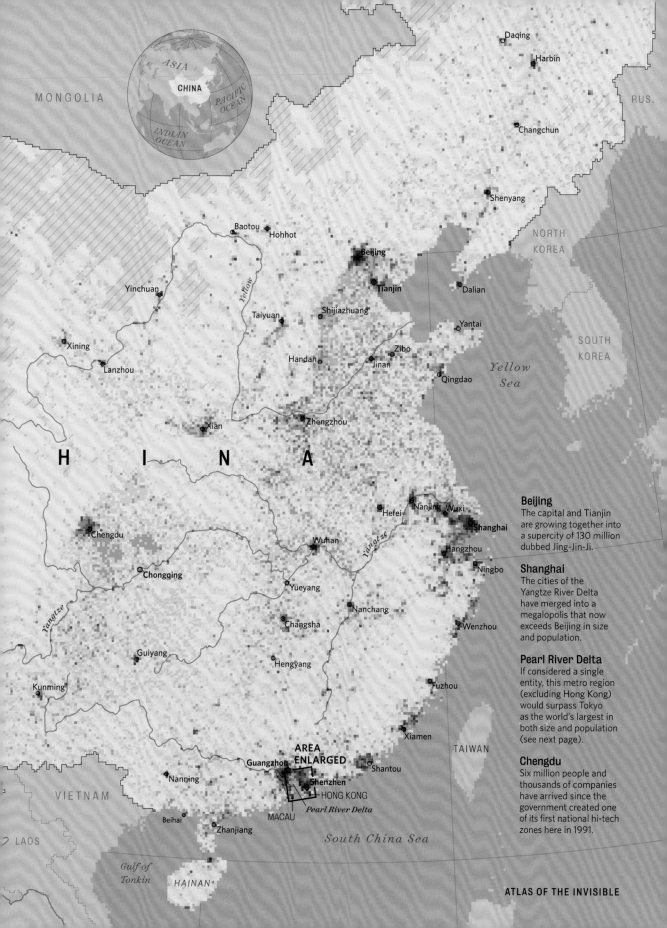

MONGOLIA

RUS.

Daqing

Harbin

Changchun

Shenyang

NORTH
KOREA

Baotou
Hohhot

Beijing

Tianjin
Dalian

Yinchuan

Yantai

SOUTH
KOREA

Yellow

Taiyuan

Shijiazhuang

Zibo

Xining

Handan

Jinan

Qingdao

*Yellow
Sea*

Lanzhou

Xi'an

Zhengzhou

H   I   N   A

Chengdu

Hefei   Nanjing   Wuxi
Shanghai

Wuhan

Yangtze

Hangzhou

Chongqing

Ningbo

Yueyang

Nanchang

Wenzhou

Changsha

Yangtze

Guiyang

Hengyang

Fuzhou

Kunming

Xiamen

TAIWAN

**AREA
ENLARGED**

Guangzhou

Shantou

Nanning

Shenzhen

HONG KONG

Pearl River Delta

MACAU

VIETNAM

Beihai

Zhanjiang

South China Sea

LAOS

*Gulf of
Tonkin*

HAINAN

Beijing

The capital and Tianjin
are growing together into
a supercity of 130 million
dubbed Jing-Jin-Ji.

Shanghai

The cities of the
Yangtze River Delta
have merged into a
megalopolis that now
exceeds Beijing in size
and population.

Pearl River Delta

If considered a single
entity, this metro region
(excluding Hong Kong)
would surpass Tokyo
as the world's largest in
both size and population
(see next page).

Chengdu

Six million people and
thousands of companies
have arrived since the
government created one
of its first national hi-tech
zones here in 1991.

ATLAS OF THE INVISIBLE

ASIA
CHINA
PACIFIC
OCEAN
INDIAN
OCEAN

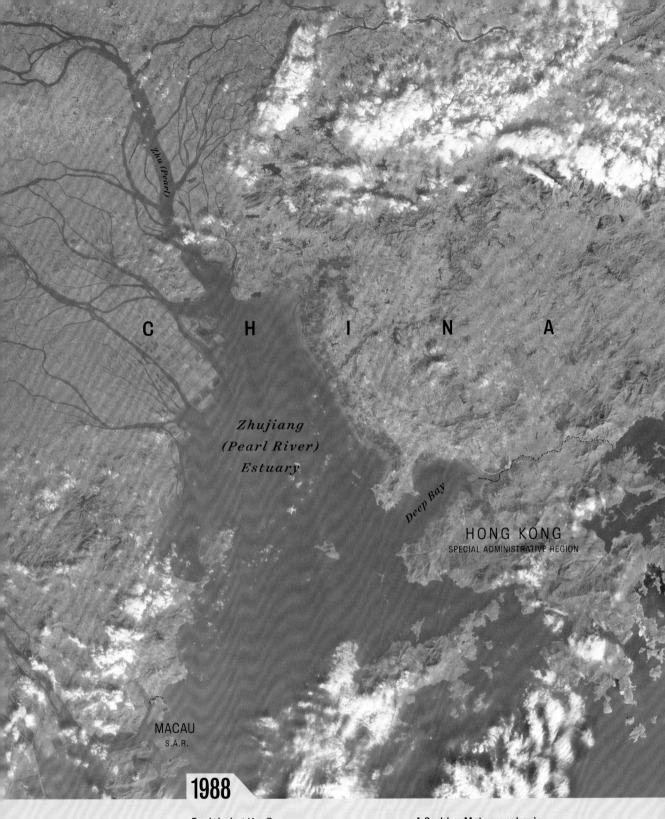

Zhu (Pearl)

C H I N A

Zhujiang (Pearl River) Estuary

Deep Bay

HONG KONG
SPECIAL ADMINISTRATIVE REGION

MACAU
S.A.R.

1988

Change in land cover
1988–2018

0 ——————— 10 km

SOURCE: NASA LANDSAT

Reclaiming the Sea
The Pearl River Delta, once a backwater of farms and wetlands, has become a hotbed for land reclamation. Developers formed angular coastlines and artificial islands, including Hong Kong International Airport, from the teal streaks of alluvial sediment in the image above.

A Sudden Metamorphosis
In 1988, urban centres of Guangzhou, Dongguan, Shenzhen and Zhongshan were still in their larval stage. As they grew, they denuded the lower elevations. Now the Guangdong–Hong Kong–Macau Greater Bay Area has more residents than Canada and Australia combined.

Guangzhou

Dongguan

Shenzhen Bao'an
International
Airport

Zhongshan

Shenzhen–Zhongshan Bridge
(UNDER CONSTRUCTION)

Shenzhen

⚓ Yantian

⚓ Shekou

Hong Kong
International Airport

Hong Kong
border crossing

Hong Kong–Zhuhai–Macau Bridge

Hong Kong
Disneyland

— TUNNEL

Zhuhai

Macau
border crossing

Macau
International
Airport

SOUTH CHINA SEA

2018

Ports of Export

The Port of Shekou opened in 1989, followed by
the Port of Yantian five years later. Together, they
made Shenzhen the third busiest container port
in the world, surpassing Hong Kong in 2013. Nine
out of ten containers leaving the port are exports,
with about half headed for North America.

Building Bridges

The delta can only function as one big city if it's
well-connected. The Hong Kong–Zhuhai–Macau
bridge-tunnel system took a 55-kilometre step to
addressing that need when it opened in 2018.
Another super span is under construction that will
cut commutes across the estuary to thirty minutes.

ATLAS OF THE INVISIBLE

REVOLUTIONARY TRANSPORT

Once a fringe idea, bike-sharing is now de rigueur.

In 1965, a group of Dutch anarchists, known as Provo, announced a plan to rid Amsterdam of cars. Envisioning streets free of the 'asphalt terror of the motorized bourgeoisie', they demanded 10,000 white bicycles, unlocked and free to ride. Provo provided the first fifty bikes, but these were immediately impounded by the police to discourage theft.

Sixty years on, it's clear that Provo were pedalling far ahead of the pack. Bike share has become a must-have for any mayor wishing to claim green city credentials. By 2020 over 3,000 sharing systems were operating worldwide, making it one of the fastest growing modes of urban transportation. As the congestion on this page suggests, not all systems are headed in the right direction. A healthy one, such as New York's, has lots of bikes that are used many times a day. These appear towards the top right of our plot. Those lagging behind have fewer bikes, which few people use. Auckland and Christchurch may want to shut theirs down, whilst with a bit more promotion middling cities could match the likes of Rio.

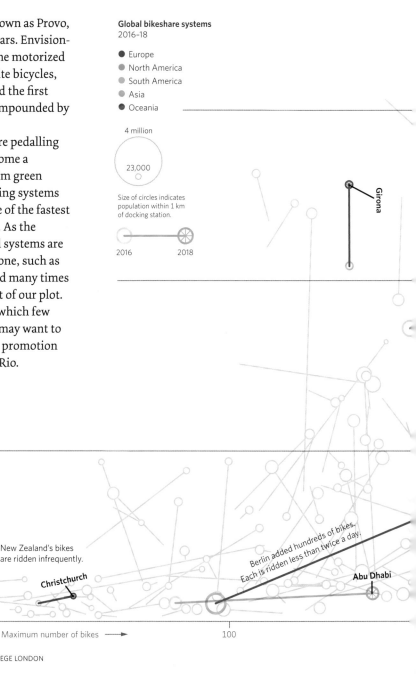

Global bikeshare systems
2016–18

- Europe
- North America
- South America
- Asia
- Oceania

4 million

23,000

Size of circles indicates population within 1 km of docking station.

2016   2018

Girona

2 trips per bike per day

1

New Zealand's bikes are ridden infrequently.

Auckland

Christchurch

Berlin added hundreds of bikes. Each is ridden less than twice a day.

Abu Dhabi

0

10   ⟵ Maximum number of bikes ⟶   100

SOURCE: JAMES TODD AND OLIVER O'BRIEN, UNIVERSITY COLLEGE LONDON

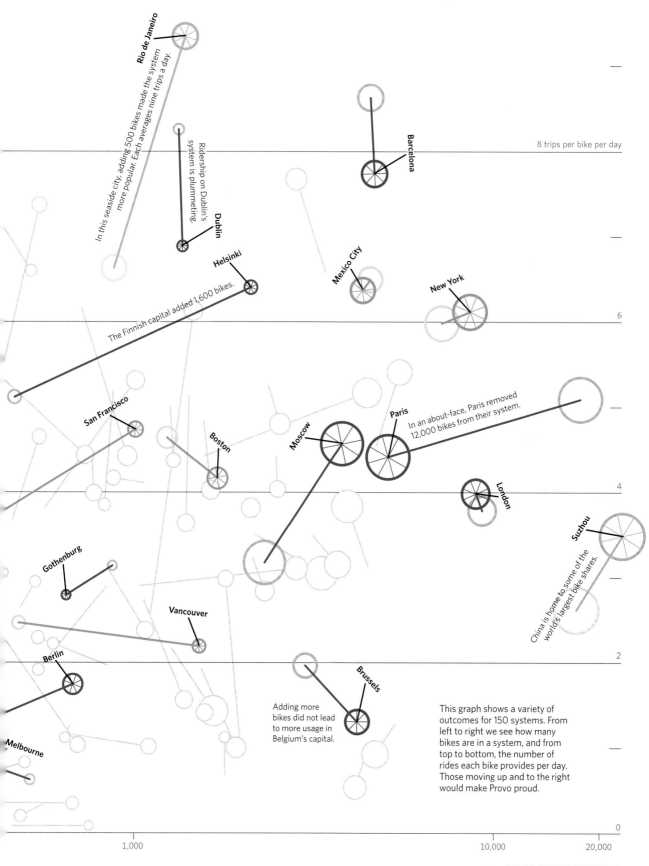

Rio de Janeiro

In this seaside city, adding 500 bikes made the system more popular. Each averages nine trips a day.

Barcelona

8 trips per bike per day

Ridership on Dublin's system is plummeting.

Dublin

Helsinki

Mexico City

New York

The Finnish capital added 1,600 bikes.

6

Paris

In an about-face, Paris removed 12,000 bikes from their system.

San Francisco

Boston

Moscow

London

4

Suzhou

Gothenburg

China is home to some of the world's largest bike shares.

Vancouver

2

Berlin

Brussels

Melbourne

Adding more bikes did not lead to more usage in Belgium's capital.

This graph shows a variety of outcomes for 150 systems. From left to right we see how many bikes are in a system, and from top to bottom, the number of rides each bike provides per day. Those moving up and to the right would make Provo proud.

0

1,000

10,000   20,000

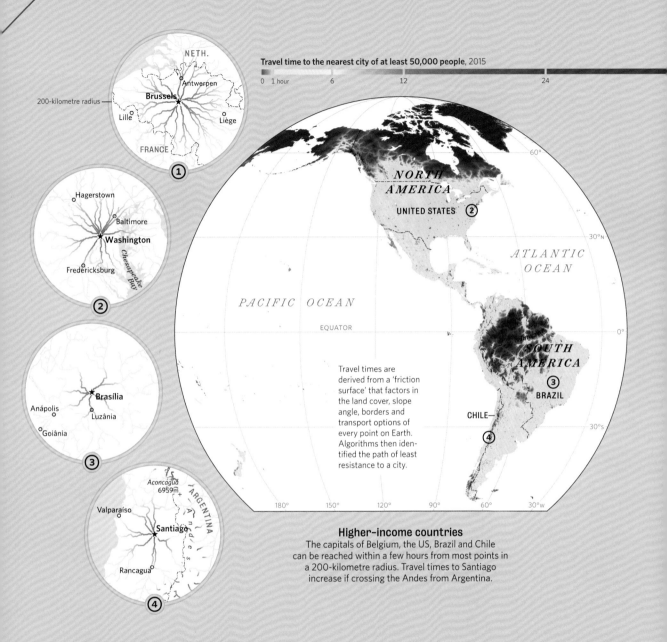

Travel time to the nearest city of at least 50,000 people, 2015

0 1 hour   6   12   24

① NETH.
Antwerpen
Brussels
Lille   Liège
FRANCE
200-kilometre radius

②
Hagerstown
Baltimore
Washington
Chesapeake Bay
Fredericksburg

③
Anápolis
★ **Brasília**
Luzânia
Goiânia

④
Aconcagua 6959m
Valparaíso
Santiago
ARGENTINA
Andes
Rancagua

NORTH AMERICA
UNITED STATES ②
ATLANTIC OCEAN
60°
30°N
PACIFIC OCEAN
EQUATOR
0°
SOUTH AMERICA
③
BRAZIL
CHILE—
④
30°S
180° 150° 120° 90° 60° 30°W

Travel times are derived from a 'friction surface' that factors in the land cover, slope angle, borders and transport options of every point on Earth. Algorithms then identified the path of least resistance to a city.

Higher-income countries
The capitals of Belgium, the US, Brazil and Chile can be reached within a few hours from most points in a 200-kilometre radius. Travel times to Santiago increase if crossing the Andes from Argentina.

EASE OF ACCESS

The best measure of proximity is time, not distance.

As teleconferencing takes over from travel, it's hard to disagree with the many futurists who have declared 'the end of geography' and 'the death of distance'. But you might think otherwise if you live in a part of the world where schools, markets and healthcare are more than a day away. These maps show some of the remotest areas on Earth, where travel time to the nearest city of at least 50,000 people can be measured in days rather than hours or minutes. Purple and

SOURCE: WEISS ET AL. (2018)

72 hours or more

Longest
travel time:
21 days

Lower-income countries
The mountains, desert and bush of Malawi, Bhutan, Sudan
and Papua New Guinea make their capitals less accessible
than in nations with more developed infrastructure.
Border crossings also add hours to a journey.

orange correspond to far-flung regions including the
Sahara, Amazon, Siberia, Australian Outback and
Himalaya; one spot in Tibet is twenty days on foot plus
one by car from the nearest city, Lhasa. (Air travel and
high-speed rail, which typically connect large cities,
are not factored in because to use these transport
modes you'd likely already be inside an urban area.)

Ninety-one per cent of people in high-income
countries live within one hour of a city compared to

fifty-one per cent of people in low-income countries.
This statistic reflects disparities in access to services
that are more likely to exist in urban areas. From
nearly two million surveys spanning fifty-two countries, the researchers who created the model behind
these maps also found a clear correlation between
access to cities and the wealth, education and health
of households. In other words, if you can get to work,
school and a doctor, your wellbeing improves.

Many nations are using mobile technology to leapfrog old barriers. In the past decade, Nigeria has switched from 1 million active fixed-line accounts to 180 million mobile subscriptions today.

We built this map from an open, crowd-sourced database of network infrastructure. While not comprehensive, it is illustrative of geopolitical realities. The row for South Korea lists a half million cells. For its authoritarian neighbour to the north? Twenty. Mobile phones are becoming more common in North Korea, but they're expensive and incapable of connecting with the wider world.

ATLANTIC OCEAN

PACIFIC OCEAN

N O R T H   A M E R I C A

UNITED STATES

S O U T H   A M E R I C A

A N D E S

PAN-AMERICAN HIGHWAY

San Juan
New York
Bogotá
Mexico City
Vancouver
Los Angeles
São Paulo
Buenos Aires

Number of cells
September 2019
- More than 10,000
- 1,001–10,000
- 101–1,000
- 11–100
- 1–10

Each hexagon is 20 kilometres wide.

0   2,000 km

RIVERS OF CONNECTIVITY

Information flows through some areas more than others.

Whenever you geotag a photo, refresh a weather app or request a ride, your device doesn't need satellites to know where you are. It can determine your location from the relative signal strength of nearby cell towers. The more towers it detects, the more accurate your location (and the stronger your connection). Zoom out to the global scale and the meanders of this invisible network come into view.

The tiny, coloured hexagons on this map indicate the varying number of cellular connection points, or 'cells', in an area. Six million-odd cells in the US reflect seemingly every road, town and city. (Turn the page for a closer look.) Densely populated places such as Japan, India and Western Europe are similarly inundated. Elsewhere internet inequality abounds: canals of coverage follow the Trans-Siberian Railway and Pan-American Highway; emergent springs in Nairobi, Lagos and Johannesburg feed Africa's digital revolution; China's streams are intermittent; and North Korea has dammed the river completely. One wonders for how long.

SOURCE: MOZILLA LOCATION SERVICE

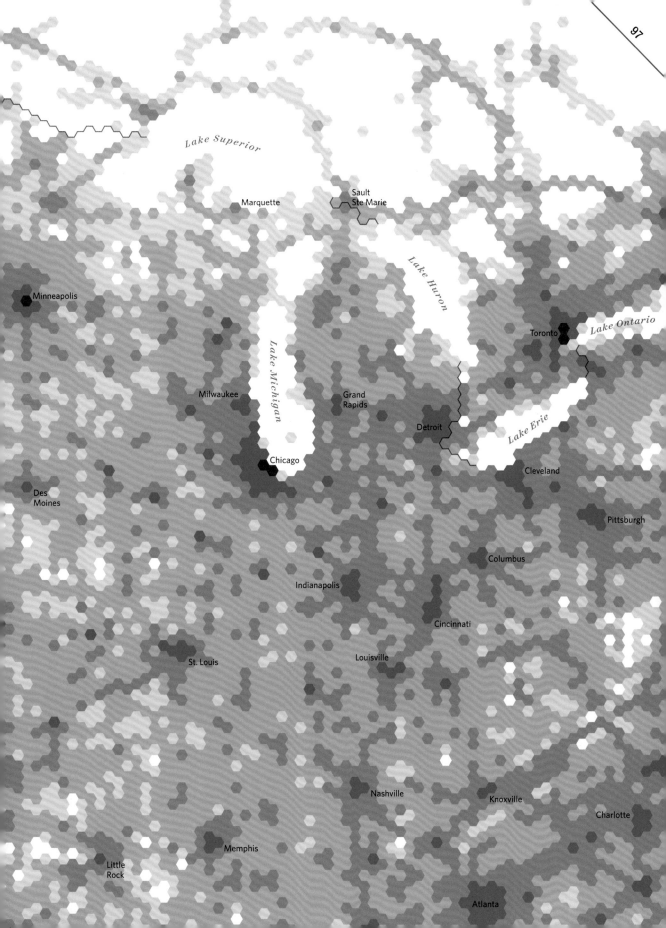

Lake Superior

Marquette

Sault
Ste Marie

Lake Huron

Lake Ontario

Minneapolis

Toronto

Lake Michigan

Milwaukee

Grand
Rapids

Detroit

Lake Erie

Chicago

Cleveland

Des
Moines

Pittsburgh

Columbus

Indianapolis

Cincinnati

St. Louis

Louisville

Nashville

Knoxville

Charlotte

Memphis

Little
Rock

Atlanta

OCTOPUS'S GARDEN

The internet lives under the sea.

On 29 October 1969, a young programmer at UCLA tried to connect to another computer at the Stanford Research Institute 350 miles away. He typed two letters of 'login'. Then the system crashed. Nevertheless, the data those two keystrokes encoded were already on their way north to Palo Alto and into the history books: the first message delivered over a computer network.

Those initial bytes travelled along copper telephone lines with a capacity for fifty kilobits per second. At that rate, the Beatles hit 'Come Together' would've taken twenty-two minutes to download when it debuted later that year. Anticipating the data demand of an increasingly interconnected planet, telecom carriers began building faster lines. Today, nearly everything we do online zips between continents through just 400 fibre-optic cables on the ocean floor. The longest, SEA-ME-WE 3 (shown in red), links 33 nations across Southeast Asia, the Middle East and Western Europe. At a scorching 200 terabits per second, the fastest cable (purple) could transfer all 280 million Beatles records ever purchased from the US to Spain in the time it took you to read this sentence.

The undersea realm is now ruled by tech titans: Google, Facebook, Microsoft and Amazon. Most submarine cable traffic services these companies, a trend that is expected to increase as more people and devices go online. Facebook is helping to fund a cable (yellow) that will nearly triple the total capacity of all subsea cables serving Africa today. When complete, it will enter the sea in England, go round the Cape of Good Hope and Horn of Africa and circle back to Europe to help another billion people come together.

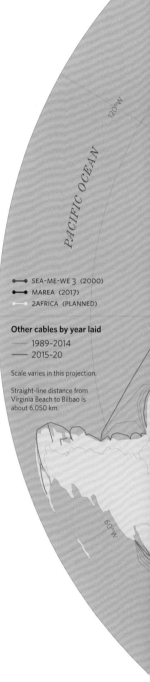

SEA-ME-WE 3 (2000)
MAREA (2017)
2AFRICA (PLANNED)

Other cables by year laid
1989–2014
2015–20

Scale varies in this projection.

Straight-line distance from Virginia Beach to Bilbao is about 6,050 km.

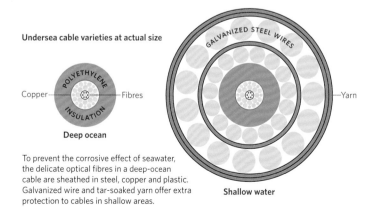

Undersea cable varieties at actual size

Copper — POLYETHYLENE INSULATION — Fibres
Deep ocean

GALVANIZED STEEL WIRES — Yarn
Shallow water

To prevent the corrosive effect of seawater, the delicate optical fibres in a deep-ocean cable are sheathed in steel, copper and plastic. Galvanized wire and tar-soaked yarn offer extra protection to cables in shallow areas.

SOURCES: TELEGEOGRAPHY; CARTER ET AL. (2009)

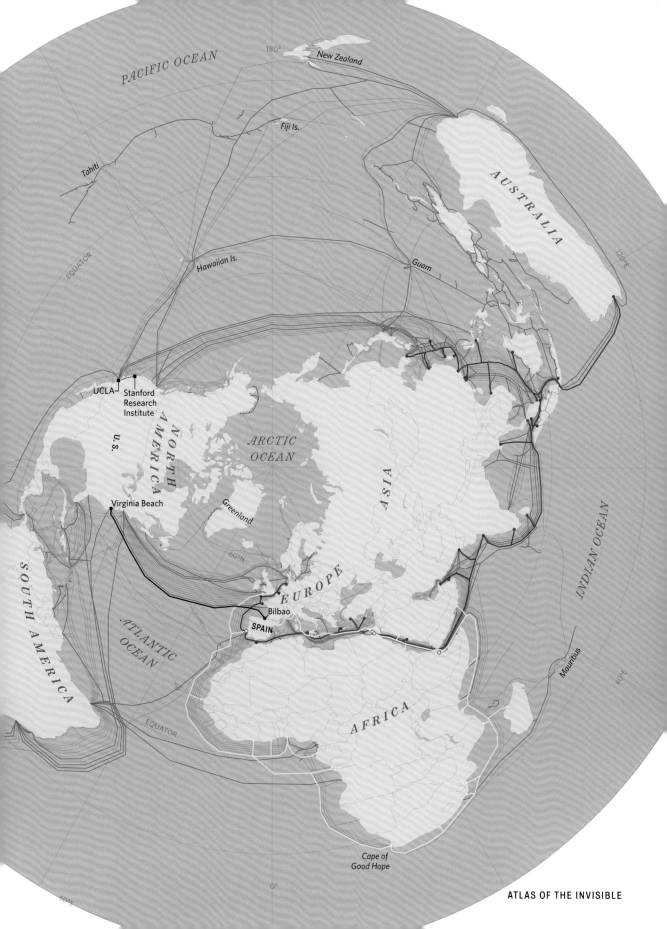

PACIFIC OCEAN

180°

New Zealand

Fiji Is.

Tahiti

AUSTRALIA

120°E

EQUATOR

Hawaiian Is.

Guam

UCLA

Stanford
Research
Institute

ARCTIC
OCEAN

NORTH AMERICA

ASIA

U.S.

Virginia Beach

Greenland

60°N

INDIAN OCEAN

SOUTH
AMERICA

ATLANTIC
OCEAN

EUROPE

Bilbao

SPAIN

AFRICA

60°E

Mauritius

EQUATOR

0°

Cape of
Good Hope

60°S

HOW WE'RE DOING

'I regarded it as axiomatic that the world wanted to learn the truth
and if the truth was sought with even approximate accuracy and
painstaking devotion, the world would gladly support the effort.'

—W. E. B. DU BOIS, in his 1940 autobiography, *Dusk of Dawn*

TRUTH TO POWER

Maps have long been thought to offer authoritative views of the world. So those with the resources to create them have often done so to cement their own advantage. Even a cursory study of the history of data collection and mapping will reveal skeletons in cartographers' closets that haunt our maps today. Whole continents were claimed with lines and labels; whole peoples subsumed. Examples range from imperialist to wilfully ignorant, from desired lands to the desired path of a storm.

Of course, maps alone don't have authority to do anything. They are only effective if people act on them. The French philosopher Bruno Latour compared a map's power to 'the way in which someone convinces someone else to take up a statement, to pass it along, to make it more of a fact'. He illustrated this with an anecdote about the French explorer Jean-François de Galaup, Comte de La Pérouse, who Louis XVI dispatched to the Far East in 1785 to chart a better map of the region. In August 1787, La Pérouse landed on present-day Sakhalin off the east coast of Russia and asked the people there if he was on an island or peninsula. An elderly man drew a map in the sand. It was clearly of little consequence to him, something ephemeral to be washed away. La Pérouse, however, saw it differently. He was on a mission for information to send back to France, where a map could be laid out and discussed in terms of imperial expansion. Though La Pérouse never made it back to France, his logbooks did. The 'discoveries' they contained appeared on a map in 1798 that asserted a definitive view of the region, including an area that now bore the label, La Pérouse Strait.

To those in power, maps were documents of ownership to be traded like properties in a global game of Monopoly. From November 1884 to February 1885, European powers gathered in Berlin to acknowledge each other's claims in Africa (right). Such cavalier cartography primed the continent for centuries of conflicts. Just one was a border dispute between Nigeria and Cameroon that wasn't resolved until 2006. Sir Claude Macdonald, a British diplomat, once regaled the Royal Geographical Society with a tale of the border's true origin: 'In those days we just took a blue pencil and a rule, and we put it down at Old Calabar and drew that blue line up to Yola,' 415 miles inland. Macdonald recalled thinking, while meeting the emir who presided over the region, that 'it was a very good thing that he did not know that I, with a blue pencil, had drawn a line through his territory.'

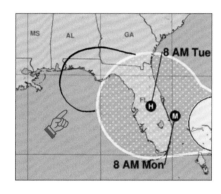

In September 2019, the President of the United States altered a map to insist Hurricane Dorian might go where he said it would.

SOURCES: MICHAEL REYNOLDS/EPA-EFE/SHUTTERSTOCK (HURRICANE); DEUTSCHES HISTORISCHES MUSEUM

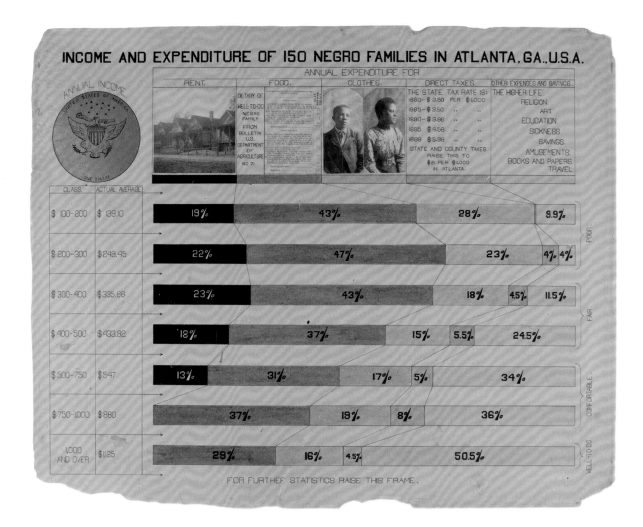

INCOME AND EXPENDITURE OF 150 NEGRO FAMILIES IN ATLANTA, GA., U.S.A.

WHILST COLONIALISTS were swapping stories about how they created divisions, W. E. B. Du Bois, a pioneering African-American sociologist and civil rights advocate, was hard at work removing them. Bisecting nearly every facet of society, from politics and commerce to intellectual and social life, he saw what Frederick Douglass had once dubbed 'the color line' – a sociological construct that kept Black and white lives apart. In his 1903 polemic, *The Souls of Black Folk*, Du Bois observed that: 'It is usually possible to draw in nearly every Southern community a physical color-line on the map, on the one side of which whites dwell and on the other Negroes.'

Those in power were almost exclusively interested in the fate of white communities, and their maps mirrored that interest. Often when maps of Black communities were drawn, the purpose was to further marginalize them. Black neighbourhoods were dismissed as areas of criminality, unworthy of study –

This visualization, part of Du Bois's exhibit at the 1900 Exposition Universelle in Paris, breaks down the budgets of 150 Black families from Atlanta, Georgia by class. Food was the greatest expense for poor families, while the 'well-to-do' spent half their income on 'the higher life'.

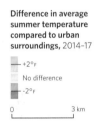

a perceptual framework that would eventually lead to policies of segregation, redlining (right) and rezoning (pp. 128–9).

Du Bois felt otherwise. He wanted to represent the Black community through the meticulous statistical analysis that theretofore benefitted white populations. Inspired by the Hull-House maps of Chicago (p. 69), he personally questioned eight thousand people in Philadelphia to create a map-filled report entitled, *The Philadelphia Negro*. Published in 1899, its purpose was to capture the geography, occupations and home lives of African Americans and 'above all, their relation to their million white fellow-citizens.' He was guided by the belief that 'we must no longer guess at [African Americans'] condition, we must know it.'

Lives were at stake. In the spring of 1899, a Georgia man named Sam Hose was being hunted by a mob. Hose had admitted to murdering his employer in self-defence but denied accusations of rape. With the full facts of the case still uncertain and the baying mob growing, Du Bois sought to calm the situation by penning a 'careful and reasoned statement' for *The Atlanta Constitution* newspaper. On his way to submit it, he heard that Hose had been caught and lynched and that parts of his charred corpse were for sale. The shock stopped Du Bois in his tracks. From that moment, he became convinced that statistics alone were not enough to change white people's minds:

> Two considerations thereafter broke in upon my work and eventually disrupted it: first, one could not be a calm, cool and detached scientist while Negroes were lynched, murdered and starved; and secondly, there was no such definite demand for scientific work of the sort that I was doing, as I had confidently assumed would be easily forthcoming. I regarded it as axiomatic that the world wanted to learn the truth and if the truth was sought with even approximate accuracy and painstaking devotion, the world would gladly support the effort. This was, of course, but a young man's idealism, not by any means false, but also never universally true.

'The cure,' he concluded, 'wasn't simply telling people the truth, it was inducing them to act on the truth.' Du Bois began to add a campaigning edge to his work and, a year later, earned a gold medal at the 1900 Exposition Universelle in Paris for a series of maps and infographics he'd produced about life across the colour line (see left). It was a hard-won achievement:

> The details of finishing these 50 or more charts, in colors, with accuracy was terribly difficult with little money, limited time and not too much encouragement. I was threatened with nervous prostration before I was done and had little money left to buy passage to Paris, nor was there a cabin left for sale. But the exhibit would fail unless I was there. So at the last moment I bought passage in the steerage and went over and installed the work.

His growing renown helped Du Bois secure funding from the US Bureau of Labor for what he would consider his 'best sociological work', a 1906 study of a single segregated county in Alabama, a former slave state that had systematically

Difference in average summer temperature compared to urban surroundings, 2014–17

+2°F
No difference
-2°F

0   3 km

In Richmond, Virginia, like many American cities, a physical 'color line' lives on in the guise of redlining. In the 1930s, the US government rated the investment risk of urban areas on a scale from 'best' to 'hazardous'. Communities of colour were disproportionately scored in the latter category. White neigh-bourhoods could petition for parks, while Black neighbourhoods became sites for heat-absorbing highways, warehouses and public housing. Today, the lack of greenery leads to higher summer temperatures and higher health risks.

disenfranchised its Black population. Despite 'being met with shotguns in certain parts of the county' Du Bois and his team surveyed over six thousand families to consider 'the distribution of Labor; the relation of landlord and tenant; the political organization and the family life and the distribution of the population'. After submitting his final report, Du Bois enquired when it would be published. To his disappointment, he was told it wouldn't be since 'it touched on political matters.' There'd been a change of leadership at the Bureau. Rather than simply storing the findings, they destroyed the only copy.

AS ONE PROJECT was hidden, another was gaining visibility. Recognizing the role of public opinion and the power of evidence to change it, American journalist Ida B. Wells had been gathering data to prove that lynchings followed the colour line. The brilliance of her work, which she first published in 'Southern Horrors: Lynch Law in All Its Phases' (1892) and then 'A Red Record' (1895), was that it presented lynchings as a national issue rather than a series of isolated events. Local laws would not suffice; injustice of this scale required federal action.

In her 1909 address to the National Negro Conference, she advanced an unequivocal, data-driven argument:

> During the last ten years from 1899 to 1908 inclusive, the number lynched was 959. Of this number 102 were white, while the colored victims numbered 857 . . . Year after year, statistics are published, meetings are held, resolutions are adopted and yet lynchings go on. Public sentiment does measurably decrease the sway of mob law, but . . . the only certain remedy is an appeal to law. Lawbreakers must be made to know that human life is sacred and that every citizen of this country is first a citizen of the United States and secondly a citizen of the state in which he belongs.

Within a year, the National Negro Conference became the National Association for the Advancement of Colored People (NAACP) with Wells and Du Bois amongst its founding members. Armed with data, they set to work on a large-scale lobbying effort for anti-lynching legislation and soon found an ally in Congressman Leonidas C. Dyer of Missouri, who took up a bill drafted by NAACP member Albert E. Pillsbury. Seeing the power of data to prove that lynchings had not ceased, Dyer invited the NAACP to share their most recent figures to bolster his case 'for the necessity of the law'.

Held up for years in committee, the bill finally came before the House of Representatives in January 1922. Southern Democrats tried to flee the chamber to prevent a vote, but the Speaker ordered the doors locked and sent the Sergeant at Arms to retrieve those missing. Hundreds of African Americans, eager to witness history in the making, gathered in the galleries. Over the course of the proceedings, congressmen taunted them from the floor as part of their increasingly desperate and contradictory arguments that the federal government should play no role in the prevention of lynching. When the bill ultimately passed 231–119, cheers echoed through the chamber. At long last, African-American voices had been heard.

Euphoria soon turned to dismay. Despite President Harding offering his full support to the bill, the Southern Democrats filibustered it out of the Senate before it could be passed into law. At the time, an NAACP advertisement described the

◆

'Year after year statistics are published, meetings are held, resolutions are adopted and yet **LYNCHINGS** go on . . . the only certain remedy is an appeal to **LAW.'**

Persons lynched by geographical division 1889-1918

The South **2,834**

The North **219**

The West **156**

Alaska and unknown places **15**

SOURCE: *THIRTY YEARS OF LYNCHING IN THE UNITED STATES, 1889-1918*

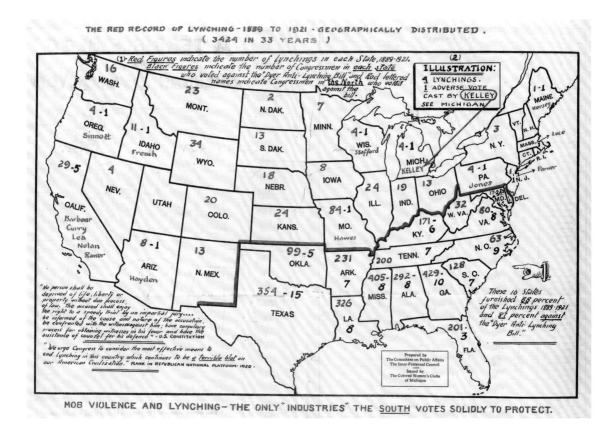

country's failure to outlaw lynching as 'The Shame of America'. The shame persists. Since 1900 there have been nearly two hundred attempts to pass anti-lynching legislation. In 2018, a Justice for Victims of Lynching Act finally passed the Senate, only for the Republican-controlled House to ignore it. Democrats, after retaking the House, tried again in February 2020. This time the Republican-led Senate failed to act. As stupefying as it may be, in the 21st-century United States, lynching is still not a federal crime.

DESPITE COUNTLESS ATTEMPTS to erase the work of Du Bois and Wells – including a federal investigation of Du Bois that concluded a) he 'does not claim to be a Communist' and b) 'the primary purpose of his efforts is the advancement of the colored people' – Du Bois is now credited as a founder of modern sociology. His innovative infographics and recently digitized papers continue to inspire new audiences. Wells was an unflinching data journalist whose legacy continues to gain greater appreciation. Whilst her peers in the national media ignored her death in 1931, *The New York Times* finally atoned for their own shameful disregard with an obituary in 2018. And in 2020, she was posthumously awarded a Pulitzer for 'her outstanding and courageous reporting'.

In 1921, the Colored Women's Clubs of Michigan created a map to show the number of lynchings per state (red) alongside counts of congressmen who had voted against a bill to outlaw the practice (black). Their focus, however, was not the southern naysayers – these were a lost cause – but the isolated few in the North who they call out by name in the same blood red as the death tolls.

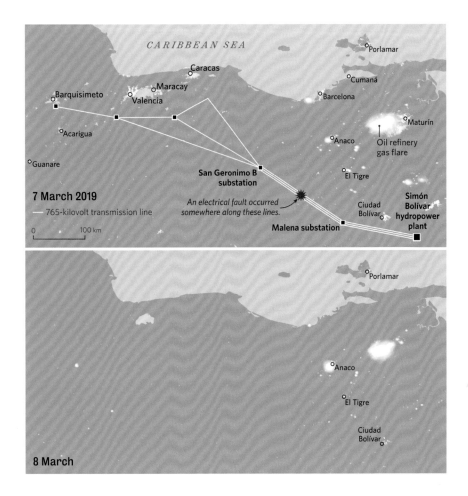

CARIBBEAN SEA

Porlamar

Caracas

Cumaná

Maracay
Valencia
Barcelona

Barquisimeto

Acarigua

Maturín

Anaco
Oil refinery
gas flare

Guanare

El Tigre

San Geronimo B
substation

7 March 2019

An electrical fault occurred
somewhere along these lines.

765-kilovolt transmission line

Ciudad
Bolívar

**Simón
Bolívar
hydropower
plant**

0   100 km

Malena substation

Porlamar

Anaco

El Tigre

Ciudad
Bolívar

8 March

★Caracas

V E N E Z U E L A
MAP AREA

Today, a proliferation of digital tools make it possible to gather and disseminate data without 'being met with shotguns'. For example, thanks to the crowd-sourced flight-tracking site ADS-B Exchange, *Buzzfeed* didn't need to have reporters on the ground at every Black Lives Matter protest in order to track where military helicopters circled overhead. Similarly, anyone researching the number of people shot and killed by police in the US – nearly three a day in 2020 – can consult the *Washington Post*'s free online database. Even satellites can hold governments to account as they did when Venezuela's power grid failed (above).

This is just the beginning. The open data movement has exposed an endless vein of stories for you to mine. By linking handwritten details from a government driver's notebooks to online public records, the Argentine newspaper *La Nación* uncovered an extensive bribery scandal involving dozens of officials, including a former President. And early in the COVID-19 pandemic, the *Financial Times*' data team became a global phenomenon when they started posting daily charts that revealed which countries were flattening the curve and which were not.

On 7 March 2019, a fault along the high-voltage lines from Venezuela's Simón Bolívar hydropower plant triggered an outage that left much of the country without power for days. Satellite imagery shows cities aglow before the blackout (top) and in the dark a day later (bottom).

SOURCE: NASA-NOAA SUOMI-NPP VIIRS

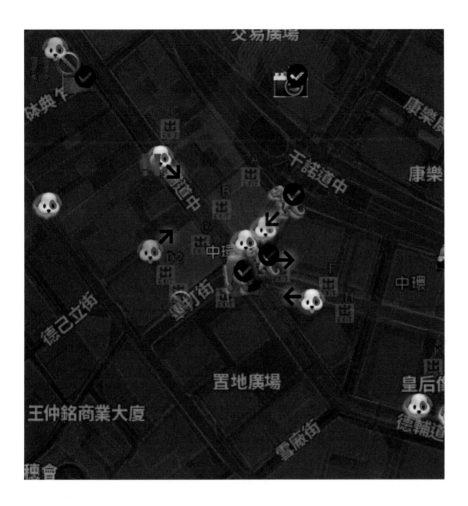

Technology is also making it easier for citizens to organize more effectively. In the early 2010s, mobile phones and social media helped rally a wave of protests that toppled governments across North Africa and the Middle East. A decade later, protestors in Hong Kong were using an online, emoji-based map to convey the location of police forces in real time (above). The Chinese government's eagerness to shut the app down was a testament to its effectiveness and a reminder that technology is no substitute for power.

Data visualization can be a great ally to democracy because it organizes information; maps and graphics gather disparate facts into memorable visuals with the power to shift public opinion. In this chapter, we examine inequalities in happiness, unpaid labour and pollution levels. We expose where eviction, gender-based violence and unexploded ordnance threaten the lives of our fellow humans. Yet, as Wells and Du Bois discovered, maps alone will not right the wrongs. That's why we devoted a spread to the women in India fighting back with historic rates of peaceful protests. To speak truth to power, people need 'to act on the truth'.

In August 2019, a crowd-sourced map of Hong Kong launched to help protestors anticipate and respond to police movements in real time. In the chaos of the streets, emoji spoke volumes: dogs and dinosaurs marked the presence of police and tactical squads; exclamation points screamed danger.

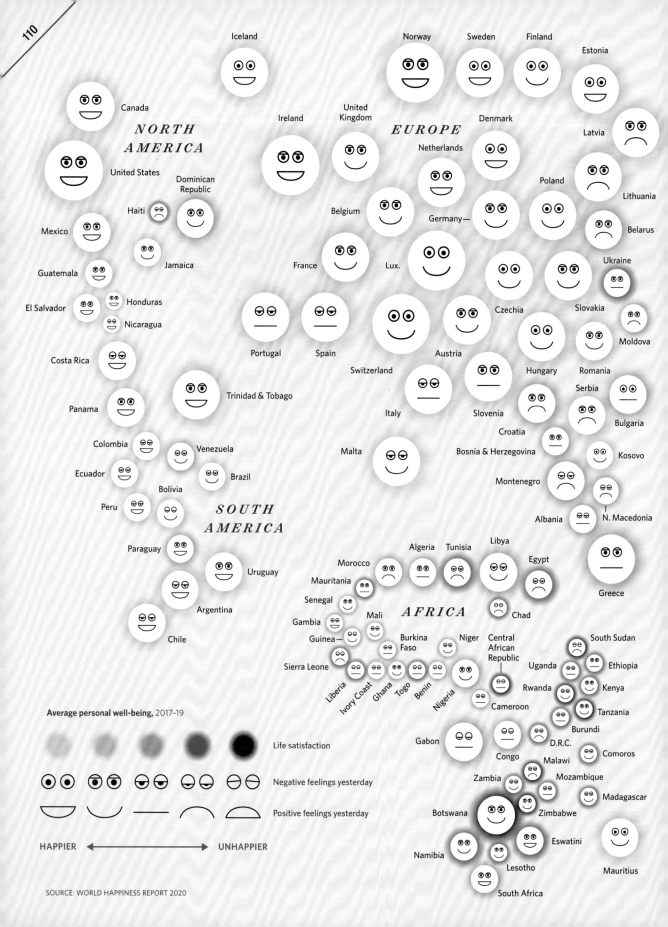

NORTH AMERICA

Iceland · Canada · United States · Dominican Republic · Haiti · Jamaica · Mexico · Guatemala · El Salvador · Honduras · Nicaragua · Costa Rica · Panama · Trinidad & Tobago

EUROPE

Norway · Sweden · Finland · Estonia · Ireland · United Kingdom · Denmark · Latvia · Netherlands · Lithuania · Belgium · Germany — · Poland · France · Lux. · Belarus · Czechia · Ukraine · Slovakia · Switzerland · Austria · Hungary · Slovakia · Portugal · Spain · Italy · Slovenia · Romania · Serbia · Croatia · Moldova · Malta · Bosnia & Herzegovina · Kosovo · Montenegro · Albania · N. Macedonia · Bulgaria · Greece

SOUTH AMERICA

Colombia · Venezuela · Ecuador · Brazil · Bolivia · Peru · Paraguay · Uruguay · Argentina · Chile

AFRICA

Morocco · Algeria · Tunisia · Libya · Egypt · Mauritania · Senegal · Chad · Gambia · Mali · Guinea — · Burkina Faso · Niger · Central African Republic · South Sudan · Uganda · Ethiopia · Sierra Leone · Liberia · Ivory Coast · Ghana · Togo · Benin · Nigeria · Cameroon · Rwanda · Kenya · Tanzania · Burundi · Gabon · Congo · D.R.C. · Comoros · Malawi · Mozambique · Zambia · Madagascar · Botswana · Zimbabwe · Eswatini · Namibia · Lesotho · Mauritius · South Africa

Average personal well-being, 2017-19

Life satisfaction

Negative feelings yesterday

Positive feelings yesterday

HAPPIER ←——→ UNHAPPIER

SOURCE: WORLD HAPPINESS REPORT 2020

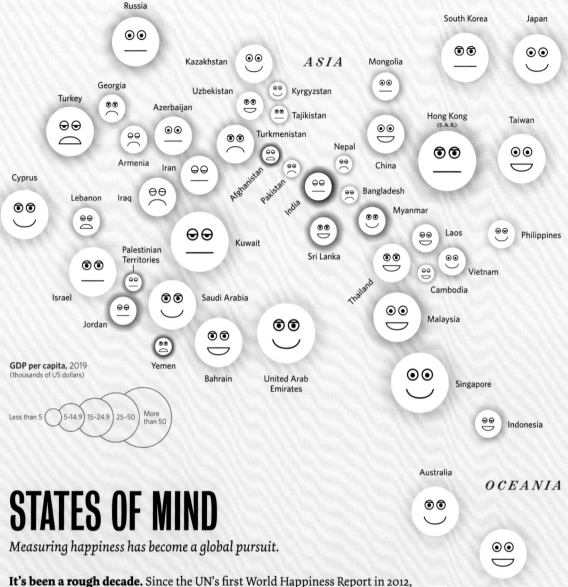

GDP per capita, 2019
(thousands of US dollars)

Less than 5 | 5–14.9 | 15–24.9 | 25–50 | More than 50

STATES OF MIND

Measuring happiness has become a global pursuit.

It's been a rough decade. Since the UN's first World Happiness Report in 2012, there's been a steady rise in worry, sadness and – to a lesser degree – anger across the globe. Each year, researchers ask individuals in more than 150 countries to rate their lives on a scale where the top represents the best possible and the bottom the worst possible life. They also ask if respondents felt happiness, laughter, enjoyment or negative emotions for much of the previous day. On this map, we have linked each country's average response over a three-year period to a different facial attribute and sized the heads by per capita income. Larger heads tend to be sunnier, reflecting an understandable link between livelihoods and life satisfaction. For example, prosperous Scandinavia radiates far more contentment than populous South Asia. Elsewhere, the mood in Eastern Europe has brightened since the 2008 financial crisis, whilst economic, political and social stress have mired Afghanistan, India, Yemen and many southern African nations in a purple gloom.

The report showed lower incomes lowered overall outlooks, but freedom and generosity were better predictors of positive feelings. As for negative emotions, those in free and trustworthy societies with a safety net of friends and relatives were less likely to worry.

PASSPORT CHECK

Some travel documents are more powerful than others.

In 445 BCE, the Persian king Artaxerxes sent his trusted aide Nehemiah to Jerusalem with an unusual document in hand. It was a 'safe conduct' letter, requesting safe passage through the region. Were Nehemiah to attempt a trek from Iran to Israel today, he might not get far. The governments of countries along his route – Iraq, Jordan and Israel – require Iranian passport holders to obtain visas in advance.

To see how twenty-first century travel documents compare, we used a database of visa requirements for 193 countries and six territories to chart passports from strongest to weakest and nations from least to most welcoming as of 2018. Circles are sized by GDP. Citizens from wealthier countries tend to enjoy greater ease of travel (see top of chart) while less affluent countries are often more welcoming (far right). Sometimes a country's openness score is more a factor of bureaucracy than hospitality. For example, Algeria (lower left) intends to introduce eVisas but hasn't yet.

Prior to the COVID-19 pandemic, Singapore's passport topped Germany's as the most powerful one to carry. Its holders could travel freely to 166 countries. Singapore was also among the most welcoming, allowing visitors from 162 countries without advance permission. With a free pass to only 30 countries and no nationalities allowed in visa-free, Afghanistan ranked at the bottom of both metrics.

Citizens can travel freely to 166 countries

UNITED STATES
AUSTRALIA

150

100
75
50
25

○ No data

GDP per capita by purchasing power parity, 2018
(thousands of international dollars)

○ Africa
○ Asia
○ Europe
○ North America
○ South America
○ Oceania

RUSSIA

PASSPORT POWER

100

↑ EASIER TO TRAVEL
↓ HARDER TO TRAVEL

SAUDI ARABIA
NAURU
CHINA

CUBA
MONGOLIA

SIERRA LEONE

BHUTAN
ALGERIA
GUINEA

TURKMENISTAN

MALI

50

A

NIGERIA

NORTH KOREA
LIBYA
YEMEN
SUDAN

SYRIA
IRAQ
PAKISTAN

AFGHANISTAN

Ⓐ **10 AFRICAN COUNTRIES**
BURUNDI
CAMEROON
CENTRAL AFRICAN REPUBLIC
CHAD
CONGO
DEM. REP. OF THE CONGO
EQUATORIAL GUINEA
ERITREA
LIBERIA
SOUTH SUDAN

Citizens can travel freely to zero countries

No countries may visit without advance permission

NORTH AMERICA
EUROPE
ASIA
AFRICA
SOUTH AMERICA
AUSTRALIA

SOURCES: PASSPORT INDEX; INTERNATIONAL MONETARY FUND (GDP DATA)

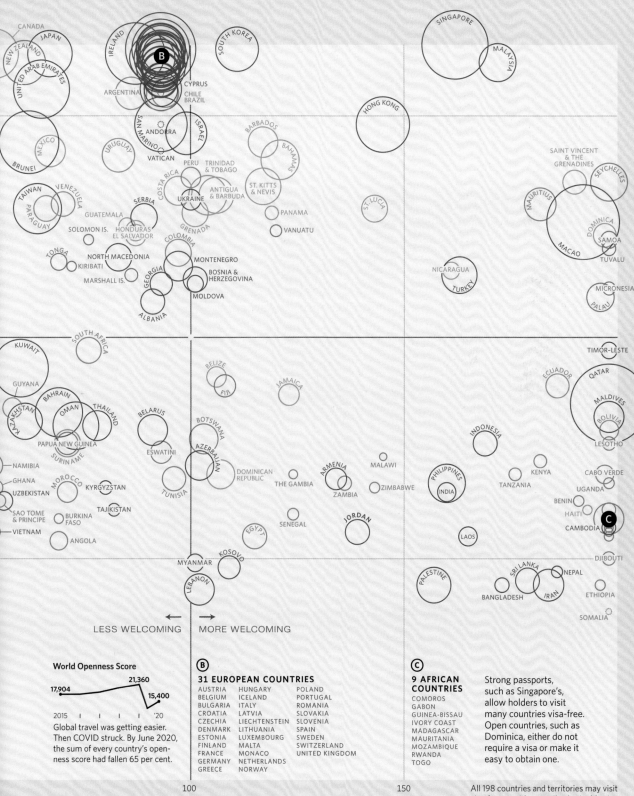

CANADA
JAPAN
NEW ZEALAND
UNITED ARAB EMIRATES
IRELAND
B
SOUTH KOREA
SINGAPORE
MALAYSIA

ARGENTINA
CYPRUS
CHILE
BRAZIL

MEXICO
SAN MARINO
ANDORRA
ISRAEL
HONG KONG
BRUNEI
VATICAN
URUGUAY
PERU
TRINIDAD & TOBAGO
BARBADOS
BAHAMAS
SAINT VINCENT & THE GRENADINES
SEYCHELLES

TAIWAN
VENEZUELA
COSTA RICA
ST. KITTS & NEVIS
ST. LUCIA
MAURITIUS
PARAGUAY
SERBIA
UKRAINE
ANTIGUA & BARBUDA
PANAMA
DOMINICA
SAMOA
GUATEMALA
GRENADA
VANUATU
MACAO
TUVALU
SOLOMON IS.
HONDURAS
EL SALVADOR
COLOMBIA
TONGA
NORTH MACEDONIA
MONTENEGRO
MICRONESIA
KIRIBATI
GEORGIA
BOSNIA & HERZEGOVINA
NICARAGUA
PALAU
MARSHALL IS.
MOLDOVA
TURKEY
ALBANIA

KUWAIT
SOUTH AFRICA
TIMOR-LESTE
GUYANA
BELIZE
ECUADOR
QATAR
BAHRAIN
FIJI
JAMAICA
MALDIVES
KAZAKHSTAN
OMAN
THAILAND
BELARUS
BOTSWANA
BOLIVIA
PAPUA NEW GUINEA
AZERBAIJAN
INDONESIA
LESOTHO
SURINAME
ESWATINI
NAMIBIA
DOMINICAN REPUBLIC
ARMENIA
MALAWI
KENYA
CABO VERDE
GHANA
MOROCCO
THE GAMBIA
PHILIPPINES
TANZANIA
UGANDA
UZBEKISTAN
KYRGYZSTAN
ZAMBIA
ZIMBABWE
INDIA
BENIN
TAJIKISTAN
TUNISIA
HAITI
SAO TOME & PRINCIPE
BURKINA FASO
SENEGAL
JORDAN
LAOS
CAMBODIA
VIETNAM
EGYPT
ANGOLA
DJIBOUTI
MYANMAR
KOSOVO
PALESTINE
SRI LANKA
NEPAL
LEBANON
BANGLADESH
IRAN
ETHIOPIA
SOMALIA

← LESS WELCOMING   MORE WELCOMING →

C

World Openness Score

17,904   21,360
15,400

2015 ┃ ┃ ┃ ┃ '20

Global travel was getting easier. Then COVID struck. By June 2020, the sum of every country's openness score had fallen 65 per cent.

(B) 31 EUROPEAN COUNTRIES

AUSTRIA	HUNGARY	POLAND
BELGIUM	ICELAND	PORTUGAL
BULGARIA	ITALY	ROMANIA
CROATIA	LATVIA	SLOVAKIA
CZECHIA	LIECHTENSTEIN	SLOVENIA
DENMARK	LITHUANIA	SPAIN
ESTONIA	LUXEMBOURG	SWEDEN
FINLAND	MALTA	SWITZERLAND
FRANCE	MONACO	UNITED KINGDOM
GERMANY	NETHERLANDS	
GREECE	NORWAY	

(C) 9 AFRICAN COUNTRIES

COMOROS
GABON
GUINEA-BISSAU
IVORY COAST
MADAGASCAR
MAURITANIA
MOZAMBIQUE
RWANDA
TOGO

Strong passports, such as Singapore's, allow holders to visit many countries visa-free. Open countries, such as Dominica, either do not require a visa or make it easy to obtain one.

100   150

All 198 countries and territories may visit visa-free or with an easily obtainable visa

OPENNESS SCORE

ATLAS OF THE INVISIBLE

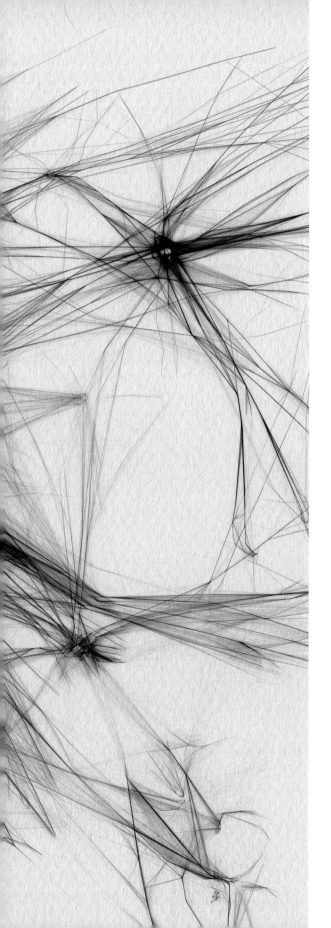

CARBON OVERHEAD

There's a web of exhaust we do not see.

When we look up into a blue sky and see a white plume trailing a silver plane, air travel can seem harmless, even pretty. A darker truth is emerging. Choosing to fly is one of the most carbon-intensive choices an individual can make. Per passenger, one trans-Atlantic return ticket carries the same atmospheric burden as two years on a meat-based diet, eight years without recycling or four lifetimes' worth of plastic bags. It gets worse. At the altitudes where most airliners fly, those plumes of water vapour and greenhouse gases trap heat, which doubles the warming effect of the plane's carbon emissions. Scientists have known this for decades. Only recently has the severity of these impacts begun to register with travellers.

In recent years, Swedish climate activist Greta Thunberg has popularized the word *flygskam* (flight shame) to guilt people into greener alternatives such as rail travel or teleconferencing. So far it's working. In 2019, passenger numbers at Swedish airports were down whilst ridership on the nation's railways reached new highs. A new term began to trend: *tagskyrt* (train bragging).

This map depicts a week's worth of flights over Europe. A return flight from London to Istanbul emits more CO_2 than the average citizen in many countries will in a year – and that's not counting the doubling effect of contrails.

Because these flight routes were recorded by receivers on the ground, the lines fade once airplanes fly out of range.

SOURCE: ADS-B EXCHANGE

ATLAS OF THE INVISIBLE

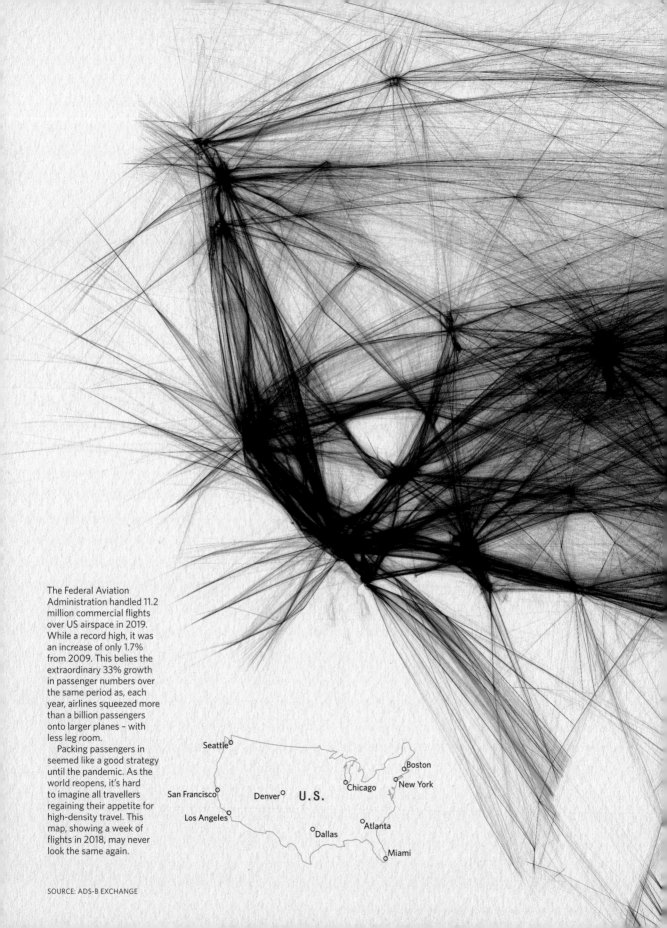

The Federal Aviation Administration handled 11.2 million commercial flights over US airspace in 2019. While a record high, it was an increase of only 1.7% from 2009. This belies the extraordinary 33% growth in passenger numbers over the same period as, each year, airlines squeezed more than a billion passengers onto larger planes – with less leg room.

Packing passengers in seemed like a good strategy until the pandemic. As the world reopens, it's hard to imagine all travellers regaining their appetite for high-density travel. This map, showing a week of flights in 2018, may never look the same again.

Seattle
Boston
San Francisco
Chicago
New York
Denver
U.S.
Los Angeles
Dallas
Atlanta
Miami

SOURCE: ADS-B EXCHANGE

Nitrogen dioxide concentration
25 July 2019, midday GMT

30e⁻⁵ mol/m²
25
20
15

Hazy summer skies are often an indication of air pollution. Here we show plumes of nitrogen dioxide on one of Northern Europe's warmest days in 2019.

10

Scale varies in this projection.

Straight-line distance from Madrid to Baghdad is about 4,300 km.

5

SOURCE: COPERNICUS SENTINEL-5

IN EXHAUSTIVE DETAIL

Satellites help us see what we're breathing.

Air pollution killed an estimated 8.9 million people in 2015, with 790,000 in Europe alone. These figures include fatal cases of bronchitis, asthma and reduced lung function. Topography and weather can make matters worse. For instance, the Alps cause industrial pollutants to pool over Northern Italy; Marseille needs a stiff breeze to dissipate the fumes from cruise liners; and high pressure conditions can keep urban exhaust swirling over the UK.

Whilst the threat may be hard for human eyes to see, it hasn't gone unnoticed. In 2018, the European Commission sued the UK, France, Germany, Hungary, Italy and Romania for repeatedly breaching legal nitrogen dioxide levels and for not implementing credible mitigation plans. The European Space Agency's Tropospheric Monitoring Instrument (Tropomi) provides added oversight. Since 2017, its daily global readings of nitrogen dioxide, sulphur dioxide and particulate levels in the atmosphere have offered a clear view of the chemicals billowing from smokestacks and trailing transport. At the local level, Tropomi can help to forecast the most toxic times for exercise outside. Its wider views give dirty industries and governments nowhere to hide.

While oil fields in the Middle East generate some of the brownest blotches on this map, air travel is largely responsible for the noxious wake between Amsterdam and London.

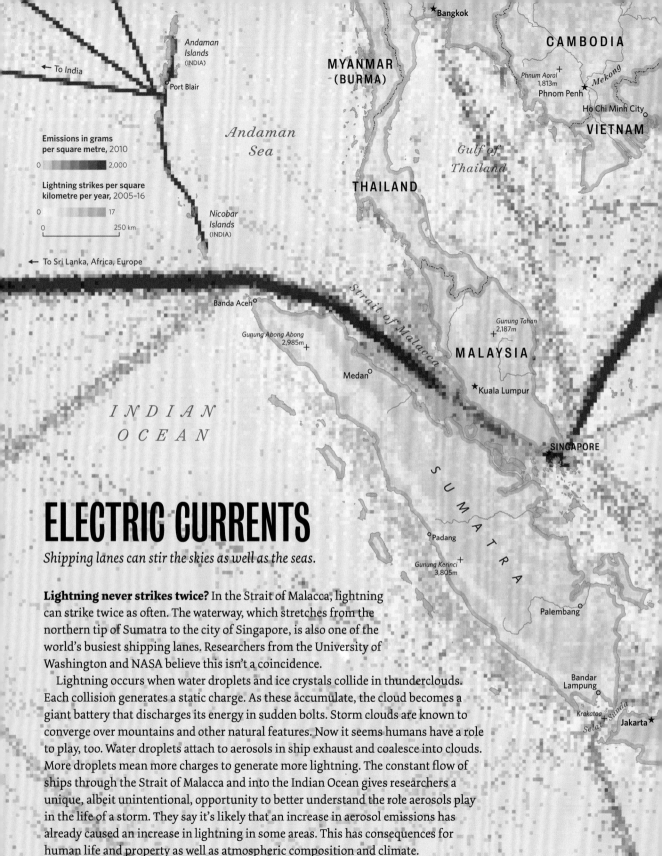

Bangkok ★

CAMBODIA

Andaman
Islands
(INDIA)

MYANMAR
(BURMA)

Phnum Aoral
1,813m
Phnom Penh +

Mekong

← To India

Port Blair

Ho Chi Minh City

VIETNAM

*Andaman
Sea*

Gulf of
Thailand

THAILAND

**Emissions in grams
per square metre, 2010**

0 ▭▭▭▭▭ 2,000

**Lightning strikes per square
kilometre per year, 2005–16**

0 ▭▭▭▭▭ 17

0 ▭▭▭▭▭ 250 km

Nicobar
Islands
(INDIA)

Strait of Malacca

Gunung Tahan
2,187m +

MALAYSIA

← To Sri Lanka, Africa, Europe

Banda Aceh ○

Gunung Abong Abong
2,985m +

Medan ○

★ Kuala Lumpur

*INDIAN
OCEAN*

SINGAPORE ★

S
U
M
A
T
R
A

ELECTRIC CURRENTS

Shipping lanes can stir the skies as well as the seas.

○ Padang

Gunung Kerinci
3,805m +

Lightning never strikes twice? In the Strait of Malacca, lightning
can strike twice as often. The waterway, which stretches from the
northern tip of Sumatra to the city of Singapore, is also one of the
world's busiest shipping lanes. Researchers from the University of
Washington and NASA believe this isn't a coincidence.

○ Palembang

Lightning occurs when water droplets and ice crystals collide in thunderclouds.
Each collision generates a static charge. As these accumulate, the cloud becomes a
giant battery that discharges its energy in sudden bolts. Storm clouds are known to
converge over mountains and other natural features. Now it seems humans have a role
to play, too. Water droplets attach to aerosols in ship exhaust and coalesce into clouds.
More droplets mean more charges to generate more lightning. The constant flow of
ships through the Strait of Malacca and into the Indian Ocean gives researchers a
unique, albeit unintentional, opportunity to better understand the role aerosols play
in the life of a storm. They say it's likely that an increase in aerosol emissions has
already caused an increase in lightning in some areas. This has consequences for
human life and property as well as atmospheric composition and climate.

Bandar
Lampung ○

Krakatoa
Selat + Sunda

Jakarta ★

SOURCES: NASA GHRC DAAC (LIGHTNING); EUROPEAN COMMISSION EDGAR (POLLUTION)

To China →

To Japan →

Sibuyan

Sea

PHILIPPINES

Iloilo ○

Cebu City

+ *Canlaon Volcano*
2,435m

Bohol Sea

South China Sea

PALAWAN

Sulu Sea

MINDANAO

Davao
+ × Mount Apo
2,954m

Zamboanga City ○

Gunung Kinabalu
+ 4,095m

Sulu
Archipelago
(PHILIPPINES)

Celebes Sea

Bandar Seri
Begawan ★

BRUNEI

Tarakan ●

MALAYSIA

Kuching ○

Kapuas

Gorontalo ○

Teluk
Tomini

Maluku
Sea

B O R N E O

+ *Bukit Raya*
2,278m

Samarinda ●

Makassar Strait

Palu ○

Balikpapan ●

SULAWESI

BURU

+ *Buntu*
Rantekambola
3,478m

Parepare ○

Java Sea

Makassar ○

I N D O N E S I A

Gunung Cereme
3,078m

Gunung Merapi
+ 2,911m   Surabaya ○

To Polynesia →

J
A + **V** **A**

Bali Sea

Flores Sea

BALI

SUMBAWA

FLORES

Dili ★ **TIMOR-LESTE**

TIMOR

SUMBA

Kupang ●

To Australia ↙

ATLAS OF THE INVISIBLE

Very fine particulate matter exposure (PM2.5)
2–17 April 2019

In early April 2019, northerly winds blew particulates from this factory toward sensors 1–3 in the image above. On 17 April, the winds reversed, causing a spike on sensor 4.

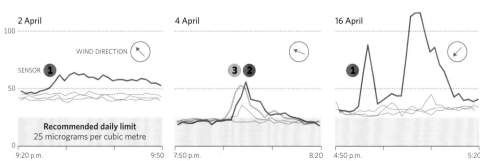

WIND DIRECTION

SENSOR ①

Recommended daily limit
25 micrograms per cubic metre

2 April

100
50
0
9:20 p.m. — 9:50

4 April

③ ②
7:50 p.m. — 8:20

16 April

①
4:50 p.m. — 5:20

SOURCES: CAMEO.TW; BING (SATELLITE IMAGE)

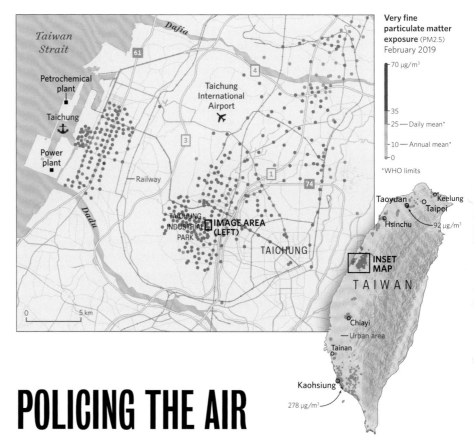

Very fine particulate matter exposure (PM2.5) February 2019

70 µg/m³

35
25 — Daily mean*
10 — Annual mean*
0

*WHO limits

92 µg/m³

Taoyuan · Keelung · Taipei · Hsinchu

INSET MAP

TAIWAN

Chiayi
— Urban area
Tainan

Kaohsiung

278 µg/m³

POLICING THE AIR

In Taiwan, thousands of air-quality sensors stand watch.

Look across a city skyline at dusk and you will likely see buildings mired in haze. From a distance, air pollution can seem a single mass, afflicting residents below in equal measure. But there are always fluctuations in toxicity. In many cities, prevailing winds blow particulates over less affluent areas while the trees and parks in wealthier neighbourhoods pull carbon from the sky. There can be big differences throughout the day, too. Roads clog with smog during rush hours, and power stations belch more at night as they labour to meet demand.

To keep tabs on a given neighbourhood, regulators typically rely on spot checks and self-reports from industry. Predictably, a lot goes undetected. In recent years, Taiwan's Environmental Protection Administration installed nine thousand air-quality sensors across the island. From their continuous pollution readings, algorithms identify peaks – even if they only last a few minutes – and flag them for further investigation. By adding other metrics, such as wind direction, authorities can target pollution at its source. In 2018, they fined a bottling factory in the Taichung City Industrial Park nearly US$8 million for submitting inaccurate air-pollution readings and exceeding local standards. After the ruling, the factory spent US$3.5 million on equipment upgrades to clean up its act – and the air.

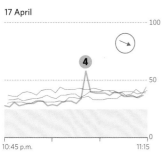

17 April

10:45 p.m.   11:15

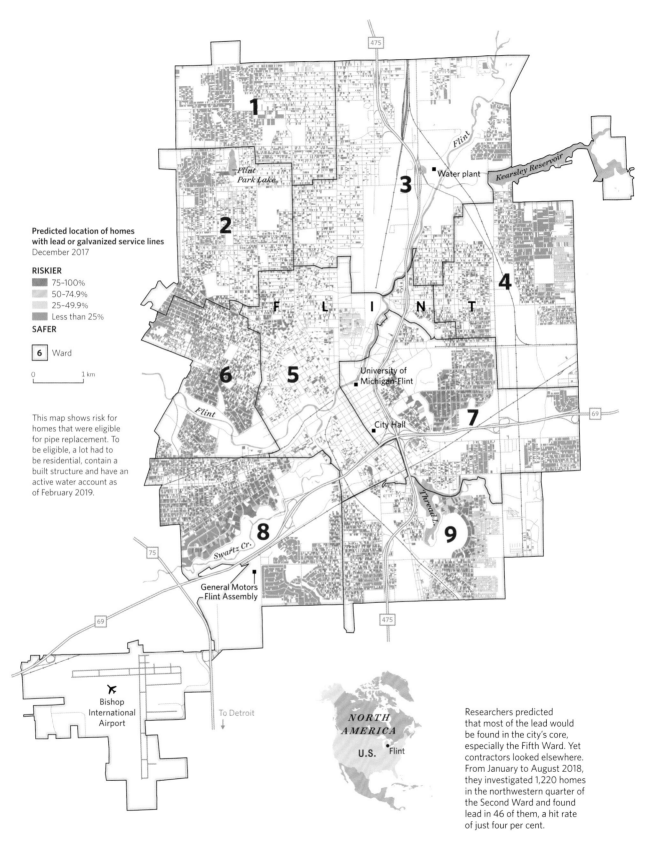

Predicted location of homes with lead or galvanized service lines
December 2017

RISKIER

75–100%
50–74.9%
25–49.9%
Less than 25%

SAFER

6 Ward

0 ——— 1 km

This map shows risk for homes that were eligible for pipe replacement. To be eligible, a lot had to be residential, contain a built structure and have an active water account as of February 2019.

1

2

3

Water plant

4

F L I N T

5

6

University of Michigan-Flint

City Hall

7

8

General Motors Flint Assembly

Swartz Cr.

9

Flint

Flint Park Lake

Kearsley Reservoir

475

69

475

75

69

To Detroit

Bishop International Airport

NORTH AMERICA

U.S. • Flint

Researchers predicted that most of the lead would be found in the city's core, especially the Fifth Ward. Yet contractors looked elsewhere. From January to August 2018, they investigated 1,220 homes in the northwestern quarter of the Second Ward and found lead in 46 of them, a hit rate of just four per cent.

SOURCE: JACOB ABERNETHY, ALEX CHOJNACKI, ARYA FARAHI, ERIC SCHWARTZ AND JARED WEBB, UNIVERSITY OF MICHIGAN

LOOKING FOR LEAD

The key to solving the Flint water crisis was to trust data over digging.

In April 2014, the state of Michigan switched Flint's water source from Lake Huron to the Flint River to save money. Untreated water, acidified from decades of industrial runoff, began to corrode the city's aging pipes. Residents soon noticed foul brown water flowing from their taps. Officials denied the problem until September 2015, when tests confirmed 'serious' levels of lead in hundreds of homes – and children.

Computer scientists at the University of Michigan proposed a solution. With the help of city record keepers, they compiled data on the age and value of homes and designed a model to predict which homes were most likely to have lead or galvanized service lines. These (shown in brown) are where the researchers recommended checking first. The city initially followed their advice with great success. But residents in low-risk areas (green) kept clamouring for new pipes, too. So in late 2017, the mayor hired a national firm to take over the mitigation effort and eventually ordered them to excavate any home with an active water account, data be damned. The predictable result: more digging, less lead found. The effective cost to replace pipes soared. Realizing this, the city reverted to the data-driven model in 2019. Every home in Flint now has safe pipes and clean water to drink.

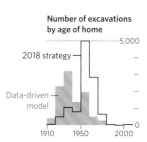

Number of excavations by age of home

2018 strategy

Data-driven model

5,000

0

1910   1950   2000

Researchers predicted risk to be highest in homes built before 1950.

Excavation results   ■ Lead or galvanized pipes found   ■ Safe materials found

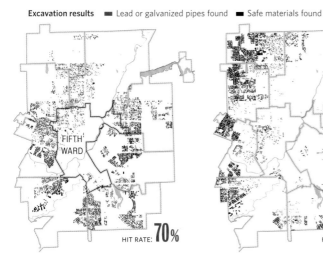

FIFTH WARD

HIT RATE: **70%**

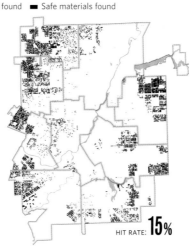

HIT RATE: **15%**

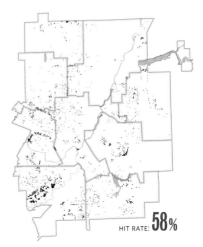

HIT RATE: **58%**

June 2016–December 2017

A University of Michigan model predicted which homes were at risk. With the model as a guide, 70% of excavations found lead.

January 2018–February 2019

Bowing to public pressure, the city excavated newer homes in more affluent outer areas with little success and enormous expense.

March–September 2019

Seeing their low hit rate, the city reverted to the data-driven model. Nearly all lead pipes were replaced by the end of 2019.

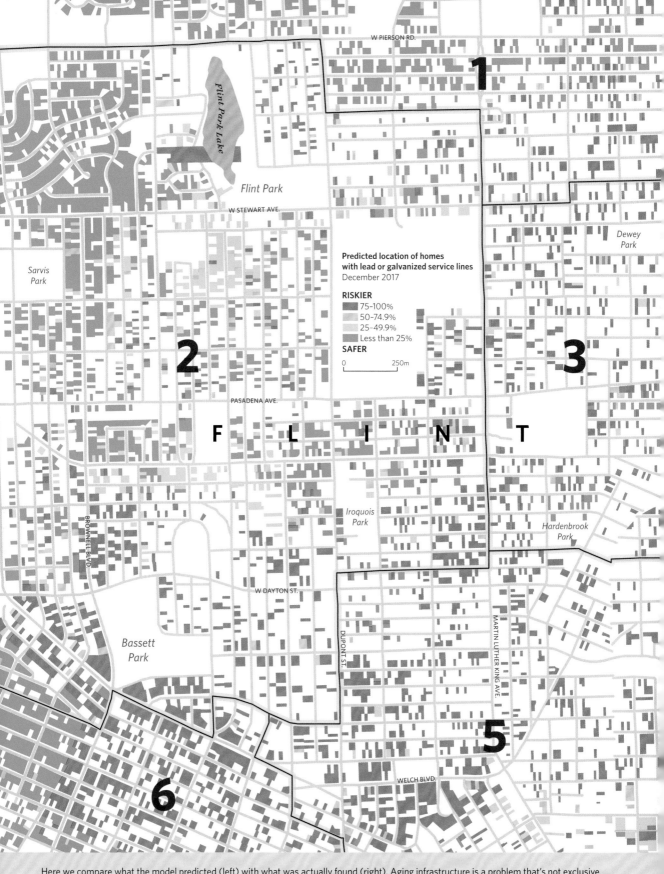

Predicted location of homes
with lead or galvanized service lines
December 2017

RISKIER

75–100%
50–74.9%
25–49.9%
Less than 25%

SAFER

0   250m

W PIERSON RD.

1

Flint Park Lake

Flint Park

W STEWART AVE.

Dewey Park

Sarvis Park

2

3

PASADENA AVE.

F L I N T

BROWNELL BLVD.

Iroquois Park

Hardenbrook Park

W DAYTON ST.

DUPONT ST.

MARTIN LUTHER KING AVE.

Bassett Park

5

WELCH BLVD.

6

Here we compare what the model predicted (left) with what was actually found (right). Aging infrastructure is a problem that's not exclusive to Flint. So mayors take heed. When it costs up to $5,000 per home to dig up and replace pipes, it pays to follow the data.

Flint Park Lake

Excavation results
June 2016 – September 2019

▪ Lead or galvanized pipes found
▪ Safe materials found

Max Brandon Park

NORTH AMERICA
U.S.

New York

MAP AREA

NEW YORK

John F. Kennedy International Airport

❶ Inwood

When the city rezoned one of Manhattan's last affordable neighbourhoods in 2018, its residents pushed back – and won. A New York judge agreed that the city 'failed to take a hard look' at the risk of racial displacement. But seven months later, an appeals court reversed the decision, arguing that the city does not have to 'parse every sub-issue framed by petitioners'.

❷ South Bronx

For years, residents have fended off realtors trying to rebrand the area with names like 'SoBro' or the 'Piano District'. After the 2018 rezoning of Jerome Avenue between Yankee Stadium and Fordham, some see the borough becoming what they fear most: another Brooklyn.

❸ Flushing

Chinese developers began investing in this largely Asian enclave during the 2008 financial crisis when American banks were hesitant to lend. The creation of 3,075 condos in the following decade drove Flushing's median sale price up 86 per cent.

❹ Bed-Stuy

This historic Black community saw the city's fourth-highest median rent and median sales price spikes of the 2010s. And since 2000, nearly 30 per cent of Bed-Stuy's population has shifted from Black to white.

❺ St. George

With fewer rentals than other boroughs, Staten Island is less susceptible to gentrification. Still, many have their sights set on the North Shore, a free ferry ride from Manhattan.

UNTENABLE CONDITIONS

For many New Yorkers, development means displacement.

Don't blame the baristas. The roots of gentrification grow from the top down, long before a single soy latte is poured. Officials rezone neighbourhoods, banks lend capital and developers raise rents to pay off those loans. Rent stabilization helps, but it hasn't stopped landlords from finding ways to force tenants out.

One way they turn the screws is through neglect. In 2018, New York City's service hotline received eleven thousand housing complaints a week, often for lack of heat or hot water. Confirmed violations enter a database, which we've used here to flag properties in need of improvement (orange) or deemed unacceptable (red). Layering those locations over census tracts of advanced (blue), ongoing (teal) and potential gentrification (yellow) reveals how closely housing conditions map to income. Twenty years after rezoning, with gentrification complete, few red flags remain in Long Island City whilst teal and yellow tracts in Brooklyn are littered with them.

Something has to change. In 2020, the mayor's office began rethinking where to rezone. One proposal is to build affordable housing in wealthy white areas such as SoHo and Gowanus. It's an approach that invites people in rather than pushing them out.

Gentrification
2016

- Advanced
- Ongoing
- Potential

Public housing

Rental grade
March 2019

- Needs improvement
- Unacceptable

0 ———— 2 km

SOURCES: RENTLOGIC
(GRADES); URBAN
DISPLACEMENT PROJECT
(GENTRIFICATION)

NORTH

East River

Upper Bay

Gravesend Bay

Newark Bay

Kill Van Kull

Map labels:
EAST NEW YORK · HIGHLAND PARK · BROWNSVILLE · BUSHWICK · BUSHWICK AVE. · ATLANTIC AVE. · EAST FLATBUSH · CROWN HEIGHTS · BEDFORD-STUYVESANT · MIDWOOD · GRAVESEND · CONEY ISLAND · BROOKLYN · KENSINGTON · BOROUGH PARK · BENSONHURST · BATH BEACH · CLINTON HILL · FORT GREENE · PARK SLOPE · GOWANUS · Prospect Park · Green-Wood Cemetery · SUNSET PARK · BAY RIDGE · WILLIAMSBURG · Barclays Center · BROOKLYN HEIGHTS · RED HOOK · Governors Island · Ellis I. · Liberty I. · EAST VILLAGE · LOWER EAST SIDE · CHINATOWN · SOHO · WEST VILLAGE · FINANCIAL DISTRICT · HOLLAND TUNNEL · STATEN ISLAND FERRY · ST. GEORGE · TOMPKINSVILLE · BAY ST. · STAPLETON · CLIFTON · Silver Lake · PORT RICHMOND · MARINERS HARBOR · STATEN ISLAND · NEW JERSEY · HOLLAND TUNNEL

278 · 278 · 27 · 278

4 · 5 · 24 · 27

SOUTHERN INHOSPITALITY

America's eviction epidemic predates the pandemic.

To solve a problem, it helps to know its extent. That's why it's vital to keep statistics on job loss, disease and other societal ills. Yet only in the past decade have researchers in the US begun to compile national data on court-ordered evictions. It's an ongoing effort since records remain incomplete in many states and counties.

According to Princeton University's Eviction Lab, at least 900,000 households were evicted in 2016 with more than a third in the ten states shown here, where laws tend to favour landlords. The scourge afflicted renters in cities of all sizes and price points. Black-majority communities, victims of domestic violence and families with children are particularly vulnerable, especially poor women of colour. As Matthew Desmond, the founder of Eviction Lab, has observed: 'If incarceration has become typical in the lives of men from impoverished Black neighbourhoods, eviction has become typical in the lives of women from these neighbourhoods.'

Mercifully, eviction moratoriums during COVID-19 kept the wolf from more than a million doors, but that does not mean the threat is gone. It will never leave until wages rise, rent gouging stops and affordable housing is accessible to all who need it. Subsidizing housing would not only keep more Americans in their homes, it'd keep them in their jobs and schools as well.

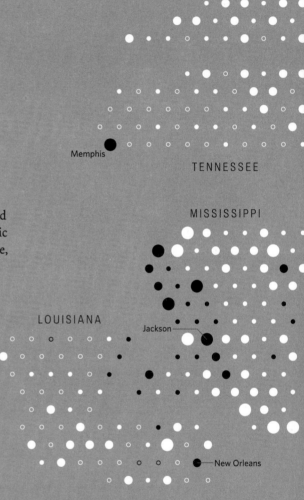

Highest eviction rates, 2016

LARGE CITIES

City	Rate
North Charleston SC	16.5%
Richmond VA	11.4
Hampton VA	10.5
Newport News VA	10.2
Jackson MS	8.8
Norfolk VA	8.7
Greensboro NC	8.4
Columbia SC	8.2
Warren MI	8.0
Chesapeake VA	7.9

MID-SIZED CITIES

St. Andrews SC	20.7%
Petersburg VA	17.6
Florence SC	16.7
Hopewell VA	15.7
Portsmouth VA	15.1
Redan GA	14.0
Horn Lake MS	11.9
Union City GA	11.7
East Point GA	11.3
Anderson SC	11.2

SMALL CITIES & RURAL AREAS

Robin Glen-Indiantown MI	40.7%
West Monroe MI	37.2
Homestead Base FL	29.2
East Gaffney SC	28.6
Wolf Lake MI	27.2
Promised Land SC	26.3
Aetna Estates CO	26.0
Falkland NC	25.7
Waterloo IN	24.4
Ladson SC	24.0

1 in 10   1 in 5

SOURCE: EVICTION LAB, PRINCETON UNIVERSITY

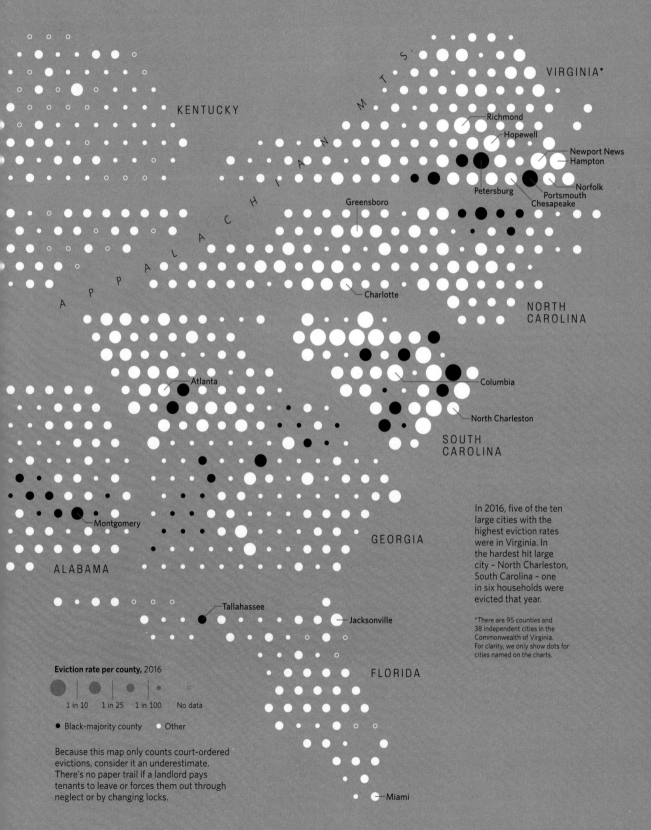

KENTUCKY

VIRGINIA*

M T S.

A P P A L A C H I A N

Richmond

Hopewell

Newport News
Hampton

Petersburg

Norfolk
Portsmouth
Chesapeake

Greensboro

Charlotte

NORTH
CAROLINA

Atlanta

Columbia

North Charleston

SOUTH
CAROLINA

Montgomery

GEORGIA

ALABAMA

In 2016, five of the ten
large cities with the
highest eviction rates
were in Virginia. In
the hardest hit large
city – North Charleston,
South Carolina – one
in six households were
evicted that year.

*There are 95 counties and
38 independent cities in the
Commonwealth of Virginia.
For clarity, we only show dots for
cities named on the charts.

Tallahassee

Jacksonville

FLORIDA

Eviction rate per county, 2016

1 in 10   1 in 25   1 in 100   No data

● Black-majority county   ○ Other

Because this map only counts court-ordered
evictions, consider it an underestimate.
There's no paper trail if a landlord pays
tenants to leave or forces them out through
neglect or by changing locks.

Miami

ATLAS OF THE INVISIBLE

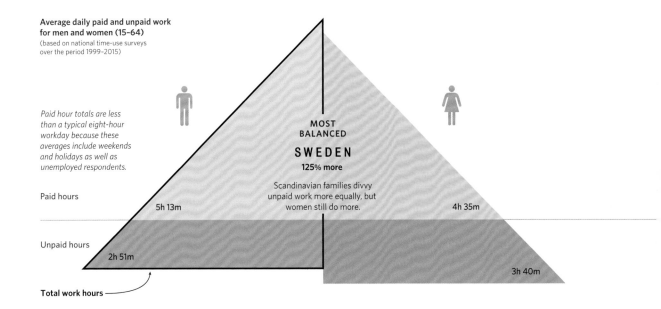

**Average daily paid and unpaid work
for men and women (15–64)**
(based on national time-use surveys
over the period 1999–2015)

*Paid hour totals are less
than a typical eight-hour
workday because these
averages include weekends
and holidays as well as
unemployed respondents.*

Paid hours

Unpaid hours

Total work hours

MOST
BALANCED
SWEDEN
125% more

Scandinavian families divvy
unpaid work more equally, but
women still do more.

5h 13m

4h 35m

2h 51m

3h 40m

UNEQUAL LOADS

Even in progressive countries, women shoulder more of the daily burden.

The piles on this page represent the average daily labour for working-age men
and women in thirty countries. Hours above the line are paid; those below are not.
In the eyes of economists at the Organisation for Economic Co-operation and Development, unpaid labour can include everything from cooking and cleaning to caring
for children and elderly relatives. If someone else could be paid to do it, it's work. By
this measure, Sweden is the most equitable nation; women there report undertaking
fifty minutes extra unpaid labour each day compared to men. In India, the offset is
more than four times larger. We list the other countries in order of gender-balance.
For instance, though women in South Korea and Japan reported few unpaid hours,
their male counterparts performed far fewer. Globally, women do three out of every
four hours of unpaid work. The only activity that skews male is home repairs.

COVID-19 exacerbated the imbalance. As schools closed and outside help
became less available, unpaid domestic duties have stacked up. In September 2020,
a UN report said the backlog amounted to months of additional work for women.
'Despite the clear gendered implications of crises,' says Papa Seck, UN Women's
Chief Statistician, 'response and recovery efforts tend to ignore the needs of women
and girls until it's too late. We need to do better.'

Women work more
unpaid hours than men,
even in countries that
log long days for both
genders, such as Latvia
and Mexico, and in
those that work fewer
hours overall, such as
France and Italy.

SOURCE: OECD

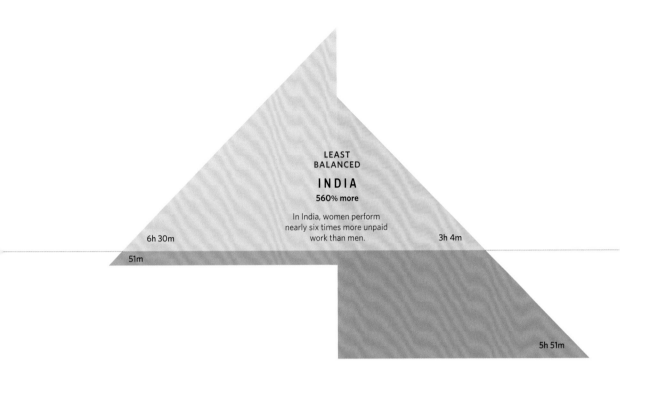

LEAST
BALANCED

INDIA
560% more

In India, women perform
nearly six times more unpaid
work than men.

6h 30m

3h 4m

51m

5h 51m

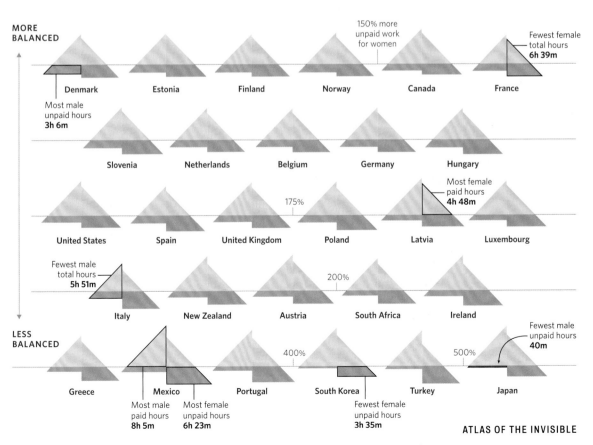

MORE
BALANCED

150% more
unpaid work
for women

Fewest female
total hours
6h 39m

Denmark

Estonia

Finland

Norway

Canada

France

Most male
unpaid hours
3h 6m

Slovenia

Netherlands

Belgium

Germany

Hungary

Most female
paid hours
4h 48m

175%

United States

Spain

United Kingdom

Poland

Latvia

Luxembourg

Fewest male
total hours
5h 51m

200%

Italy

New Zealand

Austria

South Africa

Ireland

LESS
BALANCED

Fewest male
unpaid hours
40m

400%

500%

Greece

Mexico

Portugal

South Korea

Turkey

Japan

Most male
paid hours
8h 5m

Most female
unpaid hours
6h 23m

Fewest female
unpaid hours
3h 35m

ATLAS OF THE INVISIBLE

BURSTS OF COWARDICE

Misogyny fuels a barrage of gender-based violence.

ACLED coverage area, 2019

Africa   Latin America
Asia   No data
Europe

Being a woman should not put you at risk. Yet in too many countries, rates of gender-based violence are exploding. The Armed Conflict Location and Event Data project (ACLED), an internationally funded nonprofit, keeps a database of political violence and protests in more than 150 countries and territories. Sourcing reports from international media and partners on the ground, they log dates, locations and participants for millions of events. These starbursts represent events that specifically targeted women in 2019, grouped by tactic and coloured by continent. Sexual violence was most prevalent in the Democratic Republic of the Congo; shootings riddled Mexico and Brazil; human rights petitioners frequently disappeared in China; and Indian women were most likely to be victims of mob violence. Fear of backlash, legal restrictions and psychological trauma can lead to underreporting, so the true totals are likely to be higher than even the most robust data collection efforts can reveal.

Perpetrators may believe their heinous acts will cow women from political participation; in actuality, they only expose their own cowardice. There are nearly 700 million women in India. They experience the highest gender gap of unpaid work (pp. 132–3), report some of the lowest levels of happiness (pp. 110–11), and they want change. They're organizing marches in record numbers. And, as we show on the next spread, they're calling out abuse for all the world to see.

100 reports

50

10

1

Reported instances of violence targeting women, 2019

7 Explosions
Horrific but rare: militants blew up a girls school in Afghanistan; car bombs targeted female politicians in Greece and Somalia.

17 Damaged Properties
Schools set ablaze; temples, churches and mosques razed; cars damaged and a convent robbed – all because they were owned or run by women.

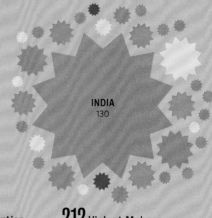

INDIA
130

212 Violent Mobs
Mobs are the most common perpetrators of gender-based violence in South Asia. It's not unusual for women or the victim's family to participate.

SOURCE: ACLED

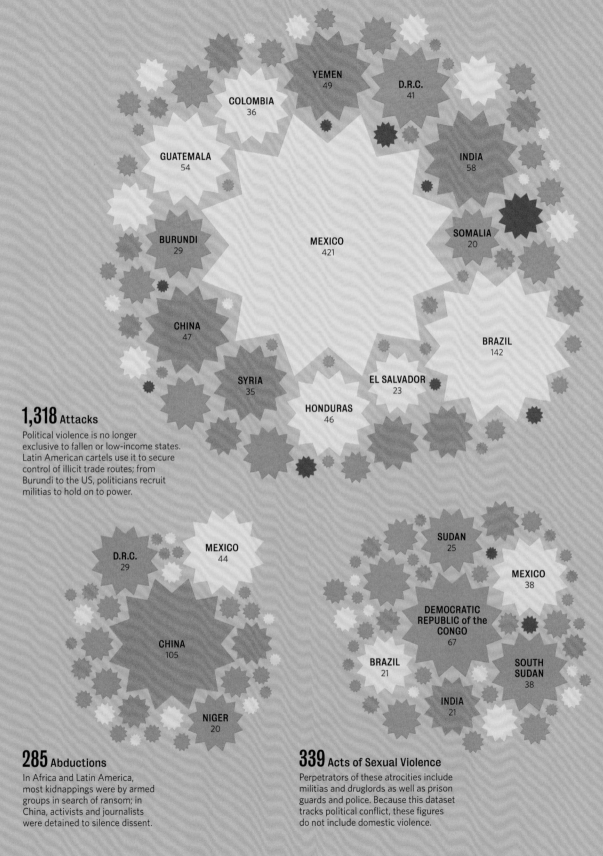

1,318 Attacks

Political violence is no longer exclusive to fallen or low-income states. Latin American cartels use it to secure control of illicit trade routes; from Burundi to the US, politicians recruit militias to hold on to power.

YEMEN 49
COLOMBIA 36
D.R.C. 41
GUATEMALA 54
INDIA 58
BURUNDI 29
SOMALIA 20
MEXICO 421
BRAZIL 142
CHINA 47
SYRIA 35
EL SALVADOR 23
HONDURAS 46

285 Abductions

In Africa and Latin America, most kidnappings were by armed groups in search of ransom; in China, activists and journalists were detained to silence dissent.

D.R.C. 29
MEXICO 44
CHINA 105
NIGER 20

339 Acts of Sexual Violence

Perpetrators of these atrocities include militias and druglords as well as prison guards and police. Because this dataset tracks political conflict, these figures do not include domestic violence.

SUDAN 25
MEXICO 38
DEMOCRATIC REPUBLIC of the CONGO 67
BRAZIL 21
SOUTH SUDAN 38
INDIA 21

More than ever, women in India are raising their voices.

1 JANUARY: demand permission to enter Sabarimala shrine • a minister's comments on the acquittal of a 2011 gang rape • 2 JAN: delays in relief for the Gaja c
Tribe status to Rajbonghis • 6 JAN: Citizenship (Amendment) Bill, 2016 • 7 JAN: a minister's comments on the acquittal of a 2011 gang rape • alleged gang
Amendment) Bill • 13 JAN: Citizenship (Amendment) Bill • 14 JAN: Citizenship (Amendment) Bill • 15 JAN: Citizenship (Amendment) Bill • 16 JAN: Citize
20 JAN: demand complete prohibition of alcohol • 21 JAN: demand complete prohibition of alcohol • failure of State Government in providing security t
23 JAN: hospital for turning away a birthing mother • demand arrest of all involved in a 2018 murder plot • demand complete prohibition of alcohol • de
complete prohibition of alcohol • 27 JAN: demand complete prohibition of alcohol • 28 JAN: demand complete prohibition of alcohol • 29 JAN: demand pol
refund from Rose Valley scam and other chit funds • alleged government takeover of state's liquor business • 31 JAN: the transfer of a teacher • Citizensh
police officers for stealing opium balls • 3 FEB: Citizenship (Amendment) Bill • 4 FEB: reinstatement of stamp duty on the purchase of property for women
cheques and a visit from a Society for Elimination of Rural Poverty minister • 5 FEB: Citizenship (Amendment) Bill • 6 FEB: Citizenship (Amendment)
Citizenship (Amendment) Bill • demand regularization for contractual nurses and ancillary staff • 8 FEB: delay in allotment of houses for the urban poor
Amendment) Bill during Prime Minister's visit • 10 FEB: Citizenship (Amendment) Bill • unfulfilled promises by the Bharatiya Janata Party, such as specia
outcomes of schoolchildren • Citizenship (Amendment) Bill • demand action against a minister who sexually assaulted a women • 12 FEB: police's baton
attack on a
shop to be
employees
evictions
in the local
Central Reserve Police F
closed • demand 33% re
from employment • 21
demand lawsuit against
distribution of rice • 3 M
communities • 8 MAR: to celebrate International Women's Day • increasing attacks on women • misery and persecution of women in the country • der
commence repairs of a road • atrocities of the Maoists • 10 MAR: the sale of spurious liquor • demand inclusion of the Meitei people • 12 MAR: demand f
past seven years • 13 MAR: demand action against the perpetrators of the Pollachi sexual abuse case • 14 MAR: demand action against the perpetrators of t
Bharatiya Janata Party's request to make voting booths 'super sensitive' • demand action against the perpetrators of the Pollachi sexual abuse case • 16 M
the Pollachi sexual abuse case • 17 MAR: alcohol abuse in the area • 18 MAR: demand speedy and impartial probe of the Pollachi case and death penalty law
scarcity • 25 MAR: drinking water shortage • 27 MAR: stale campus food that made them ill • 29 MAR: demand the release of women detained for "illegal im
University decision to move female students to another campus • demand cancellation of permits for a quarry • 4 APR: demand end to gender-based violer
of water in the village • 7 APR: candidature of congressman over allegations of sexual misconduct • 8 APR: lack of potable water • 9 APR: demand drinking
assault on a 16-year-old girl; demand local safety reforms • 15 APR: in response to the suicide of a girl who had been alleged sexually abused by father • dr
reforms • 18 APR: demand action against the culprits who attacked and injured fishermen • 19 APR: demand justice for the murder of a 11-year-old girl • 20 A
women • 23 APR: clogging of lanes by student carpools • 24 APR: demand safety measures for nearby highway, including speed limit and zebra crossings
hand grenade at the residence of a doctor • 28 APR: demand custody of a dowry harassment victim's two daughters • demand resignation of hostel superi
of a village leader • 30 APR: being asked to strip by a hostel warden to check for menstruation • 1 MAY: decision for college students to sell lucky draw tick
Sri Lanka blasts • searches conducted in connection with a murder • 4 MAY: demand either Indian citizenship or deportation • 6 MAY: exoneration of th
8 MAY: a video of a mother in labour posted online by a hospital nurse • exoneration of the Chief Justice • the procedure to deal with Chief Justice's sexu
the Chief Justice • demand drinking water • demand severe punishment for the perpetrator of a rape on a three-year-old girl • demand authorities addr
Chief Justice • demand capital punishment for the perpetrator of a rape on a three-year-old girl • demand authorities address poor distribution of dri
demand severe punishment for the perpetrator of a rape on a three-year-old girl • demand justice following the rape of a three-year-old girl • 15 MAY: dou
of a young woman domestic helper • vandalization and clashes between political party supporters • 17 MAY: demand recent rape cases be processed • 19
the Salem-Chennai eight-lane expressway • 25 MAY: demand crackdown on sale of illicit liquor and gambling • frequent and long power cuts • 27 MAY: t
on the tenth anniversary of a double rape and murder • demand crackdown on sulai (hooch) shops • 30 MAY: demand for drinking water supply to their ho
casinos and falsely issued rape charges • water scarcity in the neighborhood • 4 JUN: the construction of a Food Park • 5 JUN: demand better security ar
remarks on West Bengal migrants • hand grenades with nails in cans that were found planted in the city • 7 JUN: water scarcity in the area • shifting of Lo
minors • 11 JUN: demand action against a drug cartel after death of a 25-year-old addict • not having received water for the past eight days • an ongoing w
bribe • 17 JUN: government not releasing pending dues of compensation for irrigation projects • demand drinking water supply to all the households in t
24 JUN: to allege irregularities in payment of wages to women • demand free admission to a girls' college for students with economically weak backgroun
promised • 25 JUN: increasing attacks on nurses • sharp increase in the price of rice • 26 JUN: fake companies promoted by a conman • demand regulariz
nurses • 28 JUN: opening of a liquor vend in residential area • exclusion of a school from state government programme • 29 JUN: contaminated drinking w
police brutality • lack of water in village • 4 JUL: demand government maintain midday meal system for junior college students • demand death sente
7 JUL: scarcity of water • 8 JUL: deletion of women's names from the Below Poverty Line list • 11 JUL: intermittent supply of water • demand construction c
of rice • suspension of a lecturer who helped highlight problems for female students • 13 JUL: rising price of rice • increased duty on petrol and diesel • la
rights defenders and their families • 15 JUL: demand arrest of people responsible for a local killing • 17 JUL: gun attack on a human rights defender's daugh
at the hospital • demand strict laws to prevent mob lynching • demand raise and regularization of payment for mid-day meal workers • 21 JUL: death of
village • demand solution to the drinking water supply issue • government's use of the sedition law as an instrument of repression • protesting growing
24 JUL: shortage of drinking water • demand drinking water • poor drainage system in the area • demand drinking water • illegal liquor trade • 28 JUL: c
officials supply water properly • 30 JUL: increase of crime against women and children • government's inefficacy to find out the truth behind the death o
2 AUG: legislation to criminalize triple talaq, an instant form of Islamic divorce • 4 AUG: demand justice for N. Babysana • demand strict action against in-
of N. Babysana • 7 AUG: demand closure of liquor outlet • demand arrest of those involved in the death of N. Babysana • demand justice for N. Babysa
immediate release of detainee in connection with death of N. Babysana • demand adequate teachers and improvement of school infrastructure • 9 AUG: •
Article 370 and special status for Jammu and Kashmir • 10 AUG: demand justice in N. Babysana case • gun attack against daughter of a social activist • p
objectionable remarks made by Chief Minister about Kashmiri women • 12 AUG: demand justice in N. Babysana case • government's decision to serve
demolition of Guru Ravidas temple in Delhi • 16 AUG: demand Mumbai mayor's resignation for allegedly misbehaving with a woman • demand regulariz
Pebam Chittaranjan • demand arrests of the culprits involved in gang-rape incident • 17 AUG: increasing number of crimes against women and childrer
23-year-old male • 18 AUG: N. Babysana murder case • demand justice over N. Babysana murder case • 19 AUG: N. Babysana murder case • demand enha
N. Babysana murder case • 20 AUG: action of the Amritsar Improvement Trust to vacate flats • demand enhancement of wages • 21 AUG: contractor who sup
a case be registered against a sub-inspector for sexual assault • government's decision to repeal Article 370 • 22 AUG: government's failure to construct a
25 AUG: government's decision to repeal Article 370 • 26 AUG: poor quality of food and poor Wifi signal • cancellation of students' union election • 27 AU
shortage • service regularization for health workers • plans to locate a high-polluting industrial unit nearby • 28 AUG: Indian Nursing Council's decision
30 AUG: demand free sand for the poor and end to the sand mafia • alleged forced religious conversion and marriage of Sikh teenager • 31 AUG: to express
N. Babysana case • demand regularization of contractual health care workers • 3 SEPT: the N. Babysana Chanu case and arrests • poor condition of washr
people accused of kidnapping and murdering a teacher • 11 SEPT: demand compensation for woman's chemotherapy after wrongly diagnosed with breast c
case • 14 SEPT: the new amended Motor Vehicle Act • detention of youths amid restrictions following the repeal of Article 370 • 15 SEPT: mine deforestatic
19 SEPT: counterprotest of visit of Central Minister • 20 SEPT: decision to vacate an apartment • harassment at college • 21 SEPT: demand increase in sala
Chinmayanand on rape charges • demand formation of a self-reliant group's union • 29 SEPT: demand government shift all liquor shops to city outskir
rapist, Swami Chinmayanand • 3 OCTOBER: water shortages in town • Citizenship (Amendment) Bill • 4 OCT: various issues with university hostel • dema
justice for a woman who had been burnt alive by her husband • 11 OCT: demand justice for murder of a woman beaten to death by her police officer husba
14 OCT: demand an unconditional apology for remarks against Indian National Congress president Sonia Gandhi • chief minister over his 'dead rat' comme
punishment for suspect in death of a woman who had been pushed from a roof • delay in road construction • environmental pollution and traffic inconv
admit male postgrads • 21 OCT: delay in implementation of promotion scheme at women's college • bad road conditions • 23 OCT: demand a probe into de
of TSRTC workers be looked into • 25 OCT: denial of entry to temple • demand money deposited at bank • demand that Indo-Naga peace talks not affect
integrity of Manipur • demand increase in minimum wage, legal protection during working hours and a new helpline • 'silence' of State Commission for
Naga peace talks not affect the integrity of Manipur • 1 NOVEMBER: demand that Indo-Naga peace talks not affect the integrity of Manipur • 2 NOV: lack
sexual assault and murder of two minor girls • permission for a new liquor shop • 3 NOV: any impact to the integrity of Manipur as a result of Indo-Naga p
farm activist • 4 NOV: demand release of content of Indo-Naga peace talk agreement • any impact to the integrity of Manipur as a result of Indo-Naga pe
Cyclone Fani • demand socio-economic security and prevention of violence against women • an IED explosion in Imphal • 6 NOV: demand amicable soluti
7 NOV: demand that panchayat secretary be transferred, alleging misappropriation in the implementation of a 100-day work scheme • 8 NOV: demand am
talks that do not affect integrity of Manipur • 10 NOV: any impact to the integrity of Manipur as a result of Indo-Naga peace talks • 11 NOV: any impact to the
of Indo-Naga peace talks • 13 NOV: demand disclosure of the Framework Agreement with Naga people • 13 NOV: the results of the National Register of C
and • to proclaim the territorial integrity of Manipur • 14 NOV: demand a Special Assembly Session in support of the integrity of Manipur • demand pro
demand disclosure of the Framework Agreement with Naga people • 18 NOV: Citizenship (Amendment) Bill • 19 NOV: principal of school accused of misbe
peace talks • demand suspension of preparations for festival in Manipur • 22 NOV: Citizenship (Amendment) Bill • allegedly polluted water supply in
Citizenship (Amendment) Bill • demand creation of Zoland Territorial Council • thousands of pending auxiliary nurses and teachers posts • 26 NOV: deman
in prices • 28 NOV: demand suspension of preparations for festival in Manipur • 30 NOV: government's economic policy • demand separate state of Ka
government over a price rise and a member of Parliament's statement on Mahatma Gandhi • demand government go tough on culprits after a veterinar
capital punishment for the rape and murder of a veterinarian • recent incidents of gang rape • 2 DEC: demand security following an attack on local resid
3 DEC: demand capital punishment for the rape and murder of a veterinarian • 4 DEC: the rape and murder of a veterinarian • the gang rape of a minc
veterinarian • 6 DEC: to show solidarity with women after the rape and murder of a veterinarian • 7 DEC: demand to lodge an First Information Report ove
against women and government's failure to provide safety to girls and women • demand that authorities declare the details of the Indo-Naga peace talks •
immediate punishment for rape cases • demand local markets reduce onion prices • demand that authorities declare the details of the Indo-Naga peace •
demand immediate action against the culprits of murdered and raped girl • demand justice for the Unnao rape victim • the high prices of onions • 10 D
who raped and murdered two minor girls at police station • demand capital punishment for death of girl believed to have been sexually assaulted in a fo
gang rape and murder of a veterinarian • Citizenship (Amendment) Act • 16 DEC: Citizenship (Amendment) Act • 17 DEC: Citizenship (Amendment
20 DEC: Citizenship (Amendment) Act • 21 DEC: Citizenship (Amendment) Act • 22 DEC: Citizenship (Amendment) Act • 23 DEC: Citizenship (Amen

JAN: disruption of rituals • 4 JAN: gender-discrimination of some political parties and communal organizations • government's failure to grant Schedule
party activist's wife • 8 JAN: demand approval of Women's Reservation Bill • 10 JAN: Citizenship (Amendment) Bill • eviction notices • 11 JAN: Citizenshi
nendment) Bill • liquor sales • 17 JAN: demand release of nine jailed youth • 19 JAN: Citizenship (Amendment) Bill • demand dismissal of state minister
• 22 JAN: Citizenship (Amendment) Bill • demand exclusive bus service for students of two women's colleges • demand complete prohibition of alcoho
nission to enter Sabarimala shrine • 24 JAN: demand complete prohibition of alcohol • 25 JAN: demand complete prohibition of alcohol • 26 JAN: deman
or husband's affair • demand complete prohibition of alcohol • Citizenship (Amendment) Bill • 30 JAN: demand complete prohibition of alcohol demand
ment) Bill • 1 FEBRUARY: demand befitting punishment for a man accused of sexually assaulting his 17-year-old relative • 2 FEB: demand the suspension o
hip (Amendment) Bill • derogatory comments made towards congresswoman Priyanka Gandhia • deteriorating health care facilities • 'Pasupu Kunkuma
and regularization for contractual nurses • 7 FEB: head of Applied Arts Department over allegations of misconduct and harassment towards student
Scheduled Tribe status for the Adivasi community • demand regularization for contractual nurses • 9 FEB: Citizenship (Amendment) Bill • Citizenshi
Andhra Pradesh • visit of the Prime Minister • 11 FEB: severe drinking water shortage in the area • demand to establish a commission to monitor learnin
inst teachers on 10 Feb • demand release of the National Democratic Front of Boroland chairman • 13 FEB: Citizenship (Amendment) Bill • 15 FEB: militan
y in Pulwama • the Pulwama attack • demand Chief Minister's resignation over alleged rise in incidents of crime against women • 16 FEB: demand a liquo
n Parliament • 18 FEB: the Pulwama attack • demand rollback of recommendations on issuing permanent resident certificates • 20 FEB: dismissal of wome
r discriminatory of college hostel curfews • casteist remarks against Dalits on social media • 23 FEB: the Pulwama attack • moral policing and randon
representative for shoving a deceased policeman's kin • 24 FEB: collapse of law and order • 25 FEB: demand closure of alcohol shops • 1 MARCH: irregularitie
hed a demolition against local-made liquor dens • national 'Vijay Sankalp' pre-pool bike rally • 7 MAR: demand construction of a women's market for a
rights, wages, and benefits for women • inaction by the state government against absconding non-resident Indian husbands • prolonged inactivity t
om China in honour of Tibetan Women's Uprising Day • inaction on the Pollachi sexual abuse case; demand a probe into suicide deaths of women in th
sexual abuse case • demand free and fair investigation for the Pollachi sexual abuse case • to support media's investigation of the Pollachi case • 15 MAR
nd rights of pedestrians • demand arrest of culprits in Pollachi sexual abuse case; removal of police superintendent for revealing the identity of a victim
enders • manager of garment workers who allegedly assaulted a female worker • 19 MAR: the Pollachi sexual abuse case • 21 MAR: water dispute and wate
• 30 MAR: demand water, which has not been supplied for 20 days • 2 APRIL: demand relocation of an incinerator handling medical waste • 3 APR: Kashmi
e for change • to voice demands for the upcoming Parliamentary elections • the current environment of hate and violence against women • 5 APR: scarcit
APR: demand action to find a woman who went missing while casting her vote • 13 APR: assault on a 16-year-old girl; demand local safety reforms • 14 APR
er crisis • derogatory remarks against a female running mate • the murder of a B. Tech student • 17 APR: assault on a 16-year-old girl; demand local safet
iscrimination • police apathy towards the murder of an engineering student • 21 APR: derogatory audio message of Mukkolathor men against Mutharaiya
demand termination of their hostel contract after female student was assaulted • demand the release of Tibetan spiritual leader • militants who threw
or misbehaving with parents • to show solidarity with slain victims of blasts in Sri Lanka • 29 APR: police's failure to arrest the culprit involved in killin
ge in the number of summer days from 30 to 15 • 2 MAY: alleged errors in the final results of intermediate exams • 3 MAY: rape of an elderly woman • th
stice of India from allegations of sexual harassment • demand closure of illegal shrimp farms • 7 MAY: exoneration of the Chief Justice • a liquor vendo
ent case • 9 MAY: justification of allegations of sexual harassment by the Chief Justice of India • exoneration of the Chief Justice • 10 MAY: exoneration o
istribution of drinking water • demand action against a representative's wife for her use of terse language against protesters • 11 MAY: exoneration of th
r • 12 MAY: exoneration of the Chief Justice • the seizing of a female candidate's car by police • 13 MAY: lack of regular water supply for nearly nine day
ds and oil wells • the rapes of a three-year-old girl and a teenager • coercive action of the Canara Bank that may have led to two suicides • suspected deat
pts to brand people helping in sexual harassment cases as Maoists • 20 MAY: demand swift action against those involved in the Namakkal child sale cas
impregnation of a farm worker by farm owners • 28 MAY: rising rape cases in district and police inaction • 29 MAY: demand justice to victimized wome
AY: demand water supply • the opening of a liquor vend • 1 JUNE: offshore casino facility and a woman activist claiming molestation there • 2 JUN: offshor
at barracks for police women • undue pressure in extracting work from nurses • 6 JUN: water crisis in North Chennai • poor water supply • governor's
g bridge construction • 10 JUN: assault of female dancers, including tribal women • a school van set on fire by unknown men • increase in crimes agains
• 12 JUN: a clash between family members and doctors • 15 JUN: protest against staff shortages at the school • 16 JUN: water pump operator who demande
• 18 JUN: demand travel documents in order to return to Pakistan • opening of a liquor vend on panchayat land • 22 JUN: display of lingerie on the street
nd payment of pending scholarships to nursing students • slow distribution of groundnut seeds to farmers • denial of free laptops that government ha
vice for auxiliary nurses • 27 JUN: demand compensation from state government for killed male relatives • demand regularization of service for auxilia
ainment of 17 members of a marriage procession • exclusion of a school from state government programme • 1 JULY: contaminated drinking water • 2 JU
prit who sexually assaulted and throttled a nine-month-old child • 6 JUL: demand suspension of a professor for lewd comments and unequal treatme
n college campus • demand job regularization and salary increase • 12 JUL: demand authorities dispense drinking water to neighbourhood • rising pric
es on campus • 14 JUL: demand action against actor and politician who allegedly assaulted a journalist • failing to catch stray animals • attacks on huma
: gun attack on a human rights defender's daughter • 19 JUL: attacks on human rights defenders and their families • unavailability of ultrasound facilitie
atient due to alleged negligence from doctors • firing at human right defenders • 22 JUL: demand immediate supply of drinking water • liquor shops i
ainst women • 23 JUL: demand justice for Ningthoujam Babysana Chanu who died at a secondary school hostel • demand justice for death of N. Babysan
tice for death of N. Babysana • 29 JUL: demand relocation of a liquor shop where men make abusive comments to passing women and children • deman
na • 31 JUL: demand justice for a rape survivor • demand death sentence for an elected representative accused of rape • 1 AUGUST: rape of a 17 year old gi
oman who committed suicide due to harassment over dowry • 5 AUG: stoppage of water to canals near farms • the death of N. Babysana • 6 AUG: the deat
al of Article 370, which gave special status to Jammu and Kashmir • 8 AUG: death of a 30-year-old woman due to negligence of a duty doctor • deman
bandh over death of N. Babysana • demand arrest of the persons involved in the death of N. Babysana • death of N. Babysana • demand reinstatement o
urn hostels into a private hotel • 11 AUG: demand justice in N. Babysana case • demand an apology from Chief Minister for remarks about Kashmiri girl
notices • demand justice in N. Babysana case • 13 AUG: municipal authorities for not supplying drinking water • demand justice in N. Babysana cas
chers' work conditions • delay in action against suspect accused of molesting a teacher • to pay tribute to the 15th Death Anniversary of political activis
justice for N. Babysana murder case • demand cancellation of license of liquor shops • police station's refusal to file a molestation complaint against
wages • demand compensation in the event of death of labourers, disbursal of monetary benefits, pensions for female labourers • demand justice fo
milk packets • atrocities and hindrances meted out by 43 Assam Rifles • demand withdrawal of decision to construct a petrol pump at bus stand • deman
atrocities and hindrances meted out by 43 Assam Rifles • the accused in N. Babysana case • 23 AUG: demand swift delivery of justice in N. Babysana cas
cancellation of new liquor licenses • demand hospital be fully functional to provide healthcare to lower-income residents • demolition of shops • wate
t a General Nursing and Midwifery course • 29 AUG: late arrival of police after attacks by Trinamool Congress on Bharatiya Janata Party's office and shop
with pro-democracy agitations in Hong Kong • demand sacking of the Deputy Chief Minister who was caught watching porn at work • 2 SEPTEMBER: th
ooms at university hostels • lack of facilities at college • the N. Babysana case • 6 SEPT: demand restoration of damaged roads • 9 SEPT: demand arrest o
rtage of urea • 12 SEPT: unclean living quarters • 13 SEPT: decision to raise the minimum height limit for constables • demand swift justice for N. Babysan
dress code order at women's college • 17 SEPT: demand government declare health emergency • 18 SEPT: eviction from houses constructed on temple lan
PT: the practice of distribution of liquor to influence elections • 27 SEPT: demand First Information Report against Bharatiya Janata Party leader Swam
: demand regularization • demand swift action against water logging and reduction in power tariff • Uttar Pradesh government's patronage of accuse
wages • 6 OCT: bomb blast on 5 October • 7 OCT: conversion of Christian girls to Islam by activists of various extremist religious organizations • deman
ape of a girl and poor law enforcement • 12 OCT: water scarcity • demand full-fledged function of local police station • 13 OCT: dismissal of sports teache
dian National Congress president • 15 OCT: allegedly disrespectful comments made by chief minister • repeal Article 370 and Article 35A • 16 OCT: deman
8 OCT: prompt action regarding a rape incident • 19 OCT: demand arrest of culprits for the murder of village level worker • decision of women's college t
e level worker • 24 OCT: microfinance companies • demand that Indo-Naga peace talks not affect the integrity of Manipur • demand that labour demand
y of Manipur • 26 OCT: demand that Indo-Naga peace talks not affect the integrity of Manipur • 28 OCT: demand that Indo-Naga peace talks not affect th
arding death of a female executive officer • 31 OCT: demand payment of pay dues to call center workers • demand that Indo
pply • demand that Indo-Naga peace talks not affect the integrity of Manipur • acquittal of three men accused in allege
demand to save the political, administrative and territorial integrity of Manipur from external threat • arrest of convicte
demand minimum salary as well as government employee status • 5 NOV: demand house damage assistance for victims o
Naga peace talks that do not affect integrity of Manipur • demand immediate roll back of fee hike by educational institution
ion to Indo-Naga peace talks that do not affect integrity of Manipur • 9 NOV: demand amicable solution to Indo-Naga peac
Manipur as a result of Indo-Naga peace talks • student fee hike • 12 NOV: any impact to the integrity of Manipur as a resul
C) • results of the National Register of Citizens • transfer of helpful police inspector • demand protection of ancestra
Manipur's integrity in Naga peace talks • 17 NOV: any impact to the integrity of Manipur as a result of Indo-Naga peace talk
female students • Citizenship (Amendment) Bill • 21 NOV: any impact to the integrity of Manipur as a result of Indo-Naga
• 23 NOV: demand restoration of full statehood to Jammu & Kashmir • 24 NOV: proposal to open a liquor shop 25 NOV: th
n of violence against women • lax treatment of a sexual harassment case • privatization move by the government and a ris
Scheduled Tribe status • gang rape of a student and the rape-murder of a veterinarian • the Bharatiya Janata Party-le
s raped and killed • the rape and murder of a veterinarian • 1 DECEMBER: the rape and murder of a veterinarian deman
and capital punishment for the rape and murder of a veterinarian • the gang rape of a minor girl inside a police statio
nd a stop to crime against women • 5 DEC: objectionable sexist comments made by a teacher • the rape and murder of a
ist encounter • the Unnao rape and murder case • demand justice for the Unnao rape victim • increasing cases of violenc
woman tutor who filed a sexual harassment complaint against a medical college department head • 8 DEC: the rape and murder of a veterinarian • deman
C: Citizenship (Amendment) Bill • demand fulfilment of long-pending demands such as government employee status and fixation of salaries • inflatio
d violence against women • 12 DEC: justice for Unnao rape victim • demand death sentence for rape convicts in Delhi • 13 DEC: demand arrest of culprit
nship (Amendment) Act, 2019 • the gang rape of a college student • 14 DEC: demand daily water supply • the gang rape of a college student • 15 DEC: th
C: Citizenship (Amendment) Act • demand justice for wife of former Additional Chief Secretary of Odisha • 19 DEC: Citizenship (Amendment) Ac
• 24 DEC: Citizenship (Amendment) Act • a famous banker and singer's comments about a chief minister • 25 DEC: demand a ban on liquor shop

Protests led by women in India, 2019

Gender-based violence tops a list of concerns including water scarcity, liquor shops, public safety and widespread sexism. Of nearly 800 women-led events recorded in 2019, 89% were peaceful.

SOURCE: ACLED

**Rohingya settlements
by level of destruction**
August 2017 – March 2018

◆ Complete (>90%)
◆ Major (≥50%)
◆ Partial (<50%)

Refugee locations
December 2020

⬢ Refugee camp
⬢ Makeshift settlement
◯ Camp population
← Border crossing

0 ——————— 5 km

*Bay of
Bengal*

**MAP AREA
(RIGHT)**

Kutupalong &
Camps 1–20
704,500

BANGLADESH
MYANMAR
(BURMA)

Choukhali —
*Population data
not yet released*

N1

Camp 21
(Chakmarkul)
16,600

Camp 23
(Shamlapur)
10,600

Camp 22
(Unchiprang)
21,200

CHATTOGRAM

Naf

R A K H I N E

M A Y U   R A N G E

Nayapara &
Camps 24–27
111,400

Teknaf

Maungdaw

ASIA
**MAP AREA
(ABOVE)**
*INDIAN
OCEAN*

A VISIBLE CRISIS

The suffering of refugees is now harder to hide.

The Rohingya people trace their history in what is now
Myanmar back more than a thousand years. However, for decades
the Myanmar government has refused to acknowledge their roots in
the region, instead treating them as illegal, postcolonial immigrants
from Bangladesh. When a 1982 law stripped the Rohingya of citizenship,
the ethnic group became one of the largest stateless populations in the
world. Since then, their persecution has only intensified.

In late 2016, Myanmar's military began ravaging Rohingya villages in a
series of attacks the UN High Commissioner for Human Rights described as
'textbook ethnic cleansing'. Satellite imagery has helped human rights groups
monitor the damage (marked here with diamonds) while drones recorded
the displacement. Footage shows tens of thousands filing along roads
and riverbanks with only what they could carry. Most set out for the
Kutupalong Refugee Camp in Bangladesh, where some 34,000 Rohingya
had been living since the 1990s. To handle the influx, the Bangladesh
government allocated more land. They expected 75,000 new arrivals, but
numbers swelled to 700,000 in just three months. The sudden expansion
made Kutupalong the world's largest refugee camp, with a population
density of 8m² in some areas, far below the international standard (45m²).

Still, the Rohingya have twice rejected offers to return to Myanmar – with
good reason. The country has not guaranteed their safety or taken responsibility
for its actions. In fact, in the spring of 2020, a UN report warned that Burmese
soldiers were attacking settlements once more. It's understandable why so many
Rohingya believe a camp is the safer place to be.

SOURCES: HUMANITARIAN DATA EXCHANGE; INTER SECTOR COORDINATION GROUP; INTERNATIONAL ORGANIZATION FOR MIGRATION

Camp
1E

Kutupalong-Balukhali
Expansion Site

1W

Kutupalong
Refugee Camp

3

2W

Kutupalong
Makeshift
Settlement

2E

4

4
Extension

5

6

7

AREA ENLARGED
(NEXT PAGE)

17

8W

8E

20
Extension

20

Balukhali
Makeshift
Settlement

10

9

18

19

11

12

13

What began as a small,
planned encampment
in 1991 overflowed as
refugees arrived by
the thousands in 2017.
The Bangladesh govern-
ment has since fenced
the perimeter, restricting
further expansion.

Naf

MYANMAR (BURMA)
BANGLADESH

Refugee settlement extent
1991
August 2017
September 2017
December 2020

0   0.5 km

14

ATLAS OF THE INVISIBLE

0   100 m

To manage a city, it helps to have
a map. Georeferenced drone
photographs can be stitched
together to help aid workers
rapidly chart tens of kilometres
of roads, footpaths, and drainage
as well as thousands of new
structures, wells and latrines. In
this view alone, there are dozens
of markets, mosques, schools
and a community centre.

   Such improvements bely the
precariousness of life here. Built
on steep hillsides, shelters risk
being swept away by monsoon
rains. In July 2019, 5,600 lost
their shelters in this way. A
fire in March 2021 destroyed
thousands more. That triangular
mound in the middle of this
image is a cemetery. Because
these camps were never meant
to be permanent, the Rohingya
are running out of room to bury
their dead.

SOURCE: INTERNATIONAL
ORGANIZATION FOR MIGRATION

Mr. Kissinger/The President (tape)
December 9, 1970   8:45 p.m.

P: Well, their not only not imaginative but they are just running these things - bombing jungles. You know that. They have got to go in there and I mean really go in. I don't want the gunships, I want the helicopter ships. I want everything that can fly to go in there and crack the hell out of them. There is no limitation on mileage and there is no limitation on budget. Is that clear?

K: Right, Mr. President.

BOMBSHELL REPORTS

A trove of declassified data documents some decidedly dark ops.

Half a century after the Vietnam War, unexploded bombs haunt the fields and forests of Southeast Asia. As we show to the right, they were dropped by the US Air Force and its allies on North and South Vietnam as well as supply lines in Laos, such as the Plain of Jars and the Ho Chi Minh Trail. But as the war dragged on, President Richard Nixon secretly ordered pilots to bombard Cambodia too (see inside foldout). Operation Menu targeted border regions – each code-named after a meal – where opposition forces were thought to have bases. Then, under Operation Freedom Deal, Nixon escalated the classified campaign into a full-on carpet bombing. Roughly one in four cluster bomblets failed to detonate on impact. To date, unexploded ordnance (UXO) – including landmines from the subsequent Cambodian Civil War – have killed twenty thousand and injured forty-five thousand more.

While Nixon's secret war was a nightmare for Cambodians, the world only woke to the horror in 2000 when President Bill Clinton declassified a database detailing some 3.4 million sorties. He did so as a humanitarian gesture to help nonprofit groups locate and defuse these lethal remnants of war. We will never know the exact numbers of bombs dropped, but the data do reveal the target, weapon type and payload for most missions, all of which narrows the search. About twenty per cent of Vietnam is still contaminated by UXO while Laos remains, per capita, the most bombed country in the world. For Cambodians, the end is finally in sight. Clearing the countryside one square metre at a time, their government believes that with enough international assistance they can be 'mine-free' within the next decade.

SOURCES: THEATER HISTORY OF OPERATIONS, US AIR FORCE; NATIONAL SECURITY ARCHIVE (TRANSCRIPT); CIA (HILLSHADE); EUROPEAN COMMISSION GLOBAL HUMAN SETTLEMENT LAYER (POPULATED AREAS)

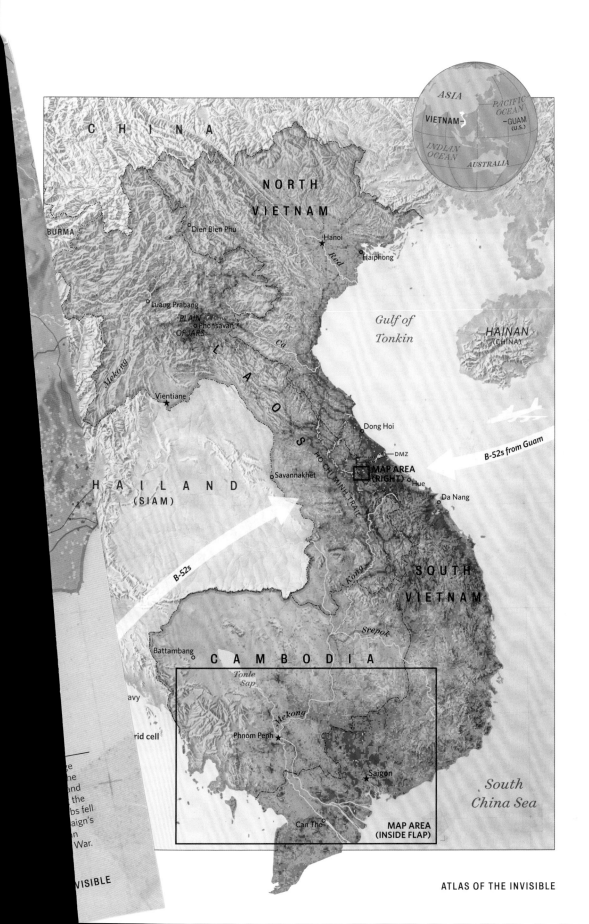

CHINA

NORTH VIETNAM

BURMA

Dien Bien Phu

Hanoi ★

Haiphong

Red

Gulf of Tonkin

HAINAN (CHINA)

Luang Prabang

PLAIN OF JARS

Phonsavan

Ca

L A O S

Mekong

Vientiane ★

Dong Hoi

DMZ

B-52s from Guam

T H A I L A N D (SIAM)

Savannakhet

HO CHI MINH TRAIL

MAP AREA (RIGHT)

Hue

Da Nang

B-52s

SOUTH VIETNAM

Kong

Srepok

avy

Battambang

C A M B O D I A

Tonle Sap

rid cell

Mekong

Phnom Penh ★

Saigon

ze
he
and
the
bs fell
aign's
n
War.

Can Tho

MAP AREA (INSIDE FLAP)

South China Sea

ASIA

VIETNAM→

PACIFIC OCEAN

GUAM (U.S.)

INDIAN OCEAN

AUSTRALIA

VISIBLE

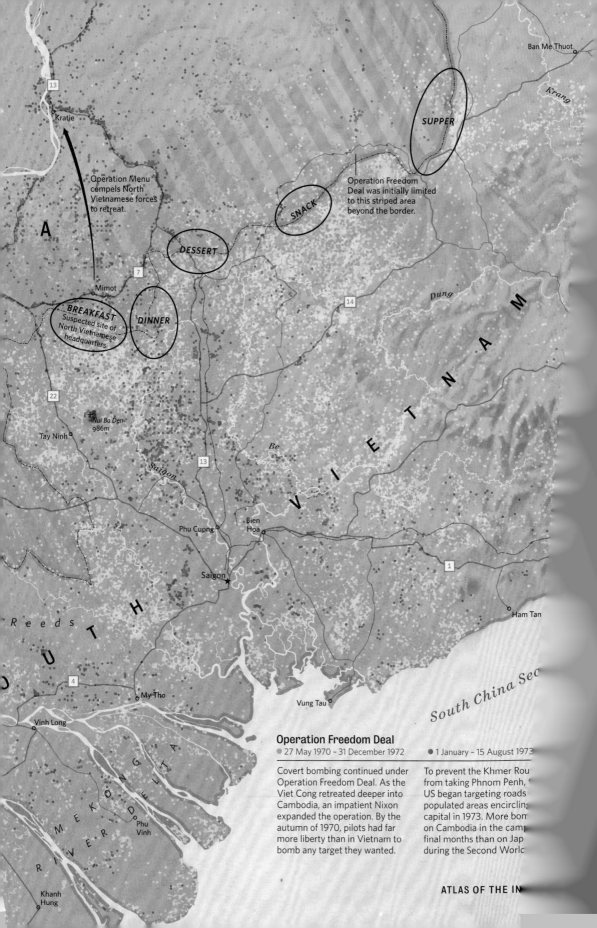

Ban Me Thuot

Krang

SUPPER

Operation Menu compels North Vietnamese forces to retreat.

Kratie

13

A

SNACK

Operation Freedom Deal was initially limited to this striped area beyond the border.

DESSERT

7

Mimot

BREAKFAST
Suspected site of North Vietnamese headquarters

DINNER

14

Dung

V I E T N A M

22

✚ *Nui Ba Den*
986m

Tay Ninh

Be

Saigon

13

Phu Cuong

Bien Hoa

1

U T H

Saigon ★

Ham Tan

Reeds

4

My Tho

Vung Tau

South China Sea

Vinh Long

M
E
K
O
N
G

D
E
L
T
A

R
I
V
E
R

Phu Vinh

Operation Freedom Deal

● 27 May 1970 – 31 December 1972   ● 1 January – 15 August 1973

Covert bombing continued under Operation Freedom Deal. As the Viet Cong retreated deeper into Cambodia, an impatient Nixon expanded the operation. By the autumn of 1970, pilots had far more liberty than in Vietnam to bomb any target they wanted.

To prevent the Khmer Rou[ge] from taking Phnom Penh, [the] US began targeting roads [and] populated areas encirclin[g the] capital in 1973. More bom[bs fell] on Cambodia in the cam[paign's] final months than on Jap[an] during the Second Worl[d War.]

Khanh Hung

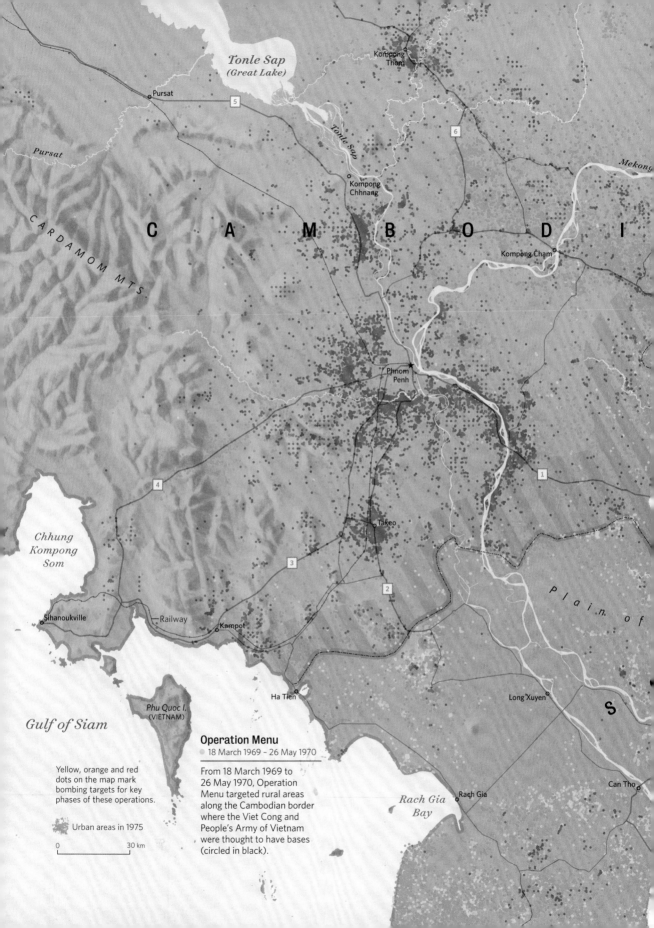

Tonle Sap
(Great Lake)

Kompong
Thom

Pursat

5

6

Mekong

Pursat

Kompong
Chhnang

C A M B O D I

Kompong Cham

Phnom
Penh

1

4

Takeo

Chhung
Kompong
Som

3

2

Railway

Sihanoukville

Kampot

Plain of

S

Ha Tien

Long Xuyen

Phu Quoc I.
(VIETNAM)

Gulf of Siam

Can Tho

Operation Menu
● 18 March 1969 – 26 May 1970

Rach Gia
Bay

Rach Gia

From 18 March 1969 to
26 May 1970, Operation
Menu targeted rural areas
along the Cambodian border
where the Viet Cong and
People's Army of Vietnam
were thought to have bases
(circled in black).

Yellow, orange and red
dots on the map mark
bombing targets for key
phases of these operations.

Urban areas in 1975

0   30 km

Operation Niagara

At 0530 on 21 January 1968, artillery shells started raining down on the US Marine base at Khe Sanh in South Vietnam. The onslaught marked the start of a 77-day siege. For the US brass, losing the base was not an option. It was the last line of defence between the North Vietnamese Army and the populated coastal region south of the demilitarized zone. So come February, when a ground attack seemed increasingly imminent, the Pentagon authorized the largest bombardment in military history. Under Operation Niagara, the US and its allies dropped nearly a hundred thousand tons of bombs between 24,000 fighter-bomber and 2,700 B-52 bomber sorties.

Today, the province of Quang Tri remains heavily contaminated with explosives, many of which are triggered inadvertently by scrap metal collectors, farmers and children. In August 2020, a man found a 900-kilogram bomb while digging a pond. Landslides and flooding unearth them too. Having suffered over 3,400 deaths and 5,100 injuries from unexploded ordnance since the war ended in 1975, Quang Tri is working to be the first Vietnamese province without a single such accident by 2025.

NORTH VIETNAM

Khe Sanh — QUANG TRI

SOUTH VIETNAM

0   200 km

The NVA fired their heaviest artillery from caves on Co Roc and from an area northwest of Hill 881 South. The caves and dense foliage made these guns hard for bombers to find.

Dansavan

Lao Bao

Xe Pon

S. VIETNAM
LAOS

L A O S

Co Roc
837m

Outposts
○ U.S. Marine Corps
● North Vietnamese Army (NVA)

Bombs dropped
January–March 1968

By fighter bombers

Jan. Feb. Mar.

150

75

0   3 km

By B-52s (Jan.–Mar.)

4,000   2,000

SOURCES: THEATER HISTORY OF OPERATIONS, US AIR FORCE

S O U T H

V I E T N A M

Hill 950
Dong Tri
1,015m

21 January
NVA attacks Hill 861;
artillery barrage strikes
Khe Sanh Combat Base.

Hill 881 North

Hill 558

Hill 861A

Hill 861

Hill 881 South

Rao Quan

3 KILOMETRES

1.2 KILOMETRES

Khe Sanh
Combat Base

O P E R A T I O N   N I A G A R A

Hill 64

1 March
Bombing thwarts
an NVA attack.

T R E N C H E S

Hill 471

Old French fort

Khe Sanh

9

Lang Vei

9

7 February
NVA tanks overrun
U.S. Special Forces Camp
to control Route 9.

January

Initially, fighter bombers
provided close air support
to a line of US outposts north
of Khe Sanh. Had the NVA
taken those hilltops, they
would have held unobstructed
perches from which to
shell the base below.

February

Bombing intensified as the NVA
encroached along Route 9, but
B-52 raids weren't yet authorized
within three kilometres of the
base. This pocket of relative safety
allowed the NVA to dig trenches.
The Pentagon had no choice but to
move the no-bomb line closer.

March

At the operation's peak, there
were B-52s over Khe Sanh every
ninety minutes. Each held 108
220-kilogram bombs. By early
March the aerial assault forced
the NVA to back off from the
base. Daily raids continued into
April to keep them at bay.

ATLAS OF THE INVISIBLE

END TIMES

Since 1947, the Doomsday Clock has chronicled our existential peril.

Amidst the fallout of World War II, two physicists from the Manhattan Project launched a magazine called the *Bulletin of the Atomic Scientists*. Its mission: 'to preserve our civilization by scaring men into rationality.' To illustrate the first cover, they enlisted a colleague's wife, artist Martyl Langsdorf. She understood the urgency to warn the world about the increasing risk of nuclear annihilation and designed an indelible metaphor for our vulnerability – the 'Doomsday Clock'. The closer the clock is to midnight, the closer we are to causing our own extinction.

Langsdorf set the initial time to 11:53 p.m. because it looked good on the page. For the next 25 years, the *Bulletin*'s editor Eugene Rabinowitch decided the minute hand's movements. Since his death in 1973, a science and security board has met each November to review the status of treaties and nuclear arsenals and to consider whether humanity is more or less imperiled than in years past. Tracing their assessments over time reveals swings of the geopolitical pendulum from deterrence to disarmament. For instance, in 1991, as Russia and the US purged their stockpiles after the Cold War, there was such relief in surviving half a century without another nuclear attack that the *Bulletin* moved the minute hand to 11:43 – off the chart of Langsdorf's original design.

Thirty years later, a new threat has us closer to midnight than ever before: climate change. Sea level rise and global heating may not be as dramatic as mushroom clouds, but they could be just as catastrophic. How do you convey this to the public and politicians? As the *Bulletin*'s editors learned decades ago, facts alone are not enough to raise alarm. Neither is an appeal to common sense. In the words of one scientist at the dawn of the atomic age, 'only one tactic is dependable – the preaching of doom.'

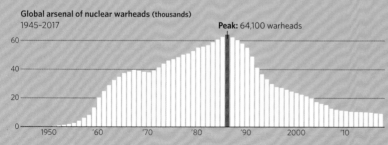

Global arsenal of nuclear warheads (thousands)
1945–2017

Peak: 64,100 warheads

The world's nuclear arsenal is a sixth the size it was at its peak in the 1980s. While far fewer nukes exist now, more countries possess them. It only takes one to cause irreparable harm.

2020

SOURCES: *BULLETIN OF THE ATOMIC SCIENTISTS; OUR WORLD IN DATA*

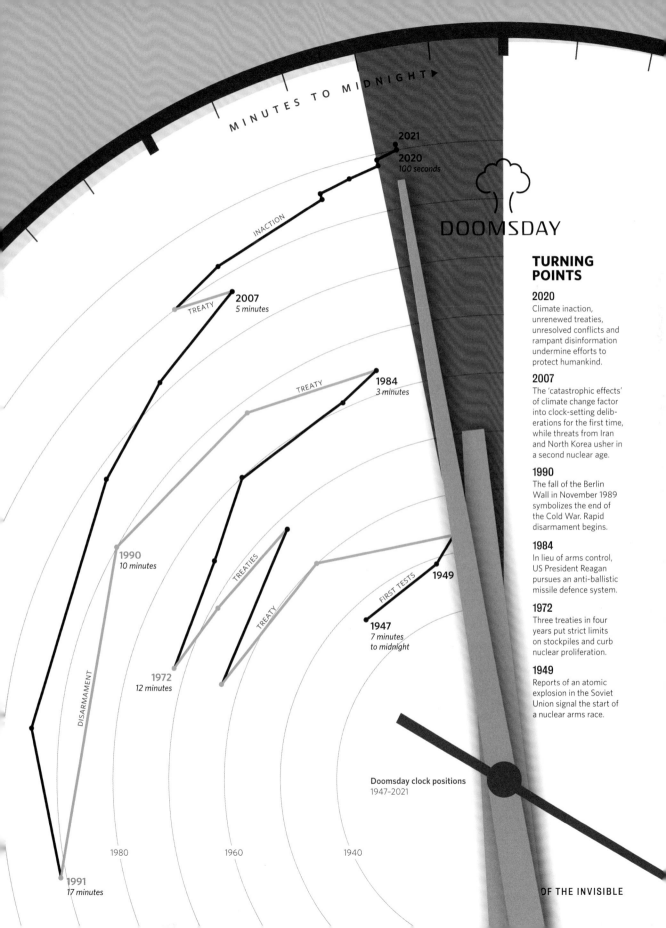

MINUTES TO MIDNIGHT ▶

2021

2020
100 seconds

INACTION

2007
5 minutes

TREATY

TREATY

1984
3 minutes

1990
10 minutes

TREATIES

FIRST TESTS

1949

TREATY

1947
*7 minutes
to midnight*

1972
12 minutes

DISARMAMENT

Doomsday clock positions
1947–2021

1980   1960   1940

1991
17 minutes

OF THE INVISIBLE

DOOMSDAY

TURNING POINTS

2020
Climate inaction, unrenewed treaties, unresolved conflicts and rampant disinformation undermine efforts to protect humankind.

2007
The 'catastrophic effects' of climate change factor into clock-setting deliberations for the first time, while threats from Iran and North Korea usher in a second nuclear age.

1990
The fall of the Berlin Wall in November 1989 symbolizes the end of the Cold War. Rapid disarmament begins.

1984
In lieu of arms control, US President Reagan pursues an anti-ballistic missile defence system.

1972
Three treaties in four years put strict limits on stockpiles and curb nuclear proliferation.

1949
Reports of an atomic explosion in the Soviet Union signal the start of a nuclear arms race.

WHAT WE FACE

'Any person, who may furnish a daily record of the face of the sky,
of the beginning and ending of rain, snow, hail, and the direction and
intensity of the wind will render valuable service . . . If sufficient data
of this kind could be obtained to complete a series of maps, comprising
one for each day in a single year, over the whole [country], the laws of
the general phenomena of our storms could be determined.'

—JOSEPH HENRY, *in the annual report of the Smithsonian Institution, 1858*

NASA'S GEOS satellite takes a portrait of the Earth every ten minutes. In this image from 4 September 2019 (17:10 Universal Time), the swirls of four tropical cyclones can be seen arcing across the Western Hemisphere.

SOURCE: NASA

THE SEARCH FOR CERTAINTY

While writing this essay in the summer of 2020, our phones lit up with weather alerts: Gonzalo. Hanna. Isaias. It was the first Atlantic hurricane season on record to have nine named storms before August. Experts issued dire warnings. Worryingly warm water, they said, was putting the ocean on pace for as many as twenty-five named storms. In retrospect, that was optimistic. By mid-November, there'd been thirty – the most ever recorded.

To storm trackers of the nineteenth century, such a prediction would have been unfathomable, not because of the number but because, until the advent of satellites and weather radar in the 1960s, storms beyond the horizon were invisible.

Consider how little we knew. Two hundred years ago, the few who studied weather deemed any atmospheric phenomenon a 'meteor'. The term, referencing Aristotle's *Meteorologica*, essentially meant 'strange thing in the sky'. There were wet things (hail), windy things (tornados), luminous things (auroras) and fiery things (comets). In fact, the naturalist Elias Loomis, who was among the first to spot Halley's comet upon its return in 1835, thought storms behaved as cyclically as comets. 'When we have fully learned the laws of storms,' he wrote in an 1848 report for the Smithsonian, 'we shall be able to *predict* them.'

He was getting ahead of himself. Before they could know the future, Loomis and the era's other leading weatherheads needed a record of what happened yesterday. So they contented themselves with weather *observations*. At a time when many still believed storms to be a form of divine retribution, they were gathering hard evidence to the contrary. Master the elements, they reasoned, and you could safely sail the seas, settle the American West, plant crops with confidence and ward off disease.

In 1856 Joseph Henry, the Smithsonian's first director, hung a map of the US in the lobby of their Washington, DC headquarters. Every morning he would affix small coloured discs to show the nation's weather: white for places with clear skies, blue for snow, black for rain and brown for cloud cover. An arrow on each disc allowed him to note wind direction too. The visualization quickly

Joseph Henry viewed his map as 'not only of interest to visitors in exhibiting the kind of weather which their friends at a distance are experiencing, but also of importance in determining at a glance the probable changes which may soon be expected.'

SOURCE: SMITHSONIAN INSTITUTION ARCHIVES

became 'an object of much interest'. For the first time, visitors could see weather conditions across the expanding country.

Although simple by today's standards, the map belies the effort and expense needed for Henry to select the correct colours each day. For starters he needed to convince telegraph companies to transmit weather reports every morning at 10 a.m. Then he had to equip each station with thermometers, barometers, weather vanes and rain gauges – no small task by horse and rail, as instruments often broke in transit. For longer-term studies of the North American climate, Henry enlisted academics, farmers and other volunteers from Maine to Mississippi and eventually from California to the Caribbean. Eager to contribute, 'Smithsonian observers' took readings three times a day on standardized forms and posted them to Washington each month.

Mapping daily weather conditions was one thing. Discerning trends from a deluge of crowd-sourced data required more processing than Henry's small team could handle. In his 1857 annual report he eloquently explained the scale of the problem: 'The records of upwards of half a million of separate observations, each requiring a reduction involving an arithmetical calculation were received . . . Allowing an average of one minute for the examination and reduction of each observation, the amount consumed will be nearly 7,000 hours.' At the rate of seven hours per day he figured it would take 'upwards of three years' to process the year's data. One bucket out, three buckets in.

As the backlog increased, volunteers grew impatient. Henry had promised them a copy of the prior year's weather report in return for their efforts. If he couldn't hold up his end of the deal, why should observers keep up theirs? One winter day in 1852, a farmer from western Massachusetts put his frustrations in writing: 'When I sow in spring,' he wrote, 'I expect to reap my bread. When I shear the fleece, I expect clothing . . . Is it right for the mind to be kept in toil and yet go in hunger and nakedness?'

Henry had created a social network on top of a weather network. He was soon swimming in missives of questionable utility. A homesteader in the Nebraska Territory shared his daughter's observation 'that a cold spell always occurs when the moon is in Aries or Taurus', whilst a Chicago resident sent in forty-three drawings of snow crystals. However, sometimes the observers made real breakthroughs. In 1853 Increase A. Lapham, a self-taught naturalist in Milwaukee, and Asa Horr, president of the Iowa Institute of Science and Arts in Dubuque, 140 miles west, began a series of telegraphic experiments in the hope of convincing the Wisconsin Legislature to establish a storm-warning service. Timing the passage of barometric troughs, they found a storm could cross the state in six to eight hours. Lapham forwarded his findings to Henry, and the two began discussing the possibility of equipping more observers along Wisconsin's western border. Then the Civil War broke out.

At its pre-war peak the Smithsonian Meteorological Project had more than 500 observers. By 1862 Henry's ranks had thinned by forty per cent as men traded barometers for bayonets. Severed telegraph lines and the priority of

Smithsonian meteorological observers and budget
1849–1874

Observers (hundreds)
Budget ($US, thousands)

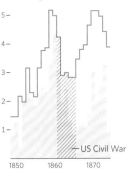

5 –

4 –

3 –

2 –

1 –

← US Civil War

1850   1860   1870

While the number of observers rebounded after the Civil War, federal funding never returned to pre-war levels. What little remained went to repairs after a fire swept through the Smithsonian in 1865. Once daily forecasting duties transferred to the US Signal Service in 1870, Henry made a final plea for funds to analyse decades of data on rain, winds, temperature and other 'peculiarities of the climate'.

SOURCE: FLEMING (1990)

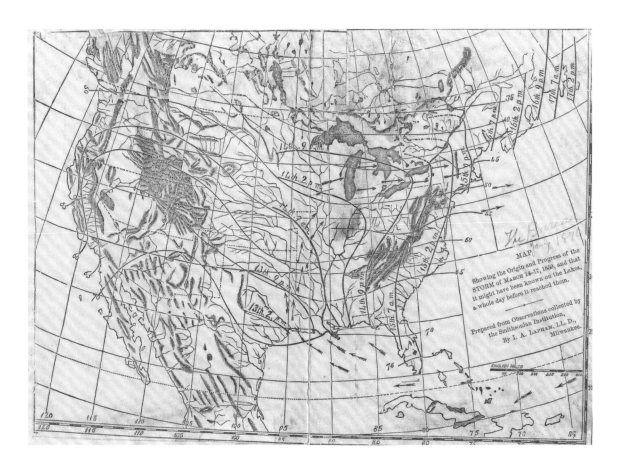

Showing the Origin and Progress of the STORM of MARCH 14–17, 1859, and that it might have been known on the Lakes, a whole day before it reached them.

Prepared from Observations collected by the Smithsonian Institution, By I. A. LAPHAM, LL. D., Milwaukee.

war messages crippled his network. Then in January 1865 a fire in Henry's office landed the fatal blow. All his efforts turned to salvaging what survived.

With a vacuum of leadership in Washington, Henry's citizen scientists picked up the slack. In September 1869 the director of the Cincinnati Observatory, Cleveland Abbe, began publishing 'Weather Synopses and Probabilities' for the Midwest. Seeing Abbe's initiative, Lapham resumed his call for a storm-warning service. Violent weather had ravaged the Great Lakes in 1868 and 1869, wrecking some 3,000 ships at a cost of $7 million. Citing these losses, successful storm prediction efforts in England and France and his earlier experiments, in December 1869 Lapham pleaded his case to anyone who would listen: the National Board of Trade, science academies, a local journal and Wisconsin Congressman Halbert E. Paine. To drive his point home, he made a map using Smithsonian data from 1859 (above):

> The map brings out, very prominently, the fact that the storm first struck our coast in Western Texas, about 2 p.m. of the 13th; from thence it moved to the northward and eastward, touching Lake Michigan twenty-four hours, and the Atlantic Coast forty-eight hours later, thus allowing ample opportunity, with the aid of the telegraph, to prepare for its dangers.

Using data collected by fellow Smithsonian observers, Wisconsin naturalist Increase A. Lapham mapped the path of storms to prove they could be tracked from east to west. His maps helped persuade the US Congress to establish a national storm warning system.

ATLAS OF THE INVISIBLE

The *Chicago Tribune* lampooned Lapham, wondering 'what practical value' a warning service would provide 'if it takes 10 years to calculate the progress of a storm'. Congressman Paine, on the other hand, who had studied storms under Loomis, needed less convincing. He rushed a bill into Congress before the winter recess. In the new year, a joint resolution establishing a storm-warning service under the US Army Signal Office passed without debate. President Grant signed it into law the following week. Joseph Henry, now in his seventies, was relieved to see someone else shoulder the burden.

THE SKIES DID NOT CLEAR immediately. Despite the mandate for an early warning system, an aversion to predictions remained. Fiscal hawks could not justify an investment in erroneous forecasts; religious zealots could not stomach the hubris; and politicians wary of a sceptical public could not bear the fallout. And so, observers were instructed to hedge. They reported 'probabilities' and 'indications' but no more than twenty-four hours in advance. The word 'tornado' was verboten for fear of inciting panic. And though observers predicted the Great Galveston Hurricane of 1900 days before it made landfall, Willis L. Moore, chief of what had become the US Weather Bureau, refused to issue a storm warning for Texas. By the time the storm had passed, eight thousand people were dead.

Data has always had doubters and deniers. So there's some reassurance to be found in knowing that the problems we face today are not new. Despite its naysayers, the Weather Bureau persisted. Science progressed. Technologies emerged. Public scepticism thawed as more people and businesses saw it was in their best interests to trust experts.

As Hurricane Carla angled across the Gulf of Mexico in September 1961, a local news team decided to broadcast live from the US Weather Bureau office in Galveston, Texas, home to the most powerful radar in the region. Leading the coverage was a young reporter named Dan Rather. 'There is the eye of the hurricane right there,' he told his audience as the radar sweep brought the invisible into view. Today we take radar weather maps for granted, but in 1961 no one had seen one before. In a stroke of genius that likely saved thousands of lives, Rather realized that for viewers to comprehend the storm's size, location and imminent danger radar alone wasn't enough. People needed a sense of scale. So he had a meteorologist draw the Texas coast on a transparent sheet of plastic, which Rather laid over the radarscope. Years later, he recalled that when he said 'one inch equals fifty miles,' you could hear people in the studio gasp. 'Anyone with eyes could measure the size of it.' The sight of the approaching buzz saw convinced 350,000 Texans to flee their homes in what was then the largest weather-related evacuation in US history. Ultimately Carla inflicted twice as much damage as the Galveston hurricane sixty years earlier. But this time only forty-six lives were lost.

Forecasts are not always accurate, of course, but they're always improving. It is no longer heresy to predict that you'll need an umbrella tomorrow or a

◆

Trust in **METEOROLOGY** has made our communities, commutes and commerce safer. The same is possible for **CLIMATE SCIENCE.**

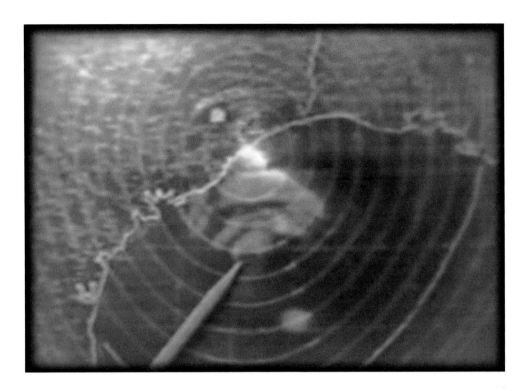

snowplough next week. Trust in meteorology has made our communities, commutes and commerce safer. The same is possible for climate science. Imagine if one day we planned careers, bought homes and passed policy based on fifty-year forecasts as routinely as we plan our weeks by five-day ones.

Current climate forecasts predict a world that's – at minimum – two degrees hotter than the pre-industrial average by 2100. Experts have stopped mincing words. It's not climate change; we're facing a climate *crisis*. In this chapter we show how global heating is influencing everything from hurricanes to the hajj; we measure glacial loss in Alaska and sea level rise in the Marshall Islands; and we show how high-tech solutions can help us monitor changes in the atmosphere and respond to problems on the ground. Gathering and visualizing data gives us the knowledge to take action, the same as it did for Joseph Henry and the early weather observers. What we do with that knowledge is a matter of political will. Yes, mitigation has a cost, but it's outweighed by the cost of inaction. Increase Lapham, the DIY naturalist from Wisconsin, put it best 150 years ago in his plea for a storm-warning service: 'Doubtless there would be failures and mistakes made; and many experiments and repeated observations would be necessary before the system could be made to work with perfection. But is not the object sought of sufficient importance to justify such a sacrifice?' It is too late to stop the coming storm, but we still have time to board our windows.

During a live broadcast on 9 September 1961, Dan Rather used a pencil, radar and a hand-drawn coastline to show the eye of Hurricane Carla off the coast of Galveston, Texas. While weather radar maps are ubiquitous today, Rather's viewers had never seen one before.

HEAT GRADIENT

Year on year, the world is warming.

One of the chief misconceptions about the climate crisis is that warming will be uniform. Deniers cite a cold front here, a blizzard there as proof that climate science is bunk. Such bad-faith arguments ignore the difference between weather and climate. Weather blows through; climate takes off its coat and stays a while. And as the tiles on this spread show, the climate we've ushered in is one tempestuous houseguest.

Each tile represents one year from 1890 to 2019, coloured by how and where temperatures deviated from a reliable baseline period (1961–90). Reading the decades left to right reveals an alarming pattern. While heat waves and cold spells speckle the grid, tiles for the current century are flush with warm tones. Including 2020, the ten hottest years on record have occurred since 2005.

Temperature anomalies (°C)
1890–2019

-2   -1   0   +1   +2   +3   Insufficient data

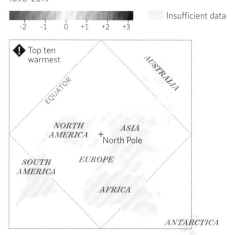

Top ten warmest

AUSTRALIA
EQUATOR
NORTH AMERICA
ASIA
+ North Pole
EUROPE
SOUTH AMERICA
AFRICA
ANTARCTICA

1890

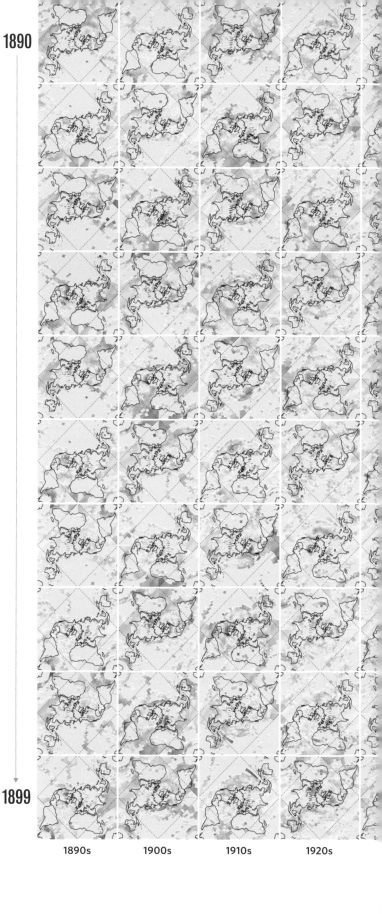

1899

1890s   1900s   1910s   1920s

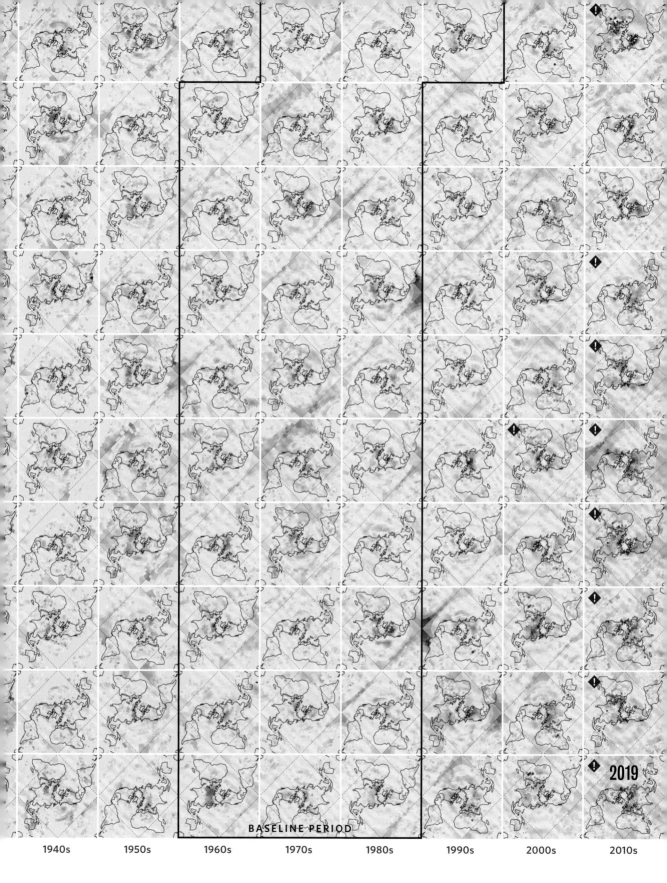

BASELINE PERIOD

1940s   1950s   1960s   1970s   1980s   1990s   2000s   2010s

2019

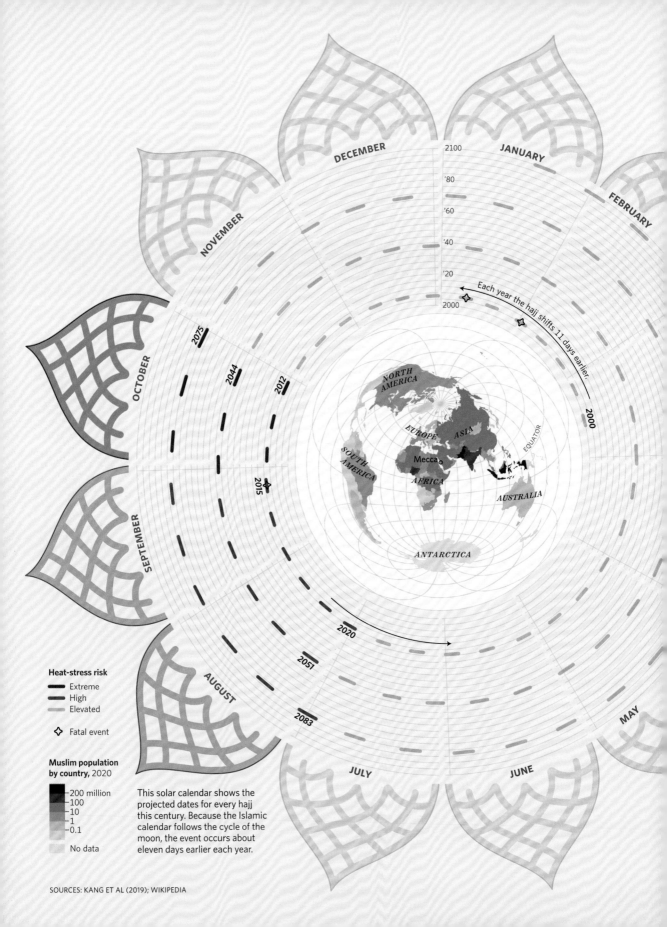

DECEMBER

JANUARY

NOVEMBER

FEBRUARY

2100

'80

'60

'40

'20

2000

Each year the hajj shifts 11 days earlier.

OCTOBER

2075

2044

2012

SEPTEMBER

2015

2000

NORTH AMERICA

EUROPE

ASIA

SOUTH AMERICA

Mecca

EQUATOR

AFRICA

AUSTRALIA

ANTARCTICA

AUGUST

2020

2051

2083

JULY

JUNE

MAY

Heat-stress risk
— Extreme
— High
— Elevated

◇ Fatal event

Muslim population by country, 2020

—200 million
—100
—10
—1
—0.1

No data

This solar calendar shows the projected dates for every hajj this century. Because the Islamic calendar follows the cycle of the moon, the event occurs about eleven days earlier each year.

SOURCES: KANG ET AL (2019); WIKIPEDIA

TOO HOT TO HAJJ?

Pandemics aren't the only threat that planners and pilgrims must consider.

For nearly fourteen centuries, pilgrims have made their way to Mecca. In adherence with the fifth pillar of Islam, all Muslims who are physically and financially able are expected to make the sacred journey at least once. As air travel has grown more affordable, attendance has skyrocketed. Two and a half million people from more than twenty countries participated in 2019 alone. But when coronavirus cases and deaths began to spike in Saudi Arabia in June 2020, the kingdom announced strict limits on who could come. When the pandemic passes, there'll still be reason to limit the crowds.

The hajj is a multi-day outdoor ritual. On the second day, pilgrims are required to walk more than a dozen kilometres in the desert. This is unsustainable. Since the 1990s, temperatures in western Saudi Arabia have risen, as has the frequency of heat stress. Perilous conditions are most common around Mecca from August through to the end of October, when winds from the Red Sea mix humid air with withering inland heat. During the 2015 pilgrimage, which took place in September, more than 2,000 hajjis died in a stampede. While the exact cause of the crush is unknown, it's possible that excessive heat exacerbated the toll; the maximum temperature that year was 48.3°C. Without a reduction in global greenhouse gas emissions, the risk in 2044–51 and 2075–83 will be as bad or worse. Adding more shade, water and vegetation along the route would help. Officials also need to ensure hajjis know they can receive medical exemptions to escape the sun.

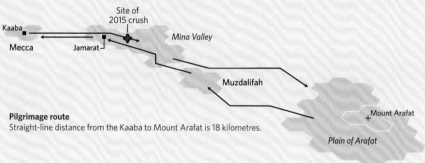

Pilgrimage route
Straight-line distance from the Kaaba to Mount Arafat is 18 kilometres.

Day 1
Upon arriving in Mecca pilgrims are bussed to a vast encampment of air-conditioned tents in the Mina Valley.

Day 2
Hajjis walk 12 kilometres to the Plain of Arafat where they stand until sunset. The night is spent in Muzdalifah.

Day 3–5
At dawn pilgrims return to Mina to 'stone the devil' before proceeding to the Kaaba in Mecca. The pilgrimage culminates in Mina with the festival of Eid Al-Adha. Some extend their stay to repeat the third day's rites before going home.

Active vegetation fires by hexagon
November 2018 – October 2019

- 750
- 500
- 250
- 200
- 150
- 100
- 50
- 30
- 10

Thermal sensors on satellites can detect heat from fires as small as a parking space. Here we show areas with multiple vegetation fires in the year following the Camp Fire, the costliest natural disaster in 2018.

BURN SCARS

Some days it can seem like the world is on fire. It is.

In November 2018, the Camp Fire incinerated Paradise, a town in northern California. Since then, the magnitude of fires in the American West has only increased, while slash-and-burn farmers and ranchers have ignited tropical forests from Amazonia to Indonesia; smoke has obscured skylines in Seattle and Singapore; and bush fires have ravaged Australia's wildlife populations. For many of these regions fire has long been part of the natural landscape, but what is happening in Siberia is unprecedented.

In Verkhoyansk, Russia temperatures hit 38°C on the longest day of 2020. It was the hottest day on record north of the Arctic Circle. Alone that would be alarming; as part of a trend it's terrifying. Six months earlier, temperatures in Siberia began reaching levels that worst-case climate models didn't expect for another eighty years. Such sustained heat turned forests to tinder; drying peatlands became underground fuel. By the summer solstice a total area larger than Moscow was ablaze in the Sakha Republic. Smoke plumes extended to Alaska, carrying more carbon into the sky that June than Belgium emits in an entire year.

It gets worse. In the data from fire-detecting satellites, atmospheric scientists have noticed an ominous pattern: the sites of Siberia's fires in 2020 align with many from 2019, which suggests that they may have never burned out. Instead these 'zombie fires' smouldered in the soil over winter and reignited come spring. If true, it means the wounds will fester for years to come.

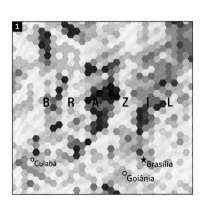

Amazonia
Brazil's rain forest is a natural carbon dioxide scrubber, yet President Bolsonaro views it as a resource to be plundered rather than protected. In 2019, his first year in office, satellites detected 21,000 more hotspots in the Amazon than the year before – data which he dismissed as 'lies.'

SOURCE: NASA FIRMS

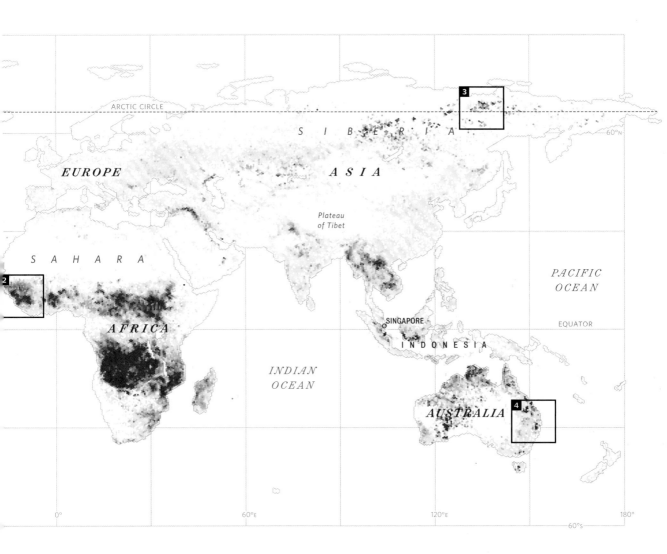

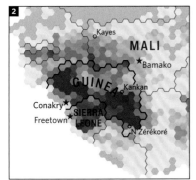

West Africa

Farmers throughout the world set fires to clear land for crops or livestock. In Africa, the red bands on the map reflect the shift of seasons across the Equator. Guinea's dry season triggers fire alerts between December and May whereas Angola's runs from May to October.

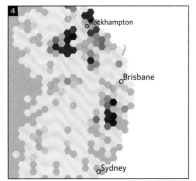

Siberia

Russia's fire season begins in April as snow melts and the tundra warms. In recent years it's been warm enough to melt permafrost too. When the carbon-rich soil thaws, greenhouse gases escape, which – along with wildfire smoke – further a tragic cycle of warming, thawing and burning.

Australia

Heatwaves and drought are creating longer and deadlier bushfire seasons down under. In 2018, the first fires started in August. A year later they began in June. By one estimate the 2019–20 fires killed at least a billion animals and nearly a third of the world's koala population.

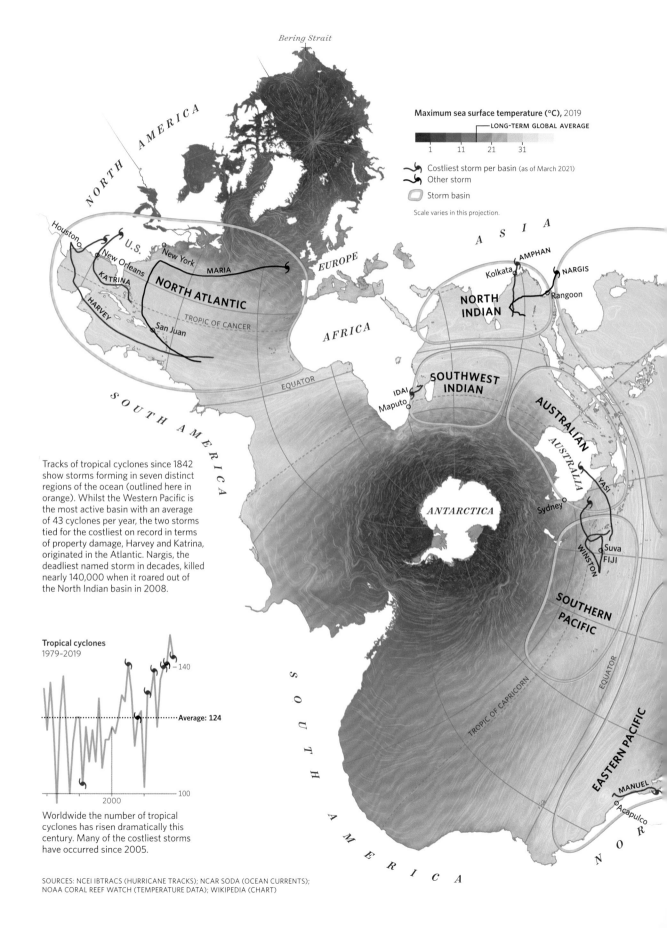

Bering Strait

NORTH AMERICA

NORTH

Maximum sea surface temperature (°C), 2019

—— LONG-TERM GLOBAL AVERAGE

1   11   21   31

Costliest storm per basin (as of March 2021)
Other storm

Storm basin

Scale varies in this projection.

A S I A

Houston
U.S.
New York
New Orleans
KATRINA
HARVEY
MARIA
NORTH ATLANTIC
TROPIC OF CANCER
San Juan

EUROPE

AFRICA

Kolkata
AMPHAN
NARGIS
Rangoon
NORTH INDIAN

S O U T H   A M E R I C A

EQUATOR

IDAI
Maputo
SOUTHWEST INDIAN

AUSTRALIAN
AUSTRALIA
YASI

Sydney

WINSTON
Suva
FIJI

Tracks of tropical cyclones since 1842
show storms forming in seven distinct
regions of the ocean (outlined here in
orange). Whilst the Western Pacific is
the most active basin with an average
of 43 cyclones per year, the two storms
tied for the costliest on record in terms
of property damage, Harvey and Katrina,
originated in the Atlantic. Nargis, the
deadliest named storm in decades, killed
nearly 140,000 when it roared out of
the North Indian basin in 2008.

ANTARCTICA

SOUTHERN PACIFIC

S O U T H

Tropical cyclones
1979–2019

– 140

Average: 124

2000

– 100

TROPIC OF CAPRICORN

EQUATOR

EASTERN PACIFIC

MANUEL
Acapulco

Worldwide the number of tropical
cyclones has risen dramatically this
century. Many of the costliest storms
have occurred since 2005.

A M E R I C A

N O R

SOURCES: NCEI IBTRACS (HURRICANE TRACKS); NCAR SODA (OCEAN CURRENTS);
NOAA CORAL REEF WATCH (TEMPERATURE DATA); WIKIPEDIA (CHART)

Bering Strait

ARCTIC
OCEAN

Sea surface temperature anomaly (°C), 2019
(as compared to long-term average)

+1   3   5   7   Negative values

ATLANTIC
OCEAN

EQUATOR

INDIAN
OCEAN

PACIFIC
OCEAN

Bering
Strait

TROPIC OF CAPRICORN

EQUATOR

TROPIC OF CANCER

ASIA

WESTERN
PACIFIC

Nagasaki

MIREILLE

Tokyo

Bering
Strait

THE

AMERICA

U.S.

ONE STORMY SEA

No shore is sheltered from the ripple effects of global heating.

Sit in the sun in a dark suit and you will feel the ocean's burden. All day, every day, this singular mass absorbs solar energy. In the past fifty years it has also soaked up more than its fair share of the excess heat trapped by greenhouse gas emissions. This map views the world's oceans as an interconnected body of water – one whose surface temperatures are increasing rapidly. In 2019, waters in the Arctic exceeded their historical average by seven degrees Celsius (see above).

Like heads of a hydra the effects multiply. Melting sea ice and sea level rise, the ones you hear about most, we examine on pages 166–71. Other consequences are more insidious. Warmer water holds less oxygen, kills heat-sensitive species, pumps more moisture into the air and disrupts ocean and atmospheric currents. In turn hundreds of hypoxic 'dead zones' have jeopardized fisheries and food chains; half of Australia's Great Barrier Reef has died; storms have swelled in size, force and saturation; and these monster storms are lingering longer after landfall. Hurricane Harvey, the wettest storm in US history, hung around Houston for four days in 2017, dumping well over a metre of rain and costing $125 billion in damage.

Berners Bay

ICE FLOWS

A glacial pace is no longer slow.

The Juneau Icefield, North America's fifth largest,
straddles the boundary between the US and Canada.
To the west it meets primeval rainforest; to the east
it fills tributaries of the Yukon River. From the centre
of it all flows the mighty Taku Glacier, which, despite
global heating, was still advancing until 2018. Then
the retreat began.

Glaciers act like giant conveyor belts. Snow piles up
at the top, compacts into hard ice and then gradually
slides down valley to the glacier's snout where it
melts away. Scientists participating in the Juneau
Icefield Research Program use a simple formula called
'mass balance' to gauge the health of this system.
Advancing glaciers have a positive mass balance
value because there's more snow and ice entering the
glacier at the top than exiting at the snout. In the case
of the Taku (and most other glaciers on the planet
now) that ratio has inverted. So much snow is melting
each summer that it can't accumulate. Essentially,
the glacier starves. With less snow and ice to reflect
the sun's rays and more exposed rock to absorb them,
temperatures in the region will increase and hasten
the retreat. According to some scenarios, the Icefield
will be gone in just 200 years.

Eagle Gl.

Favorite Channel

One way to measure the
speed of a glacier is to use
satellite imagery to track the
movement of surface features
on the ice. In the multihued flows
to the right, warmer colours
indicate faster movement. While
not as precise as ground surveys,
the technique provides a rapid
global view of glacier health.

Juneau •

NORTH
AMERICA

U.S.

Average glacier surface velocity, 2018
(metres per year)

| 0 | 200 | 400 |

| 0 | 5 km |

Stephens Passage

SOURCES: NASA/JPL-CALTECH; POLAR GEOSPATIAL CENTER; NASA LCLUC

Bucher Gl.

Gilkey Glacier

Tulsequah Gl.

Nelles Peak

BRITISH COLUMBIA, CANADA
ALASKA, U.S.

Devils Paw

J U N E A U

Matthes Gl.

West Branch Taku Gl.

2018 snow line

Hades Highway

I C E F I E L D

The Snow Towers

Demorest Glacier

East Twin Gl.

T A K U

Taku Towers

2013 snow line

West Twin Gl.

Emperor Peak

Accumulation above the snow line feeds the glacier; snowfall below it melts. In 2018, the snow line was too high for the glacier to keep advancing.

Taku Gl.

G L A C I E R

Twin Glacier Lake

Herbert Gl.

Mendenhall Towers

Southwest Branch Taku Gl.

Taku

Mendenhall Gl.

Norris Glacier

Juneau International Airport

Lemon Creek Gl.

Because the first 45 kilometres of the Taku Valley are below sea level, its glacier is especially vulnerable. Currently a wall of ice and sediment keeps the inlet at bay. When that collapses the valley will flood and melt the glacier from below too.

Gastineau Channel

Juneau

Taku Inlet

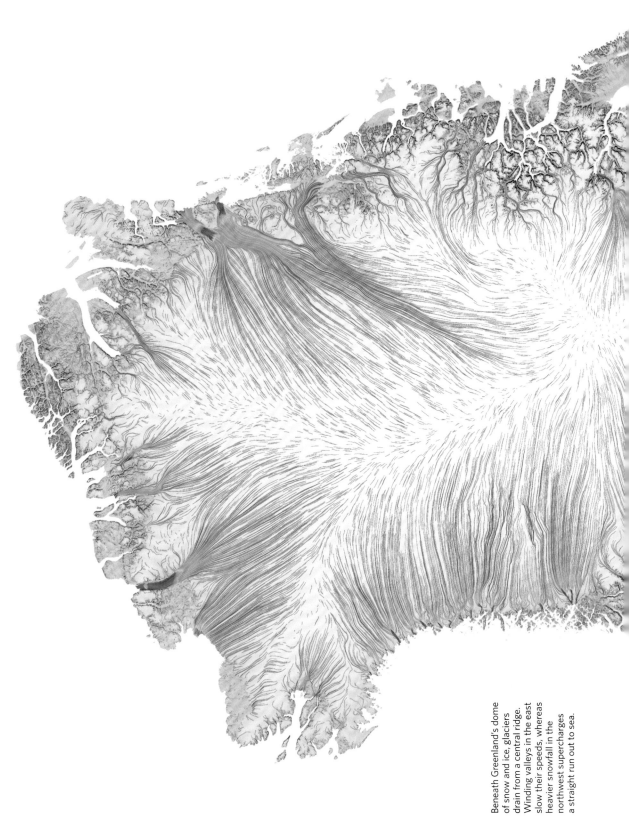

Beneath Greenland's dome of snow and ice, glaciers drain from a central ridge. Winding valleys in the east slow their speeds, whereas heavier snowfall in the northwest supercharges a straight run out to sea.

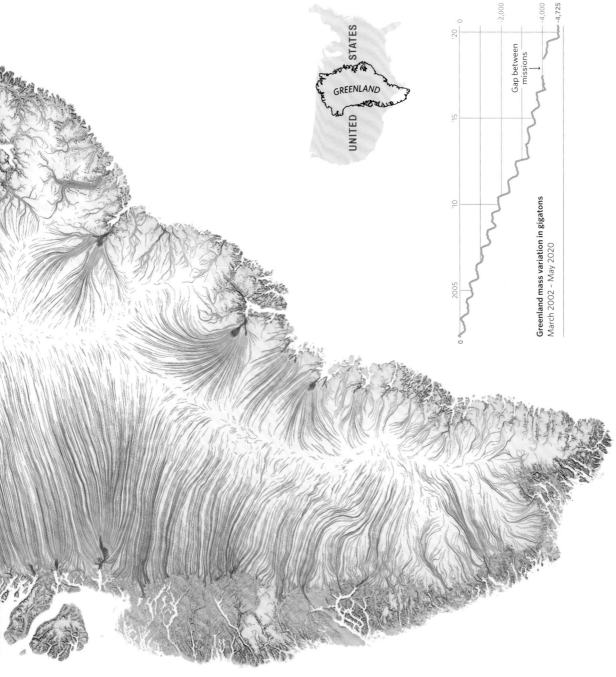

While the loss of the Juneau Icefield will have little effect on the world's sea levels, the loss of Greenland's ice sheet would be catastrophic. Sea levels would rise seven metres and submerge entire nations (see pp. 170–71).

Alas, the big melt is already underway. Greenland lost another 600 gigatons of ice in 2019, leaving it with about 5,000 gigatons less than it had twenty years ago. Part of the problem is that it is hard to stop. Pools of warm melt-water eventually seep into the glacier. This softens and lubricates its base, speeding its slide to warmer elevations where the ice softens further and slides even faster.

Average surface velocity, 2018

0   500m   1 km/year

0   200 km

UNITED STATES

GREENLAND

Greenland mass variation in gigatons
March 2002 – May 2020

Gap between missions

2005   '10   '15   '20

0   −2,000   −4,000   −4,725

SOURCES: NASA; POLAR GEOSPATIAL CENTER

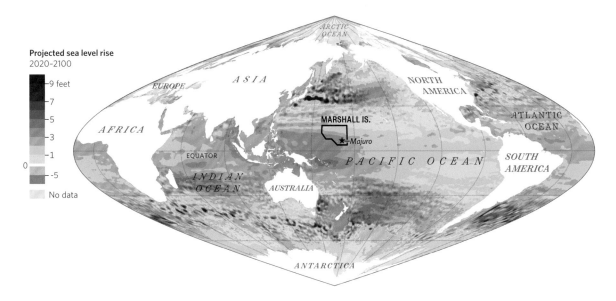

Projected sea level rise
2020–2100

9 feet

7

5

3

1

0

–5

No data

TREADING WATER

In the South Pacific, island nations are fighting for survival.

The Marshall Islands are resilient. Still reeling from the consequences of the US military's nuclear testing programme, which detonated 67 nuclear weapons on the archipelago between 1945 and 1958, the nation of more than a thousand islands is now contending with the cascading onslaught of the climate crisis: ever stronger typhoons, deadly algal blooms, severe drought, dengue fever and the relentless creep of sea level rise. There's only so much the Marshallese can take.

Roughly a third already live in the US. Those who remain sense that their future is being stolen. In an address to the 2019 UN Climate Change Conference, then President Hilda Heine summed up the seriousness of the situation: 'It's a fight to the death for anyone not prepared to flee. As a nation, we refuse to flee. But we also refuse to die.' Without significant change in the projected rate of sea level rise and huge investment in sea defenses, by the end of the century areas of the nation's capital coloured here in blue will most likely be lost to the sea.

Sea level rise doesn't happen uniformly across the Earth (see above). Ocean currents, weather patterns and variable rates of warming can all make a difference. Island groups in the western Pacific Ocean face a greater threat than those in the eastern half of the Pacific.

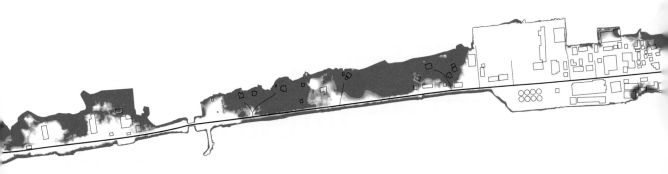

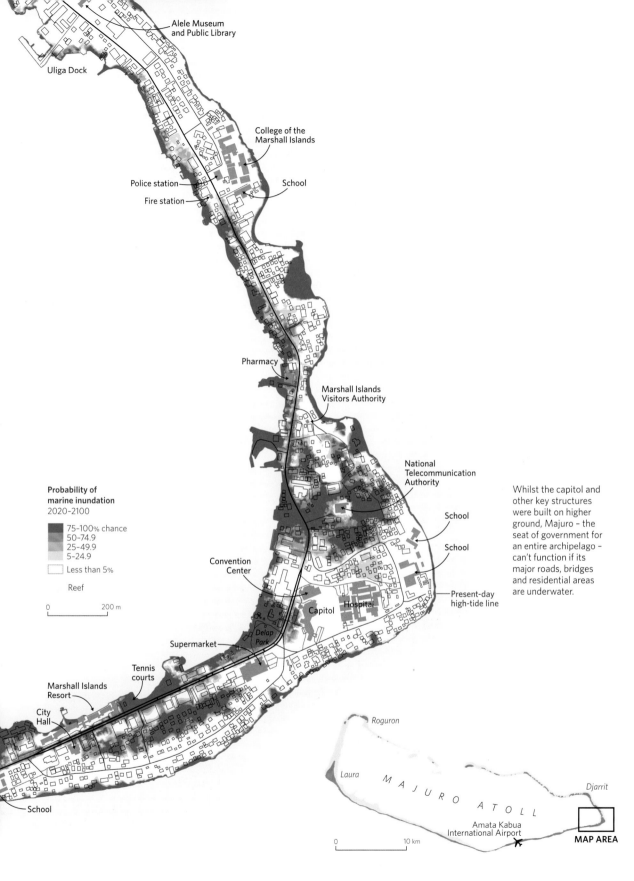

Uliga Dock

Alele Museum
and Public Library

College of the
Marshall Islands

Police station

Fire station

School

Pharmacy

Marshall Islands
Visitors Authority

National
Telecommunication
Authority

School

School

Present-day
high-tide line

**Probability of
marine inundation**
2020–2100

75–100% chance
50–74.9
25–49.9
5–24.9
Less than 5%

Reef

0   200 m

Convention
Center

Capitol

Hospital

*Delap
Park*

Supermarket

Tennis
courts

Marshall Islands
Resort

City
Hall

School

Whilst the capitol and
other key structures
were built on higher
ground, Majuro – the
seat of government for
an entire archipelago –
can't function if its
major roads, bridges
and residential areas
are underwater.

Roguron

Laura

M A J U R O   A T O L L

Djarrit

MAP AREA

Amata Kabua
International Airport

0   10 km

SOURCES: GESCH ET AL. (2020); NOAA

Fishing hours per grid cell, 2012–16

- More than 1,000
- 500–1,000
- 100–499
- Less than 100

Exclusive economic zone

Each grid cell measures 0.5 x 0.5 degrees.

Likely rendezvous with a refrigerated cargo ship, 2012–17

- ◆ Drifting longliner
- • Other fishing method
- → Route of reefer

Range of four Chinese longliners (May–August 2017)

0   3,000 km

7 July 2017
Reefer leaves Fuzhou.

5–7 August
Reefer meets longliners.

13 Aug.
Ecuadorean Navy detains reefer.

Galápagos Is.
(ECUADOR)

ECUADOR

30°N

EQUATOR

120°E

180°

120°W

30°S

PACIFIC OCEAN

ASIA

CHINA

NORTH AMERICA

AUSTRALIA

SOUTH AMERICA

ANTARCTICA

Transshipment

Drifting longliner   Reefer

In August 2017, a Chinese refrigerator ship was found carrying thousands of sharks and fins illegally in the protected waters of the Galápagos. Tracking data showed the reefer alongside four longliners a week earlier. Ecuador fined the ship's owner $5.9 million and sentenced the captain to four years in prison.

CAUGHT AT SEA

The tracks of fishing vessels reveal illegal activity.

For the world's fisheries, the effects of climate change are already here. A global survey of sea temperatures and fish populations found that yields began to decrease last century as oceans began to warm. If fish continue to flee for cooler waters, island nations whose diets and economies depend on seafood will be gutted. Overfishing compounds the damage. When there are fewer fish in the sea, it's harder for them to reproduce because, well, there are fewer fish in the sea.

SOURCE: GLOBAL FISHING WATCH

ARCTIC OCEAN

NORTH AMERICA

ASIA

CHINA

EUROPE

ATLANTIC OCEAN

AFRICA

EQUATOR

ECUADOR

SOUTH AMERICA

MAURITIUS

INDIAN OCEAN

120°

30°N

30°S

AUSTRALIA

0°

60°W

60°E

After a rendezvous, reefers in the Indian Ocean often head to Mauritius; in the Atlantic many go to port in West Africa.

ANTARCTICA

Longliners tow lines of baited hooks that can stretch for more than a hundred kilometres.

Fortunately we have new weapons in the fight to eliminate overfishing. Satellites and land-based receivers record the tracks of ships, allowing organizations such as Global Fishing Watch to isolate and study the unique movement signatures of different fishing methods. Longliners stalk the high seas (above) while trawlers and squid jiggers operate on or near continental shelves (see following pages). In analyzing some 37 billion data points since 2012,

Global Fishing Watch has also learned to spot when a refrigerated cargo ship, or 'reefer', sidles alongside a fishing vessel. This pattern often indicates an offloading of illegal catch, especially in international waters. Fishing vessels do this in order to bypass regulations and to get fish to market quickly while remaining at sea. Historically these transfers would have gone unseen. Now that we're able to connect the dots, an ocean of criminality is coming into view.

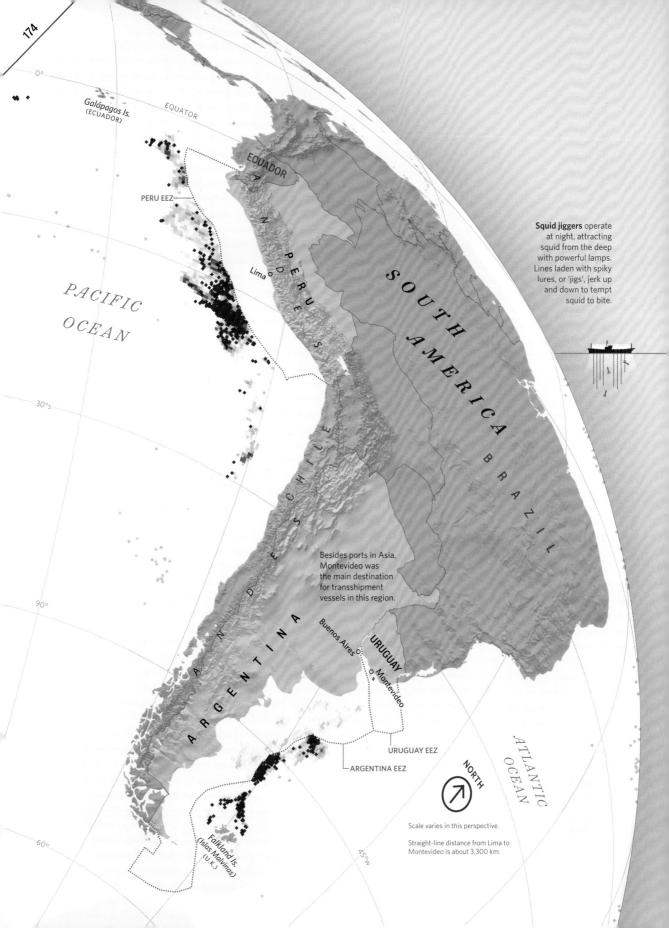

0°

Galápagos Is.
(ECUADOR)

EQUATOR

PACIFIC

OCEAN

ECUADOR

PERU EEZ

A
N

Lima

P
E
R
U

D
E

S
O
U
T
H

A
M
E
R
I
C
A

B
R
A
Z
I
L

Squid jiggers operate
at night, attracting
squid from the deep
with powerful lamps.
Lines laden with spiky
lures, or 'jigs', jerk up
and down to tempt
squid to bite.

30°S

C
H
I
L
E

Besides ports in Asia,
Montevideo was
the main destination
for transshipment
vessels in this region.

90°

A
N
D
E
S

A
R
G
E
N
T
I
N
A

Buenos Aires

URUGUAY

Montevideo

URUGUAY EEZ

ARGENTINA EEZ

ATLANTIC

OCEAN

NORTH

Scale varies in this perspective.

Straight-line distance from Lima to
Montevideo is about 3,300 km.

60°

Falkland Is.
(Islas Malvinas)
(U.K.)

45°W

Fishing hours per grid cell, 2012–16

- More than 1,000
- 500–1,000
- 100–499
- Less than 100

Each grid cell measures 0.5 x 0.5 degrees.

○ Exclusive economic zone (EEZ)

Likely rendezvous with a refrigerated cargo ship, 2012–17

- ◆ Squid jigger
- ◆ Trawler
- ◆ Other fishing method

Trawlers tow a funnel-shaped net either along the seafloor to gather groundfish such as cod and flounder or higher in the water to catch mackerel and other midwater species.

Svalbard (NORWAY)

Barents Sea Loophole

Barents Sea

Novaya Zemlya

RUSSIA EEZ

○ **Murmansk**
Most transshipment vessels in this region were tracked back to Murmansk.

ICELAND

ARCTIC CIRCLE

Faroe Is. (DENMARK)

NORWAY   SWEDEN   FINLAND

60°

North Sea

IRELAND   U.K.   DENMARK

Baltic Sea   ESTONIA   LATVIA   LITHUANIA

RUSSIA

RUSSIA   Moscow ○

NETH.   GERMANY   POLAND   UKRAINE

BELG.

EUROPE

ATLANTIC OCEAN

FRANCE   ROMANIA   *Black Sea*

SLOV.   CROATIA   BOSN. & HERZG.   MONT.   BULGARIA

PORTUGAL   SPAIN   *ITALY*   ALBANIA   GREECE   TURKEY

Corsica

Sardinia   Sicily

Mediterranean Sea   MALTA

0   500 km

30°N

MOROCCO   ALGERIA   TUNISIA   LIBYA   EGYPT

A F R I C A

Areas of Concern

Squid thrive in the upwelling waters off the coast of Peru and Argentina. So does suspicious activity. Global Fishing Watch detected hundreds of likely rendezvous there between squid jiggers and reefers, most of which hurried their hauls home to ports in China. An ocean away in Russian waters and a pocket of high seas known as the 'Barents Sea Loophole', the researchers found hundreds of meetups between reefers and trawlers. In principle, transshipment makes sense: use a mother ship to aid a fleet of smaller vessels. In practice, however, transfers on the high seas obscure the legality of catch and enable trafficking and other abuses.

SOURCE: GLOBAL FISHING WATCH

FASTEN YOUR SEATBELTS

Climate models predict pukier skies ahead.

Clear air turbulence comes out of the blue. One minute you're sipping a drink above the clouds, the next you've spilled it over yourself and your neighbour – or worse if you're not buckled in. Severe jolts have hurled passengers from their seats.

While the Federal Aviation Administration reported only nine serious injuries from turbulence out of a billion passengers in 2018, the risk persists because neither captains nor their onboard instruments can see rough air ahead; instead they rely on other pilots and flight dispatchers to warn them.

In recent years meteorologists have alerted aviatiors to bigger bumps coming this century. Simulations show that as climate change makes jet streams more erratic, the chances of encountering turbulent airspace will soar, especially in autumn and winter along the busiest routes. What does this mean for your flight plans in thirty years? Travellers in the tropics, where routes are less congested, may not notice a difference. However, frequent fliers over North America, the North Atlantic and Europe may become increasingly green in the face.

Projected change in risk of encountering moderate turbulence while flying at 34,000 feet, 2050–80

-75% 0 125 250 375 500%

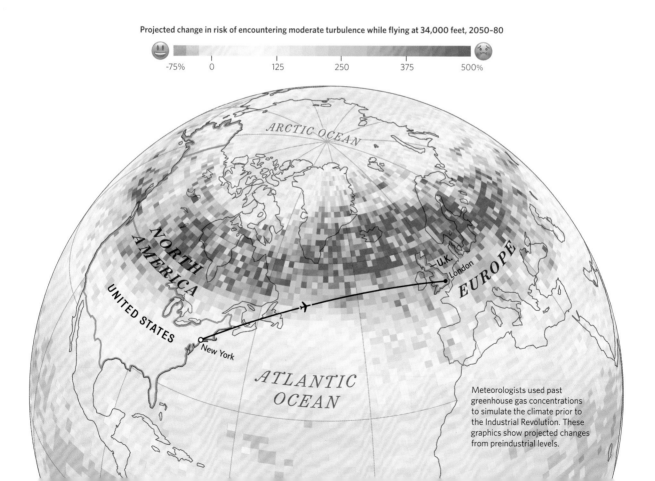

Meteorologists used past greenhouse gas concentrations to simulate the climate prior to the Industrial Revolution. These graphics show projected changes from preindustrial levels.

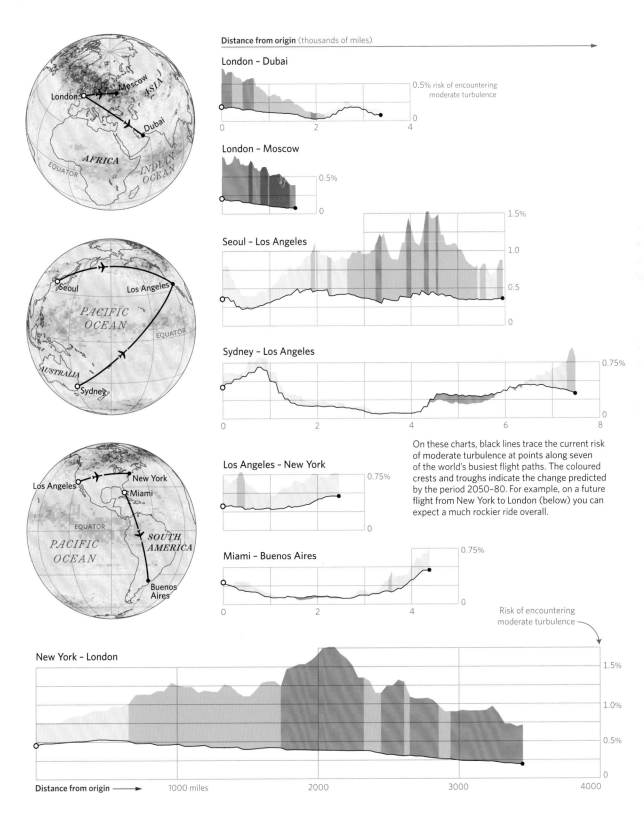

Distance from origin (thousands of miles)

London – Dubai

0.5% risk of encountering moderate turbulence

0

London – Moscow

0.5%

0

1.5%

Seoul – Los Angeles

1.0

0.5

0

Sydney – Los Angeles

0.75%

0

On these charts, black lines trace the current risk of moderate turbulence at points along seven of the world's busiest flight paths. The coloured crests and troughs indicate the change predicted by the period 2050–80. For example, on a future flight from New York to London (below) you can expect a much rockier ride overall.

Los Angeles – New York

0.75%

0

Miami – Buenos Aires

0.75%

0

Risk of encountering moderate turbulence

New York – London

1.5%

1.0%

0.5%

0

Distance from origin ⟶   1000 miles   2000   3000   4000

SOURCE: LUKE STORER, PAUL WILLIAMS AND MANOJ JOSHI, UNIVERSITY OF READING

ATLAS OF THE INVISIBLE

ALL-SEEING EYES

Satellites are now among our first responders.

On 28 September 2018 a magnitude 7.5 earthquake shook the island of Sulawesi in Indonesia. Undersea landslides sent six-metre waves into the city of Palu. Photos from the scene show a hellscape: twisted metal, toppled minarets, miles of rubble awash with seawater. Amongst such widespread destruction, how did rescuers know where to begin?

Within hours of the quake, the European Union's Copernicus Emergency Management Service processed new satellite imagery to give local officials and rescue teams a literal overview of the damage: thousands of buildings destroyed, bridges out, entire neighbourhoods erased. Comparing before-and-after images, geologists calculated how far the earth had shifted. As the small map to the right shows, land west of the fault slipped south (orange) while some areas to the east lurched north by as much as seven metres (red). Because ground displacement can sever roads, dams and gas lines, such maps were critical for helping emergency responders identify risks and prevent further casualties.

As of March 2021, the EU's Rapid Mapping service has generated more than 5,000 near real-time maps of floods, fires, storms and other crises worldwide. During the 2014–16 West African Ebola epidemic, satellites were even tasked with identifying potential roosts for bats, a known transmission vector. As global heating increases the risk of extreme weather events, it's reassuring to know that *when* disaster strikes, at least something will be watching over us.

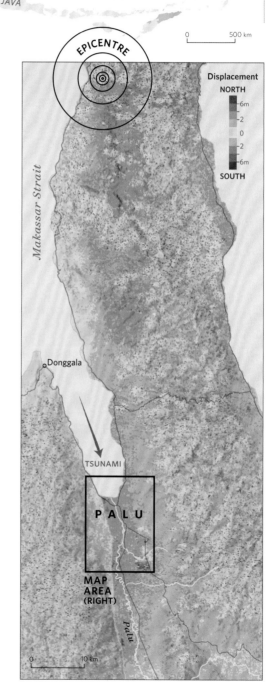

SOURCE: FRENCH GEOLOGICAL SURVEY (BRGM). MAP ACTION CONTAINS MODIFIED COPERNICUS SENTINEL DATA (2018).

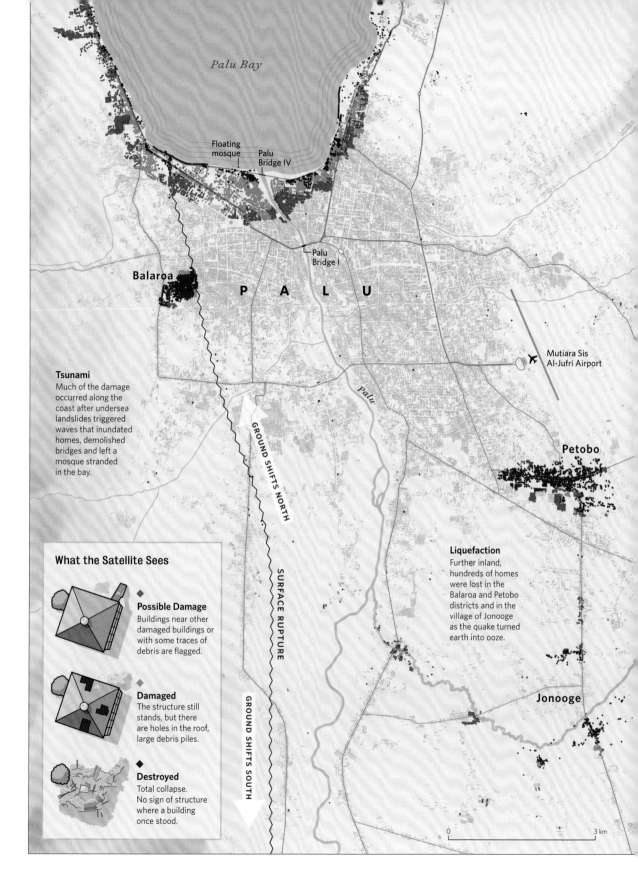

Palu Bay

Floating mosque

Palu Bridge IV

Balaroa

Palu Bridge I

P A L U

Mutiara Sis Al-Jufri Airport

Tsunami
Much of the damage occurred along the coast after undersea landslides triggered waves that inundated homes, demolished bridges and left a mosque stranded in the bay.

Palu

GROUND SHIFTS NORTH

SURFACE RUPTURE

GROUND SHIFTS SOUTH

Petobo

Liquefaction
Further inland, hundreds of homes were lost in the Balaroa and Petobo districts and in the village of Jonooge as the quake turned earth into ooze.

Jonooge

What the Satellite Sees

◆ **Possible Damage**
Buildings near other damaged buildings or with some traces of debris are flagged.

◆ **Damaged**
The structure still stands, but there are holes in the roof, large debris piles.

◆ **Destroyed**
Total collapse. No sign of structure where a building once stood.

0   3 km

MOVE FAST, BREAK MAPS

Facebook wants to digitize every road on Earth. What could go wrong?

Every month around forty thousand contributors sign on to OpenStreetMap to map their neighbourhoods or to trace the roads and buildings in satellite images of faraway places. The result is one of the most detailed maps of the world. By one estimate, users had mapped 83% of the global street network in 2016. Even with this huge effort, the contributors aren't working fast enough to fill in the blanks for the tech companies, who now rely upon the free service instead of costly commercial alternatives. For example, Facebook, which has become an internet provider as well as a social network, needs to know where roads are in order to lay cabling, and to speed the mapping process it has developed artificial intelligence that can trace satellite imagery faster than humans. This approach generates millions of updates, but they are not always helpful; as we show in the insets of Indonesia below, quantity does not guarantee quality. Artificial intelligence still needs OpenStreetMap's seasoned local users to ground-truth its blue-sky thinking.

Difference in road density
per digitization method
November 2019

MORE BY OSM CONTRIBUTORS

▮ 0.6–5 roads per km²
▮ 0.1–0.5
☐ No difference
▮ 0.1–0.5
▮ 0.6–5

MORE BY FACEBOOK AI

0 ————— 500 km

Filling the map . . .

OpenStreetMappers have urban areas covered. It's the harder-to-reach rural parts with few local contributors that see the greatest benefit from machine mapping.

Facebook's method quickly sketches in backroads missing from OpenStreetMap. Adding these to the map may aid emergency responders or optimize delivery routes.

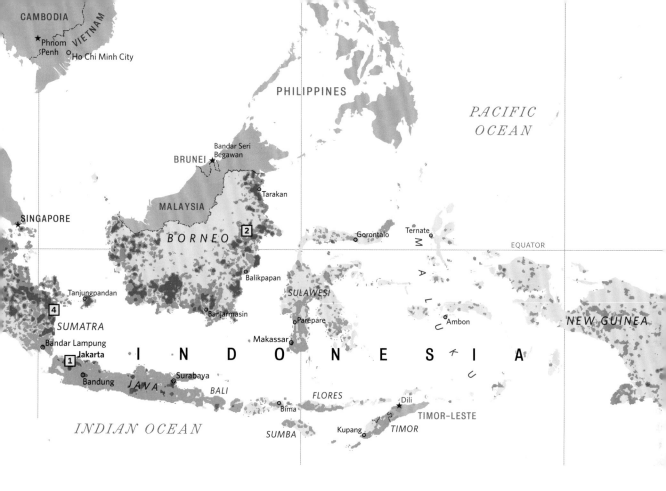

. . . with noise?

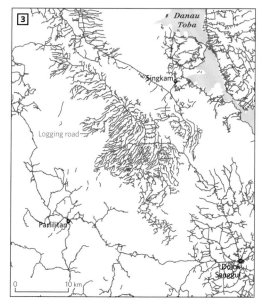

But AI is no substitute for local knowledge. It can mistake logging tracks or intermittent river beds for permanent roads. False positives cause confusion and require manual removal.

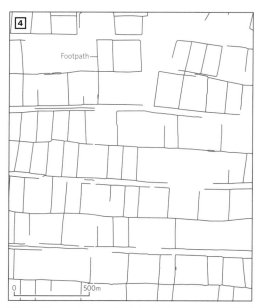

Worse still, the software extracts footpaths around agricultural areas, generating a jangle of unconnected lines. As any GPS user can attest, a bad map can be worse than no map at all.

SALT IT WHERE THE SUN DON'T SHINE

Solar data can help cities weather a snowpocalypse.

Knoxville, Tennessee isn't a particularly snowy place. Its sixteen centimetres per year is a sixth of Chicago's average, yet thanks to scientists at the nearby Oak Ridge National Laboratory the city has become a model for how others can get through a winter with their budgets intact.

As the planet warms, winters are forecast to be shorter and milder. However, regions that do get snow may get a ton. That could be crippling for many US states and cities, which already spend a combined $2.3 billion on winter road maintenance. Typically that involves trucks that dispense de-icing brine uniformly. Scientists at Oak Ridge invented a way to treat roads more efficiently. First they divided Knoxville's road network into 50-metre segments. Then using a lidar model of trees and buildings, they mapped how much sunlight each segment receives on a given day. Smart salt trucks follow this map, spilling brine only as needed. Steep, shaded roads (shown in teal) get more while flat, sunny stretches (yellow) get less.

Saving salt for the most vulnerable roads creates other savings too. It protects our watersheds from unnecessary saline runoff, protects our cars and bridges from excessive corrosion and keeps more tax dollars salted away for the next snowy day.

NORTH AMERICA

U.S.

•Knoxville

To Lexington

75

9

Beaver Ridge

PLEASANT RIDGE

62

City limit

CUMBERLAND ESTATES

K N

DOWELL SPRINGS

169

WEST HILLS

BEARDEN

To Oak Ridge

162

75 40

CEDAR BLUFF

WESTMORELAND

To Nashville

11

ROCKY HILL

140

SOURCE: BUDHENDRA BHADURI AND OLUFEMI OMITAOMU, OAK RIDGE NATIONAL LABORATORY

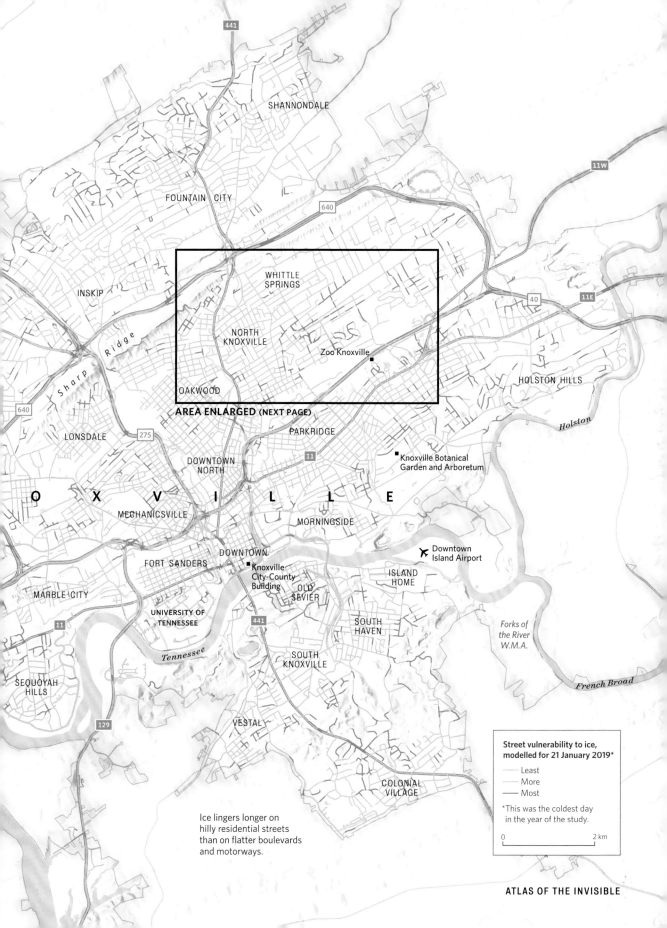

441

SHANNONDALE

11W

FOUNTAIN CITY

640

INSKIP

40

11E

WHITTLE
SPRINGS

NORTH
KNOXVILLE

Zoo Knoxville ■

HOLSTON HILLS

OAKWOOD

Holston

AREA ENLARGED (NEXT PAGE)

PARKRIDGE

LONSDALE

275

11

DOWNTOWN
NORTH

Knoxville Botanical ■
Garden and Arboretum

640

Sharp Ridge

O X V I L L E

MECHANICSVILLE

MORNINGSIDE

✈ Downtown
Island Airport

DOWNTOWN

FORT SANDERS

■ Knoxville
City-County
Building

ISLAND
HOME

MARBLE CITY

OLD
SEVIER

Forks of
the River
W.M.A.

UNIVERSITY OF
TENNESSEE

11

441

SOUTH
HAVEN

Tennessee

SOUTH
KNOXVILLE

French Broad

SEQUOYAH
HILLS

129

VESTAL

COLONIAL
VILLAGE

Ice lingers longer on
hilly residential streets
than on flatter boulevards
and motorways.

**Street vulnerability to ice,
modelled for 21 January 2019***

— Least
— More
— Most

*This was the coldest day
 in the year of the study.

0   2 km

ATLAS OF THE INVISIBLE

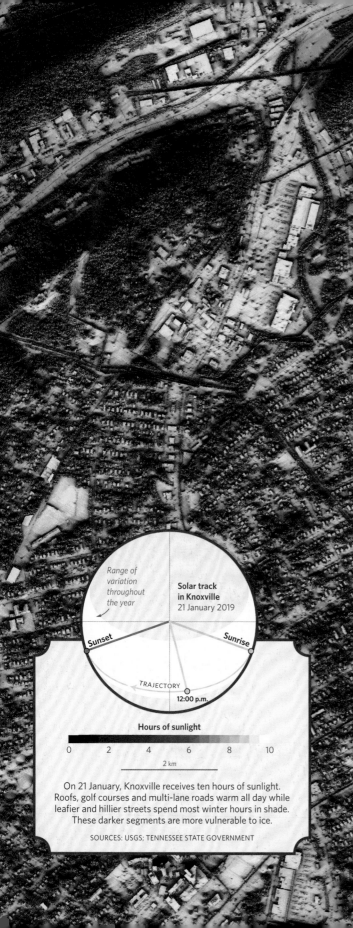

Range of variation throughout the year

Solar track in Knoxville
21 January 2019

Sunset

Sunrise

TRAJECTORY

12:00 p.m.

Hours of sunlight

0   2   4   6   8   10

2 km

On 21 January, Knoxville receives ten hours of sunlight. Roofs, golf courses and multi-lane roads warm all day while leafier and hillier streets spend most winter hours in shade. These darker segments are more vulnerable to ice.

SOURCES: USGS; TENNESSEE STATE GOVERNMENT

THE NEW AGES

Lower birth and death rates are reshaping society.

Of all the coming changes this century, the hardest to predict may be population. In a world beset by disease, war and a climate crisis, how are we supposed to make estimates eighty years out? Nevertheless, every two years, demographers at the United Nations run the numbers to help governments plan ahead. Factoring in longer life expectancy, lower child mortality and smaller family sizes, their 2019 report sees the globe swelling to 10.9 billion people by century's end.

Perhaps more consequential than the total number is the age structure of a population. The population pyramid to the left shows how the world stacked up in 2020. As has been the case throughout history, there were far more children than seniors. By 2100 that ratio will flip for the first time.

The imbalance could jeopardize economies if more people are exiting the workforce than entering it. Seeing the writing on the wall, Japan is enacting uncharacteristically pro-migrant policies in the hope of welcoming nearly 350,000 workers by 2024 to fill essential jobs vacated by its elderly population. Even countries that now consider themselves youthful such as Brazil and Colombia may need to prepare for a top-heavy pyramid.

Current and predicted populations by age and region

----- Life expectancy at birth

Growth will slow in every region on Earth this century except Africa, where the sub-Saharan population could triple by 2100.

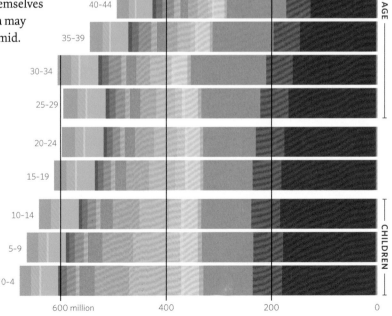

2020

7.7 billion

95-99
90-94
85-89
80-84
75-79
70-74 ---- 72.6
65-69
60-64
55-59
50-54
45-49
40-44
35-39
30-34
25-29
20-24
15-19
10-14
5-9
0-4

SENIORS

WORKING AGE

CHILDREN

600 million   400   200   0

SOURCE: UN POPULATION DIVISION

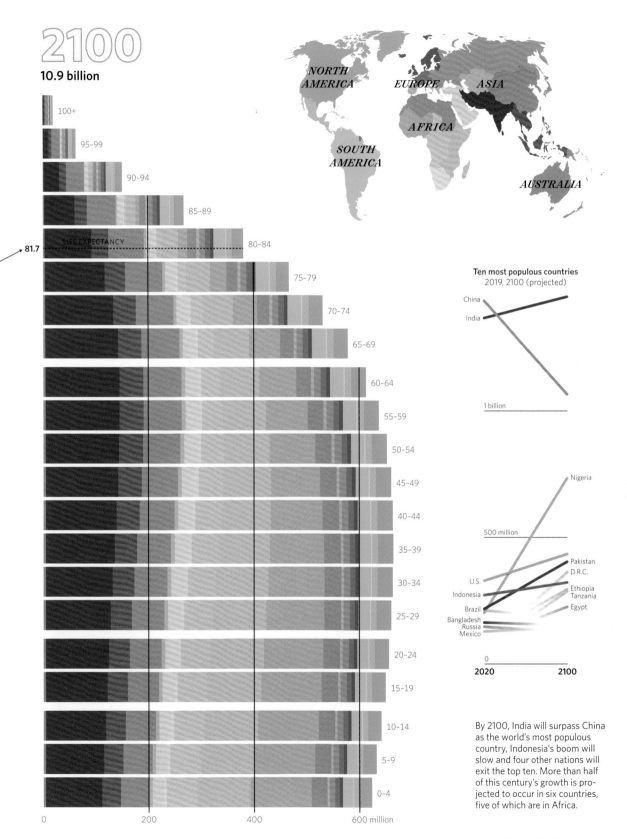

2100

10.9 billion

100+

95-99

90-94

85-89

LIFE EXPECTANCY ·········· 80-84
81.7

75-79

70-74

65-69

60-64

55-59

50-54

45-49

40-44

35-39

30-34

25-29

20-24

15-19

10-14

5-9

0-4

0   200   400   600 million

NORTH AMERICA

EUROPE   ASIA

AFRICA

SOUTH AMERICA

AUSTRALIA

Ten most populous countries
2019, 2100 (projected)

China

India

1 billion

Nigeria

500 million

U.S.

Indonesia

Brazil

Bangladesh
Russia
Mexico

Pakistan
D.R.C.

Ethiopia
Tanzania

Egypt

0

2020   **2100**

By 2100, India will surpass China as the world's most populous country, Indonesia's boom will slow and four other nations will exit the top ten. More than half of this century's growth is projected to occur in six countries, five of which are in Africa.

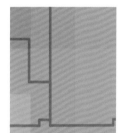 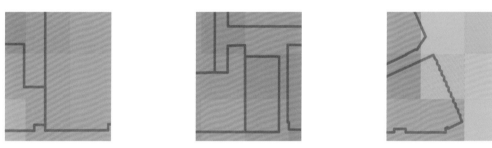 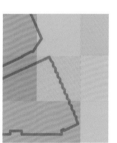

EPILOGUE

'*That you cannot navigate a ship without charts, however,
does not mean that you can navigate it by charts alone.
Rudders and helmsmen are also necessary.*'

—JOHN K. WRIGHT, 1942

by James Cheshire

Data have the power to increase our understanding of the world. In our first book, *London: The Information Capital,* we showed what open data can reveal about life in cities. Then in *Where the Animals Go,* we tracked the journeys of dozens of species from killer whales to bumblebees to explore what data can teach us about the natural world. In its epilogue entitled 'Where the Humans Go', we noted how technologies and techniques pioneered by ecologists could be used to understand human behaviour too.

When we wrote that in 2016, we were imagining the many upsides of a greater respect for the planet. We had no idea that a virus spawned through the exploitation of animals would soon confine us to our homes. Nor could we have anticipated how it would catalyse a broader awareness of the role of data in a crisis. As we completed this book under lockdown, it was clear we had reached a profound moment in the history of data analysis and visualization. People were becoming increasingly conversant in statistical concepts like case rates and death counts per capita. Charts led the front pages of newspapers. And for many, sound data was seen to be as vital to stopping the pandemic as healthcare and vaccine research.

Additionally, scientists and policymakers were eager to see how behaviour was changing in near real time. The ability to do this from mobile phone data had existed for years. On pages 72–3 we show how it can help aid workers estimate evacuations after a hurricane. There have also been clear commercial purposes such as targeted advertising. China has taken this technology to the extreme, feeding detailed behavioural data into everything from credit scores to online dating profiles. But for the most part, backlash over legitimate privacy concerns kept these datasets in the shadows, that is until a virus spreading through human contact – and movement – became the greater evil. Within days of the World Health Organization's declaration of a pandemic, watchdog groups began approving the use of tracking technologies.

The biggest sources of such data are call detail records (CDRs) and the GPS in a phone. CDRs are generated every time a phone pings a cell tower (pp. 94–7). If you know how many phones are in an area, you can guess how many people are there too (pp. 70–71). CDR data will capture all phones that are switched on in a given area, but their locations can be quite generalized if there aren't many cell towers around. Conversely, GPS provides positions

GENERAL

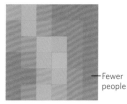
Fewer people

One person

SPECIFIC

Tracking can provide generalized data on crowd size in an area or the specific path of an individual.

SOURCE: KATHLEEN STEWART AND JUNCHUAN FAN, UNIVERSITY OF MARYLAND

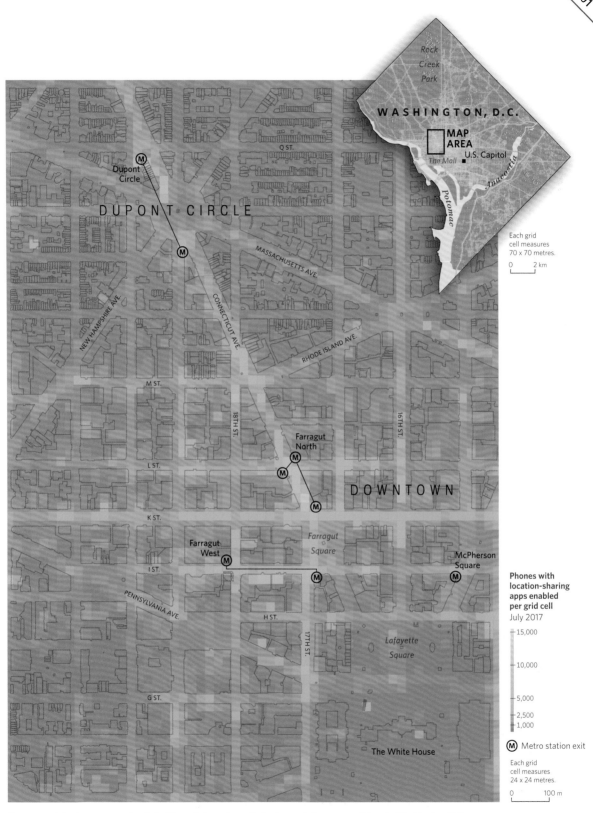

Rock
Creek
Park

WASHINGTON, D.C.

MAP
AREA

The Mall   ■ U.S. Capitol

Anacostia

Potomac

Each grid
cell measures
70 x 70 metres.

0   2 km

Q ST.

Dupont
Circle

D U P O N T   C I R C L E

MASSACHUSETTS AVE.

NEW HAMPSHIRE AVE.

CONNECTICUT AVE.

RHODE ISLAND AVE.

M ST.

18TH ST.

16TH ST.

Farragut
North

L ST.

D O W N T O W N

K ST.

Farragut
West

Farragut
Square

McPherson
Square

I ST.

17TH ST.

PENNSYLVANIA AVE.

H ST.

Lafayette
Square

**Phones with
location-sharing
apps enabled
per grid cell**
July 2017

15,000

10,000

5,000

2,500
1,000

G ST.

Ⓜ Metro station exit

Each grid
cell measures
24 x 24 metres.

0   100 m

The White House

App usage data shows commuters in traffic and streaming out of subway stations on weekdays in Washington, D.C.

accurate to within a few metres, but only from phones with location-sharing apps enabled. Because such phones collect GPS points constantly, they can be followed to your doorstep like a trail of breadcrumbs, depending on how the data is processed. Summing the points in grid squares can reveal patterns without oversharing personal data (see previous page). Using this approach in the early weeks of the pandemic, I was able to create maps of Londoners' activity from in-app phone data and worked with epidemiologists to investigate if Facebook data could indicate the effectiveness of localized lockdowns.

The case for using the most granular data available to tackle disease isn't new. When bubonic plague was sweeping the globe near the end of the nineteenth century, no one knew its source or how to treat it. However, through a strict regimen of transparency, disinfection, quarantine and contact tracing, Japanese officials slowed an outbreak in Osaka and traced it to infected rats in cotton warehouses (see pp. 194–5). A century later, South Korea took similarly aggressive measures to quell a MERS outbreak in 2015. Despite some pushback, especially from businesses worried about reputational damage if they were sites of infection, the government amended its Infectious Disease Prevention and Control Act to allow certain agencies to collect and share highly personal mobility data. When COVID struck, not only were Koreans experienced with prophylactic measures, the legal framework for intensive contact tracing was already in place.

For each positive case in the country, South Korea's COVID-19 National Emergency Response Center undertook a detailed investigation to determine a patient's close contacts. They extracted phone location information (including GPS), trawled credit card transactions and reviewed surveillance footage. From this information, investigators were able to reconstruct itineraries of patient behaviour, which they published online (see example, right). Text messages and app alerts went out to anyone who may have been nearby. The idea of revealing the particulars of a person's movements made many Westerners uncomfortable, but it garnered support in Korea because it worked. By May 2020, South Korea had 250 confirmed COVID deaths. The UK, with a similarly sized population, had 27,454.

The UN concurred. In a joint statement with the World Health Organization and countless other agencies, they said, 'Mounting evidence demonstrates that the collection, use, sharing and further processing of data can help limit the spread of the virus and aid in accelerating the recovery, especially through digital contact tracing.' Specifically, they emphasized the utility of mobility data derived from people's mobile phones, emails, banking, social media and postal services.

There are tradeoffs. After hearing how Japan combated the plague, the French director of public health Émile Vallin thought 'that all these measures, most assuredly right and desirable in themselves, [would] be considered as so many attacks on the liberty of the individual.' Indeed, when Korean officials linked a cluster of cases publicly to gay clubs and bars in the Itaewan district

We're constantly creating digital breadcrumbs. For example, the metadata of one of my tweets contains when and where I posted it and the device I used (right). In aggregate, this information is enough to reveal my daily schedule.

To combat COVID-19, South Korea was more direct. Officials combed phone records, transaction histories and CCTV footage to compile detailed accounts of where infected patients had been:

27 December 2020
Restaurant
1:50-3pm
Home
3:10pm-
28 Dec.
Bakery
2:15-2:25pm
Home
2:30-4pm
Café
4:10-4:15pm
30 Dec.
Hospital
8:40-9:13am
Pharmacy
9:15-9:17am
Salon
10:00-10:30am

Cumulative confirmed COVID-19 deaths, 2020
in thousands

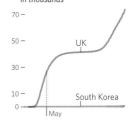

70 –
50 –   UK
30 –
10 –   South Korea
0 –
         May

SOURCES: SEOUL METROPOLITAN GOVERNMENT (ITINERARY); JOHNS HOPKINS UNIVERSITY, OUR WORLD IN DATA (CHART)

↺
JAMES CHESHIRE RETWEETED

{ "contributors": null, "coordinates": null, **"CREATED_AT": "THU JUL 12 16:36:11 +0000 2018"**, "entities": { "hashtags": [], "symbols": [], "urls": [], "user_mentions": [{ "id": 389673270, "id_str": "389673270", "indices": [3, 14], "name": "Guy Lansley", "screen_name": "GuyLansley" }] }, "favorite_count": 0, "favorited": false, "geo": null, "id": 1017447539199619072, "id_str": "1017447539199619072", "in_reply_to_screen_name": null, "in_reply_to_status_id": null, "in_reply_to_status_id_str": null, "in_reply_to_user_id": null, "in_reply_to_user_id_str": null, "is_quote_status": false, "lang": "en", "place": null, "retweet_count": 38, "retweeted": false, "retweeted_status": { "contributors": null, "coordinates": null, "created_at": "Thu Jul 12 15:16:07 +0000 2018", "entities": { "hashtags": [], "symbols": [], "urls": [{ "display_url": "twitter.com/i/web/status/1/u2026", "expanded_url": "https://twitter.com/i/web/status/1017427389075337217", "indices": [117, 140], "url": "https://t.co/RmTAyk6gXp" }], "user_mentions": [] }, "favorite_count": 82, "favorited": false, "geo": null, "id": 1017427389075337217, "id_str": "1017427389075337217", "in_reply_to_screen_name": null, "in_reply_to_status_id": null, "in_reply_to_status_id_str": null, "in_reply_to_user_id": null, "in_reply_to_user_id_str": null, "is_quote_status": false, "lang": "en", "place": null, "possibly_sensitive": false, "retweet_count": 38, "retweeted": false, "source": "<a href=\"http://twitter.com\" rel=\"nofollow\">Twitter Web Client</a>", "text": "Here is a free online tutorial on creating a geodemographic classification using multivariate clustering in R. Avai\u2026 https://t.co/RmTAyk6gXp", "truncated": true, "user": { "contributors_enabled": false, "created_at": "Wed Oct 12 20:27:18 +0000 2011", "default_profile": false, "default_profile_image": false, "description": "Research associate at UCL, Department of Geography and the Consumer Data Research Centre", "entities": { "description": { "urls": [] }, "url": { "urls": [{ "display_url": "geog.ucl.ac.uk/about-the-depa\u2026", "expanded_url": "http://www.geog.ucl.ac.uk/about-the-department/people/research-staff/guy-lansley", "indices": [0, 23], "url": "https://t.co/epN4cY1FEh" }] } }, "favourites_count": 84, "follow_request_sent": false, "followers_count": 389, "following": false, "friends_count": 272, "geo_enabled": true, "has_extended_profile": false, "id": 389673270, "id_str": "389673270", "is_translation_enabled": false, "is_translator": false, "lang": "en", "listed_count": 11, "location": "London", "name": "Guy Lansley", "notifications": false, "profile_background_color": "131516", "profile_background_image_url": "http://abs.twimg.com/images/themes/theme14/bg.gif", "profile_background_image_url_https": "https://abs.twimg.com/images/themes/theme14/bg.gif", "profile_background_tile": true, "profile_banner_url": "https://pbs.twimg.com/profile_banners/389673270/1476096672", "profile_image_url": "http://pbs.twimg.com/profile_images/794517796445110272/xAKeLrWl_normal.jpg", "profile_image_url_https": "https://pbs.twimg.com/profile_images/794517796445110272/xAKeLrWl_normal.jpg", "profile_link_color": "009999", "profile_sidebar_border_color": "FFFFFF", "profile_sidebar_fill_color": "EFEFEF", "profile_text_color": "333333", "profile_use_background_image": true, "protected": false, "screen_name": "GuyLansley", "statuses_count": 106, "time_zone": null, "translator_type": "none", "url": "https://t.co/epN4cY1FEh", "utc_offset": null, "verified": false } }, "source": "<a href=\"http://twitter.com/download/iphone\" rel=\"nofollow\">**TWITTER FOR IPHONE**</a>", "text": "RT @GuyLansley: Here is a free online tutorial on creating a geo-demographic classification using multivariate clustering in R. Available vi\u2026", "truncated": false, "user": { "contributors_enabled": false, "created_at": "Fri Jan 15 13:05:39 +0000 2010", "default_profile": false, "default_profile_image": false, "description": "Senior Lecturer at the UCL Department of Geography. Co-author of Where the Animals Go (@whereanimalsgo) & London: The Information Capital (@theinfocapital).", "entities": { "description": { "urls": [] }, "url": { "urls": [{ "display_url": "spatial.ly", "expanded_url": "http://spatial.ly", "indices": [0, 22], "url": "http://t.co/h0Zdp1cX1I" }] } }, "favourites_count": 566, "follow_request_sent": false, "followers_count": 9534, "following": false, "friends_count": 1592, "geo_enabled": true, "has_extended_profile": true, "id": 105132431, "id_str": "105132431", "is_translation_enabled": false, "is_translator": false, "lang": "en", "listed_count": 615, **"LOCATION": "LONDON"**, "name": "James Cheshire", "notifications": false, "profile_background_color": "131516", "profile_background_image_url": "http://abs.twimg.com/images/themes/theme14/bg.gif", "profile_background_image_url_https": "https://abs.twimg.com/images/themes/theme14/bg.gif", "profile_background_tile": true, "profile_banner_url": "https://pbs.twimg.com/profile_banners/105132431/1511557134", "profile_image_url": "http://pbs.twimg.com/profile_images/776001406838898688/a3C9FUfA_normal.jpg", "profile_image_url_https": "https://pbs.twimg.com/profile_images/776001406838898688/a3C9FUfA_normal.jpg", "profile_link_color": "009999", "profile_sidebar_border_color": "EEEEEE", "profile_sidebar_fill_color": "EFEFEF", "profile_text_color": "333333", "profile_use_background_image": true, "protected": false, "screen_name": "spatialanalysis", "statuses_count": 3061, "time_zone": null, "translator_type": "none", "url": "http://t.co/h0Zdp1cX1I", "utc_offset": null, "verified": false } }

The dots on this map mark 661 cases of plague in Osaka, Japan between September 1906 and December 1907. Cases clustered near cotton factories, warehouse districts and waterways. Investigators ultimately traced the disease back to infected fleas on rats on cotton-bearing ships from India.

SOURCE: TOMOKI NAKAYA, TOHOKU UNIVERSITY

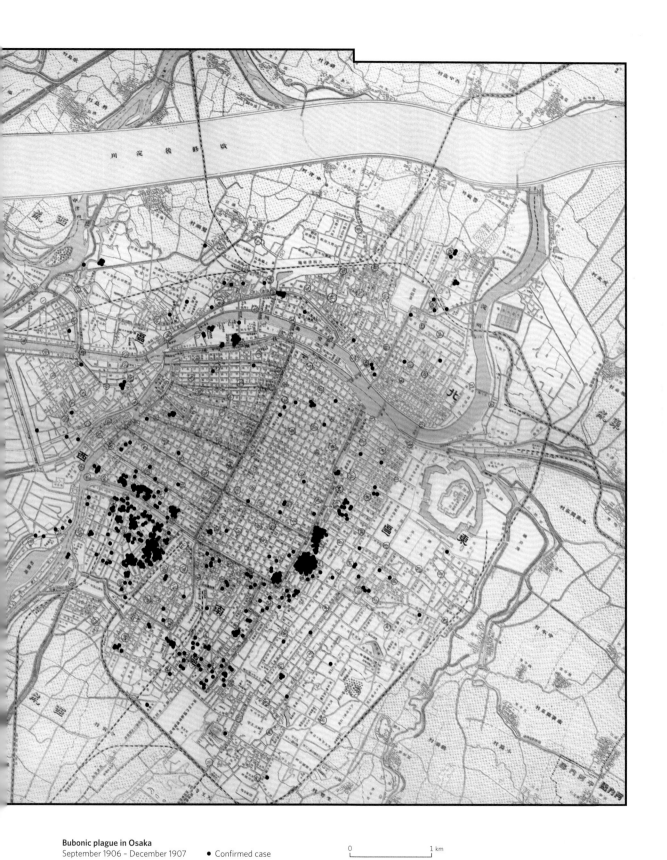

Bubonic plague in Osaka
September 1906 – December 1907   ● Confirmed case

0   1 km

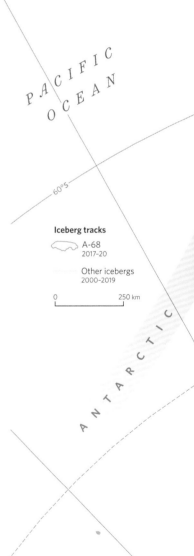

of Seoul in May 2020, many feared for their safety. Using published contact tracing information, the media reported the movements, home neighbourhood, age and employer of the first recorded case in the district. This information outed the person to a country where 92% of the LBGTQ community fear being a victim of hate crimes. Next time, the government may reconsider how much they need to share to manage an outbreak.

So how should we strike a balance between the pros and cons? In an era when a single tweet contains more data than text, it'd help if our policymakers understood the technology they're meant to regulate. In 2018, the US Congress held a hearing after Cambridge Analytica was found to have harvested data from 87 million Facebook users. Then 84-year-old Senator Orrin Hatch introduced himself to Facebook's 33-year-old CEO, Mark Zuckerberg, as chair of the 'Senate Republican High-Tech Task Force'. He then asked Zuckerberg how he sustains a business model in which users don't pay for the service. 'Senator, we run ads,' Zuckerberg replied with a smile. After a few seconds, pause, Hatch nodded and said, 'I see.'

Did he though? In four words, Zuckerberg made it sound simple, benign even. One wonders if Senator Hatch saw that it is, of course, the *targeting* of those ads based on user data that has proved so controversial. There has been more progress across the Atlantic. That same year, the EU enacted its General Data Protection Regulation (GDPR), which enshrined into law the right of Europeans – and anyone whose data is being processed within the EU – to deny a company from using their data. After all, your data is *your* data. You are generating it, so you're entitled to have some control over how or if it's used. We can't count on companies or politicians to oversee themselves. It's up to all of us to keep them honest. To do so, we need to be data literate.

The American geographer John K. Wright knew this when he made the plea for rudders and helmsmen that introduced this essay. The line comes from a paper entitled 'Map Makers Are Human'. Wright wrote it in 1942, a time when maps were being used to wage war. He saw how maps would 'contribute to shaping the thought and action of those responsible for the reconstruction of a shattered world.' But because both maps and their creators are fallible, society needed readers to use their 'qualities of integrity, judgement and critical acumen' to ensure maps are acted upon responsibly. Oliver and I couldn't agree more.

We hope this book gives you hours of enjoyment, looking, discovering, seeing. But we hope it provides more than entertainment. Whilst I write I'm watching satellite imagery of a giant iceberg swirling away from Antarctica at the end of the joint hottest year on record. What good is such knowledge if we all remain spectators? We hope that at least one of our stories will have inspired you to act.

Iceberg tracks

A-68
2017-20

Other icebergs
2000-2019

0   250 km

SOURCES: BRITISH ANTARCTIC SURVEY (A-68); THE ANTARCTIC ICEBERG TRACKING DATABASE (OTHER ICEBERGS)

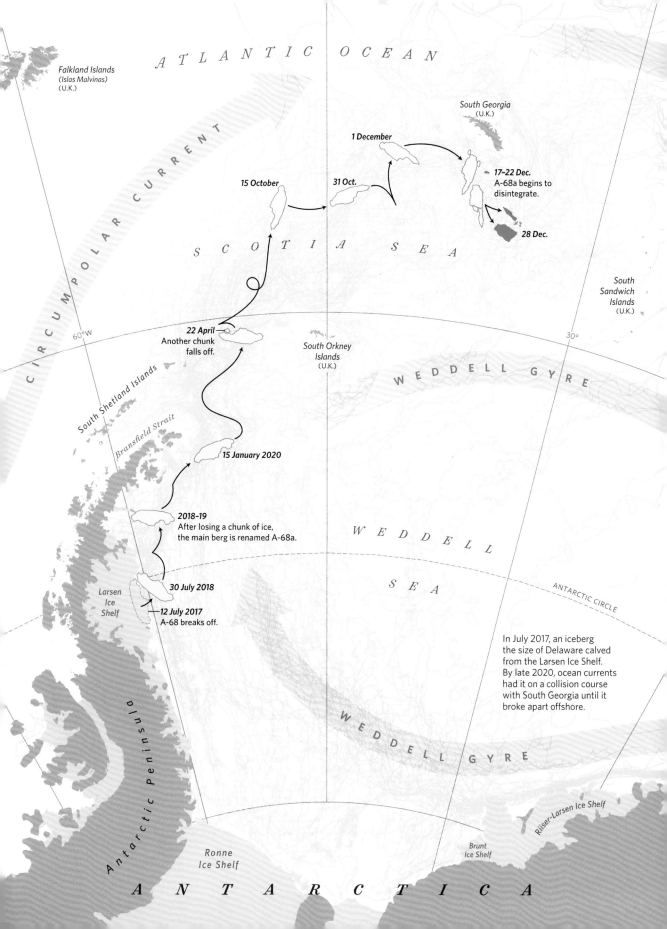

ATLANTIC OCEAN

Falkland Islands
(Islas Malvinas)
(U.K.)

South Georgia
(U.K.)

1 December

17–22 Dec.
A-68a begins to
disintegrate.

15 October

31 Oct.

SCOTIA SEA

28 Dec.

CIRCUMPOLAR CURRENT

South
Sandwich
Islands
(U.K.)

60°W

30°

22 April
Another chunk
falls off.

South Orkney
Islands
(U.K.)

WEDDELL GYRE

South Shetland Islands

Bransfield Strait

15 January 2020

WEDDELL

2018–19
After losing a chunk of ice,
the main berg is renamed A-68a.

SEA

ANTARCTIC CIRCLE

30 July 2018

Larsen
Ice
Shelf

12 July 2017
A-68 breaks off.

In July 2017, an iceberg
the size of Delaware calved
from the Larsen Ice Shelf.
By late 2020, ocean currents
had it on a collision course
with South Georgia until it
broke apart offshore.

Antarctic Peninsula

WEDDELL GYRE

Riiser-Larsen Ice Shelf

Ronne
Ice Shelf

Brunt
Ice Shelf

ANTARCTICA

FURTHER READING

Aside from the works we list in our endnotes, we drew inspiration from many cartographers, data scientists, designers, activists and writers.

W. E. B. Du Bois was best known to us for his data visualizations, collated by Whitney Battle-Baptiste and Britt Rusert in *W. E. B. Du Bois's Data Portraits: Visualizing Black America*. Reading Aldon D. Morris's *The Scholar Denied* revealed how much we didn't know about his ideas, his life and those around him. You can't go wrong reading any of Du Bois's original books and papers. Start with *The Souls of Black Folk*.

Another hero of the book is Alexander von Humboldt, whose adventurous life is brilliantly told in Andrea Wulf's *The Invention of Nature*. Susan Schulten's *Mapping the Nation* will introduce you to a number of American mapping pioneers, whilst the first three volumes of *The History of Cartography* from University of Chicago Press are free to read online. James Rodger Fleming's *Meteorology in America, 1800–1870* was our window into the cutthroat world of the early weather forecasters. For those interested in the intellectual history of computerized mapping and some of the theoretical debates surrounding it, Matthew Wilson's *New Lines: Critical GIS and the Trouble of the Map* is a helpful guide. Shoshana Zuboff's *The Age of Surveillance Capitalism* offers a comprehensive (yet very readable) primer on the new era in which personal data have become an economic resource to be exploited. For glass-is-half-full readers, *Data Action* by Sarah Williams offers a series of principles about how data can be used for social good. And for those who just love perusing maps, we recommend the websites of the David Rumsey Historical Map Collection or the Leventhal Map and Education Center.

We read the late Barry Lopez's story 'The Mappist' after the North American Cartographic Information Society (NACIS) presented us with a prize in honour of the lead character, Corlis Benefideo. It's an inspiring read for map enthusiasts; for budding cartographers, NACIS is an equally inspiring organization.

Finally, the quality of maps and graphics from magazines and news outlets have never been better. Our favourites include *National Geographic*, *New York Times*, *Washington Post* and *Financial Times*.

FLATTENING the EARTH

Cartographers are the original Flat Earthers. For millennia, they have peeled the continents and oceans from our lumpy planet and transposed them onto sheets of paper through different projections. Some distort the shape of countries; others distort their size. Some preserve accurate distance between places at the expense of accurate direction and vice versa. All cartographers have a favourite. In *Atlas of the Invisible*, we found more than a dozen ways to flatten the Earth.

ORTHOGRAPHIC

We use 'globes' throughout the book to locate areas of interest on the Earth's surface.

CONIC

Take a pen and draw lines of latitude and longitude on an orange. Before the ink dries, place a cone-shaped paper hat on top of the orange to transfer the ink. Uncurl the cone and look inside. That's how you get this projection. It preserves area but not shape, a compromise favoured by the EU and US for their continental maps.

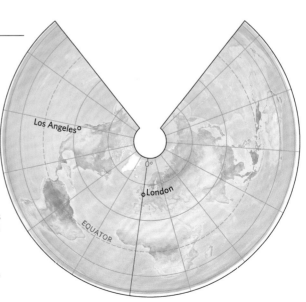

SOURCE: JOSHUA STEVENS, NASA (BASEMAP)

CYLINDRICAL

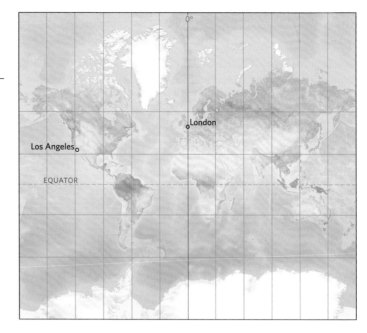

This family of projections are so-called because they wrap a cylinder around the Earth, not a cone. This creates horizontal lines of latitude and vertical lines of longitude – and a lot of distortion near the poles. Most web maps use the Mercator projection (above right). It was also favoured by mariners, so we chose it to track the ways of the whalers (pp. 46–9). We used an equirectangular version (right) to show fires worldwide (pp. 162–3).

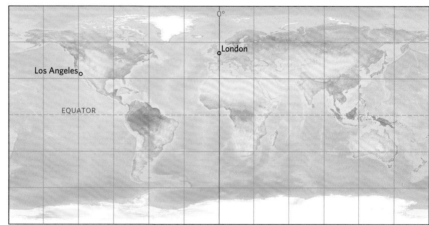

PSEUDO-CYLINDRICAL

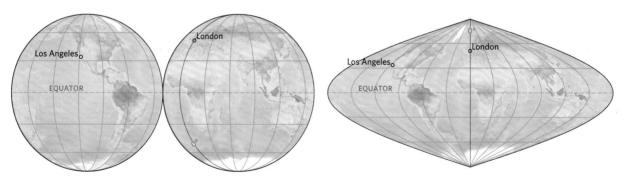

Bending lines of longitude can fix the polar distortion in cylindrical projections. Interruptions can help too. An interrupted Mollweide projection helped us contrast the accessibility of two hemispheres (pp. 92–3); a top-like sinusoidal (right) showed sea level rise spinning out of control (pp. 170–71).

AZIMUTHAL

The projections on this spread use creative geometry to emphasize different parts of the planet. As if looking through a fishbowl, the distortion changes as you change your point of view. Some things bulge; others appear to shrink.

In 1979, Athelstan Spilhaus pioneered one (right) that allowed us to plot hurricanes on one contiguous ocean (pp. 164–5). We tiled another funky arrangement (below) to create the repeating pattern on the book's endpapers and our time series of global heating (pp. 158–9).

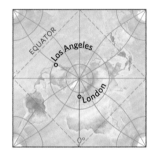

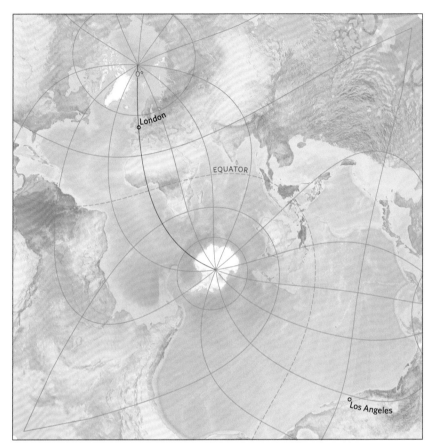

POLAR STEREOGRAPHIC & AZIMUTHAL

A stereographic view of the South Pole let us track an iceberg off Antarctica (pp. 196–7); an azimuthal view of the North Pole allowed us to connect all seven continents with undersea cables (pp. 98–9).

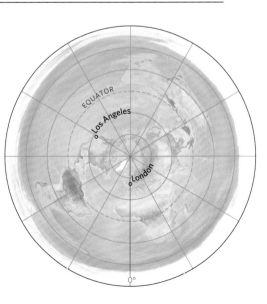

SOURCE: JOSHUA STEVENS, NASA (BASEMAP)

AZIMUTHAL EQUIDISTANT

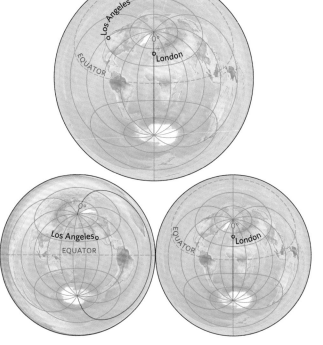

Because azimuthal projections show correct directions to their central point, they're used to make Islamic *qibla* maps with Mecca at the centre. That suited our story on the hajj (pp. 160–61). To highlight the overfishing of our oceans, we took another cue from Spilhaus and placed two side by side (pp. 172–5).

DYMAXION

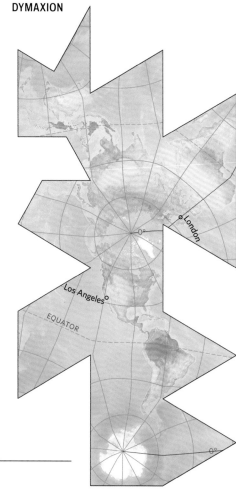

MODIFIED AZIMUTHAL

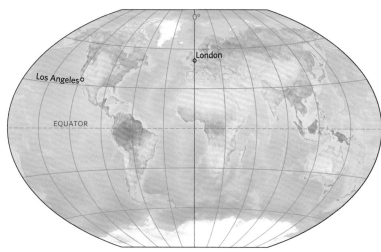

In 1946, Buckminster Fuller patented this view (above) to reveal 'a One-World Island in a One-World Ocean.' Like the polar azimuthal projection, it's helpful when you're trying to show unbroken connections between continents. We used it for our map of cell phone networks (pp. 94–5).

The adaptation at left, also known as the Winkel Tripel, minimizes distortion of area, shape and direction. It's perfect for indicating regions of the world as we did for surnames, passports and life expectancy (pp. 56, 112, 187).

NOTES

To build the contextual layers underpinning our maps (roads, rivers, borders and so on), we used Natural Earth as our primary source, tweaking manually where necessary. For our most detailed maps, we used OpenStreetMap. These two sources were invaluable; we are grateful to those who maintain and contribute to them. In addition, we obtained terrain data from NASA's SRTM. Other map sources are listed below and on the graphics themselves.

PREFACE

The data for COVID-19 deaths in the UK were downloaded from the Office for National Statistics. See: *bit.ly/3uAwh4l*

INTRODUCTION

'We can draw conclusions': Richter, G. & Obrist, H. U. (1995). *The Daily Practice of Painting: Writings and Interviews, 1962-1993.* Cambridge, Massachusetts: MIT Press, p. 11.

'to observe things': Bouman, K. L. (2017). Extreme imaging via physical model inversion: seeing around corners and imaging black holes.

imaging methods they developed: The Event Horizon Telescope Collaboration et al. (2019). *Astrophys. J. Lell.* 875: L1-6. *bit.ly/3s3TvOB*

more than sixty hours: BBC News (2012). *The most important photo ever taken?*

DNA was inferred: Medical Research Council (2013). *Behind the picture: Photo 51.*

'scientist' was not in use until 1833: *wikipedia.org/wiki/Scientist*

last great polymaths: the *Guardian* (2019). Weatherwatch: the Prussian polymath who founded modern meteorology.

'that included art': Wulf, A. (2015). *The Invention of Nature.* London: John Murray, p. 335.

Humboldt was most himself: de Botton, A. *The Art of Travel.* New York: Pantheon Books, pp. 106-14.

'send out letters': Wulf, A. (2015); Deutsche Welle (2019). *Alexander von Humboldt: A 19th century German home story.*

enlisted his friend: Humboldt was a pioneering cartographer himself. He invented the technique of isotherms to show variations in temperature.

'[M]aps for the world-wide distribution': Camerini, J. R. (2000). Heinrich Berghaus's map of human diseases. *Medical History* 44(S20): 186-208.

'seventy-five maps': David Rumsey Map Collection, image no. 2515048.

'a collection of maps': Ormeling Snr, F. J. (1986). Tribute to Justus Perthes. *GeoJournal* 13(4): 413-6.

'perfect storm': Friendly, M. (2008). The Golden Age of Statistical Graphics. *Statistical Science* 23(4): 502-35.

'coxcomb diagrams': *Mortality of the British army: at home and abroad, and during the Russian war, as compared with the mortality of the civil population in England; illustrated by tables and diagrams.* (1858) London: Printed by Harrison and Sons.

John Snow: Snow, J. (1855). *On the Mode and Communication of Cholera.* London: John Churchill.

Charles Booth: *booth.lse.ac.uk*

Du Bois in Philadelphia: *dubois-theward.org/resources/mapping*

The lidar data for the Mississippi River are part of the USGS 3D Elevation Program: *doi.org/10.3133/fs20143066*

To see more from the French statistical atlases, search for 'Imprimie Nationale' at *davidrumsey.com*

'Pictures of data': Friendly, M. (2008), p. 530.

For more on SYMAP: Chrisman, N. (2006). *Charting the Unknown: How Computer Mapping at Harvard Became GIS.* Redlands: ESRI Press.

eleven million tracks: Ordnance Survey (2020). *Ordnance Survey reveals ten years of walking and cycling data.*

'just a bunch of lines': Glynn, C. (2019, Sept. 17). Interview.

six thousand five hundred: BBC News (2016). *The trig pillars that helped map Great Britain.*

Ordnance Survey was founded on 21 June 1791 with a mission to accurately map England under the threat of a French invasion. Back then its surveyors walked the country, dividing it into a series of triangles and marking the vertices with landmarks or small stacks of stones. In 1936, the Ordnance Survey replaced those informal markers with concrete pillars.

a global map of where people exercise: *strava.com/heatmap*

keen eyes of Nathan Ruser: *twitter.com/Nrg8000/status/957318498102865920*

Strava claims: Strava Press (2018). *A Letter to the Strava Community.*

Neither did the Pentagon: *The Washington Post* (2018). U.S. soldiers are revealing sensitive and dangerous information by jogging.

All websites were live as of March 2021.

WHERE WE'VE BEEN

'In striving to drain': Ginsburg, R. B. (2004). Speech at the US Holocaust Museum on the National Commemoration of the Days of Remembrance. *supremecourt.gov/publicinfo/speeches/viewspeech/sp_04-22-04*

The Lives of Others

Tens of thousands: Hitchcock, T. et al. (2014). Loose, idle and disorderly: vagrant removal in late eighteenth-century Middlesex. *Social History* 39(4): 509–27.

still allows courts to prosecute: *Criminal Justice Act 1982, c. 48.* (UK) *legislation.gov.uk/ukpga/1982/48/section/70*

'in the open air': *Vagrancy Act 1824, c. 83.* (UK) *legislation.gov.uk/ukpga/Geo4/5/83/section/4*

'rogue and vagabond': *Berkshire Overseers' Papers, vol. 9.* (2005). Wallingford St Mary, 106. [CD]. Berkshire Family History Society.

by cart: *bit.ly/3tDiDMi*

Vagrant Lives project: Crymble, A. et al. (2015). Vagrant Lives: 14,789 Vagrants Processed by the County of Middlesex, 1777-1786. *Journal of Open Humanities Data* 1: e1.

Anyone caught living: *Poor Relief Act 1662, 14 Car. 2 c. 12.* (UK)

an obligation: Beier, A. L. & Ocobock, P. (Eds.). (2008). *Cast Out: Vagrancy and Homelessness in Global and Historical Perspective.* Athens, Ohio: Ohio University Press, p. 11.

ninety-two per cent: Crymble et al. (2015), p. 2.

Few hailed: Hitchcock et al. (2014), p. 515.

that year: BBC News (2015). *Third of homeless Londoners moved out of their boroughs.*

'sadly unfavourable light': the *Guardian* (2018). Windsor council leader calls for removal of homeless before royal wedding.

foreign rough sleepers: the *Guardian* (2020). Foreign rough sleepers face deportation from UK post-Brexit.

Survey of 458 rough sleepers: Sander, B. & Albanese, F. (2017). *An examination of the scale and impact of enforcement interventions on street homeless people in England and Wales.* London: Crisis.

'often left them feeling': Ibid., p. 48.

71 per cent in ten years: *The Salt Lake Tribune* (2020). Utah was once lauded for solving homelessness – the reality was far more complicated.

cost the shelter system less too: CBC News (2020). *A B.C. research project gave homeless people $7,500 each – the results were 'beautifully surprising'.*

some 216,000 homes: Action on Empty Homes (2019). *Empty Homes in England 2019,* p. 8.

4,700 people slept out: Homeless Link (2019). *2019 Rough Sleeping Snapshot Statistics.*

83,700 took shelter: Ministry of Housing, Communities & Local Government (2019). *Statutory Homelessness in England: October to December 2018.*

14,500 people: BBC News (2020). *Coronavirus: Thousands of homeless 'back on streets by July'.*

'The natural limits . . . someone from Essex': Crymble, A. (2019, September 19). Interview.

African Names Database: *slavevoyages.org/resources/names-database*

educational outreach: *ushmm.org/information/about-the-museum*

'questions of *where*': Knowles, A. K., Cole, T. & Giordano, A. (Eds.). (2014). *Geographies of the Holocaust.* Indiana: Indiana University Press, p. 2.

'transformed the meaning': Ibid., p. 4.

'god's-eye perspective': Knowles, A. K. et al. (2015). Inductive Visualization: A Humanistic Alternative to GIS. *GeoHumanities* 1(2): p. 242.

'the most dramatic stories': Ibid., p. 254.

'I was a bit limited': Westerveld, L. (2019, May 24). Interview.

Jacob Brodman: Interview of Jack Brodman by the National Council of Jewish Women Sarasota-Manatee Section, Holocaust Oral History Project, on 13 April 1989. *collections.ushmm.org/search/catalog/irn510728*

Anna Patipa: Interview of Anna Patipa (23 February 1989) is from the archives of the Tauber Holocaust Library of the Jewish Family and Children's Services Holocaust Center. *collections.ushmm.org/search/catalog/irn513095*

Eyewitness Cartography

SS camp network as of June 1943: Supplied by Anne Kelly Knowles

some 250,000 Jews: *encyclopedia.ushmm.org/content/en/article/the-aftermath-of-the-holocaust*

I Was There: The original version of this map: *visionscarto.net/i-was-there* ; the process behind its creation is detailed in Westerveld, L. & Knowles, A. K. (2020). Loosening the grid: topology as the basis for a more inclusive GIS. *International Journal of Geographical Information Science. doi: 10.1080/13658816.2020.1856854*

Partial Inheritance

30 million people: *blogs.ancestry.com/ancestry/2020/02/05/our-path-forward*

We adapted this graphic from one Oliver designed for: Reich, D. (2018) *Who We Are and How We Got Here: Ancient DNA and the New Science of the Human Past.* New York: Pantheon, p. 12.

Pure Myth

We adapted this map from one we created for: Narasimhan et al. (2019). The formation of human populations in South and Central Asia. *Science* 365(6457): eaat7487.

not yet entered the picture: Reich (2018), pp. 106–9.

tamed horses, built wagons: Anthony, D. W. (2007). *The Horse, the Wheel, and Language: How Bronze-Age Riders from the Eurasian Steppes Shaped the Modern World.* Princteon, NJ: Princeton University Press.

last Sarsen stone: Nash, D. J. et al. (2020). Origins of the sarsen megaliths at Stonehenge. *Science Advances* 6(31): eabc0133.

Ancestralia

millions: White, J. Peter. & Mulvaney, D. J. (1987). *Australians to 1788.* Broadway, N.S.W., Australia: Fairfax, Syme & Weldon Associates. On page 117, the authors conclude that it's reasonable to estimate the Indigenous population in 1788 to be 750,000. Therefore, we reason that the cumulative total would reach millions over fifty thousand years.

sea levels were 75 metres lower: Bird, M. I. et al. (2019). Early human settlement of Sahul was not an accident. *Scientific Reports* 9: 8220.

DNA from hair samples: Tobler, R. et al. (2017). Aboriginal mitogenomes reveal 50,000 years of regionalism in Australia. *Nature* 544: 180–84.

policy of child removal: Nogrady, B. (2019). Trauma of Australia's Indigenous 'Stolen Generations' is still affecting children today. *Nature* 570: 423–4

You can explore Native Land Digital's map at: *native-land.ca*

first major sea crossings: Australian Museum (2021). The spread of people to Australia.

Common Ground is an invaluable resource for those who want to find out more about Aboriginal and Torres Strait Islander cultures: *commonground.org.au*

Oceans of Data

More than a thousand compiled: Maury, M. F. (1856). *The Physical Geography of the Sea* (6th ed.). London: T. Nelson and Sons, p. v.

'as though he himself': Ibid., p. iii.

from 250 days to 160: Ibid., p. iv.

began digitizing: *icoads.noaa.gov*

Scientists now use them: NPR (2014). *Old Ship Logs Reveal Adventure, Tragedy And Hints About Climate.*

possible in 80 days: *bit.ly/3lA7vNA*

halved the sailing time: National Library of Australia (2006). *The Seynbrief. bit.ly/3ejGYCv*

Seeing Red

Value of whale products: Kerry Gathers has a brilliant map called 'Oil and Bone' that charts American ports during the golden age of Yankee whaling. *kgmaps.com/oil-and-bone*

For information on the creation of the whaling data see here: Lund et al. (n.d.). American Offshore Whaling Voyages: a database. *nmdl.org*

New Bedford fleet: New Bedford Whaling Museum (2016). Yankee Whaling. *bit.ly/3qnABR4* two disasters: *wikipedia.org/wiki/Whaling_Disaster _of_1871* and *sanctuaries.noaa.gov/whalingfleet/ history.html*

some 2.9 million whales: Rocha Jr, R. C. et al. (2015). Emptying the Oceans: A Summary of Industrial Whaling Catches in the 20th Century. *Marine Fisheries Review* 76(4): 37–48.

more sperm whales were killed: Ibid., p. 47.

Inhumane Flows
Venture Smith quotes: Smith, V. (1798). *A Narrative of the Life and Adventures of Venture, a Native of Africa: But Resident above Sixty Years in the United States of America. Related by Himself.* New London, CT: C. Holt, at the *Bee* office, pp. 13–4. *docsouth.unc. edu/neh/venture/venture.html*

Broteer Furro: Ibid., p. 5.

the details on: *slavevoyages.org/voyage/about# variable-list/2/en*

obscured by its own leaders: Chazkel, A. (2015). History Out of the Ashes: Remembering Brazilian Slavery after Rui Barbosa's Burning of the Documents. In C. Aguirre and J. Villa-Flores (Eds.). *From the Ashes of History: Loss and Recovery of Archives and Libraries in Modern Latin America.* Raleigh, NC: University of North Carolina Press, pp. 61–78.

previously overlooked voyages: Phys.org (2019). *Project adds 11,400 intra-American journeys to Slave Voyages database.*

import labour for them: The Colonial Williamsburg Foundation (n.d.). *Iberian Slave Trade. bit.ly/3s72IFN*

Nomenculture
because the law requires: *en.wikipedia.org/wiki/ Thai_name*

the surname, Nguyen: Atlas Obscura (2017). *Why 40% of Vietnamese People Have the Same Last Name.*

Half the population: Louie, E. W. (2008). *Chinese American Names: Tradition and Transition.* Jefferson, NC: McFarland & Co., p. 35.

Graced by Genius
the sunburst: The form of this chart was inspired by Bernini's *Ecstasy of St. Teresa*, which he completed in 1652 at age 53.

Infinity Mirror Rooms at 91: New York Botanical Garden (2021). *Kusama: Cosmic Nature.*

countless hours: *The New Yorker* (2013). Complexity and the Ten-Thousand-Hour Rule.

reach mastery fastest: Simonton, D. K. (2017, January 19). Personal communications.

'the exaltation and passion of youth' . . . tinkerers: Fry, R. (2015). *The Last Lectures.* Cambridge: Cambridge University Press, p. 14. For more on 'two types of artists', see: Galenson, D. W. (2006). *Old Masters and Young Geniuses: The Two Life Cycles of Artistic Creativity.* Princeton, NJ: Princeton University Press.

Les Desmoiselles: Picasso, P. (1907). *Les Desmoiselles d'Avignon* [oil on canvas]. Museum of Modern Art, New York, NY.

Large Bathers: Cézanne, P. (1906). *The Large Bathers* [oil on canvas]. Philadelphia Museum of Art, Philadelphia, PA.

WHO WE ARE
'A Bill for taking a census': US National Archives. *From James Madison to Thomas Jefferson, 14 February 1790.*

Drawing Lines
Historically, censuses: Whitby, A. (2020). *The Sum of the People: How the Census Has Shaped Nations, from the Ancient World to the Modern Age.* New York: Basic Books.

six census questions: *Census Act of 1790, § 1.* (US)

sixteen US marshals: US Census Bureau (2020). *Who Conducted the First Census in 1790?*

three-fifths of the enslaved: *US Const. art. I, § 2.*

post a 'correct copy': *Census Act of 1790, § 7.* (US)

more than any other public project: The entire cost of the census was $44,377 [United States (1908). *Heads of Families at the First Census of the United States Taken in the Year 1790.* Washington, DC: Government Printing Office, p. 4.], more than the allocation of $38,976.36 for lighthouses, beacons, and buoys described in: Kierner, C. A. (2019). First United States Census, 1790. In *The Digital Encyclopedia of George Washington. bit.ly/3qrZv1V*

'our present growing importance': US National Archives. *From George Washington to Gouverneur Morris, 28 July 1791.*

five million: US National Archives. *From George Washington to Gouverneur Morris, 17 December 1790.*

'it appears . . . numbers are omitted': US National Archives. *From George Washington to Gouverneur Morris, 28 July 1791.*

the final results: United States (1791). *Return of the Whole Number of Persons within the Several Districts of the United States.* Philadelphia, PA: Childs and Swaine.

Data for the apportionment table comes from: *US Const. art. I, § 2* and the *Apportionment Act of 1792.*

Hamilton initially prevailed: US National Archives. *Introductory Note: To George Washington, 4 April 1792.*

first-ever presidential veto: Ibid.

Jefferson's method: US Census Bureau (1990). *Apportionment of the U.S. House Of Representatives. census.gov/prod/3/98pubs/CPH-2-US.PDF*

four different formulas: Ibid.

a process called gerrymandering: For the best – and most entertaining – explanation, see: Maurer, J. (Writer), Oliver, J. (Writer), Twiss, J. (Writer), Weiner, J. (Writer) & Werner, C. (Director). (2017, April 9). Gerrymandering (Season 4, Episode 8) [TV series episode]. In Taylor, J. (Executive Producer), *Last Week Tonight with John Oliver.* Sixteen String Jack Productions. *youtube.com/ watch?v=A-4dIImaodQ*

'sweetheart gerrymander': Policy Map (2017). *A Deeper Look at Gerrymandering.*

'Don't bring out the maps': Hofeller, T. B. (2011). *What I've Learned about Redistricting – The Hard Way!* [PowerPoint slides]. National Conference of State Legislatures. *ncsl.org/documents/legismgt/ The_Hard_Way.pdf*

hatched a plan: NPR (2019). *Emails Show Trump Officials Consulted With GOP Strategist on Citizenship Question.*

as recently as 1950: *Department of Commerce v. New York, 588 U.S. 2561* (2019)

feared the addition: Brown, J. D. et al. (2019). Predicting the Effect of Adding a Citizenship Question to the 2020 Census. *Demography* 56: 1173–94.

population increased (2.1%) . . . overall (9.7%): New York City Department of City Planning (2011). *NYC2010, Results from the 2010 Census: Population Growth and Race/Hispanic Composition. on.nyc.gov/3emO7IK*

New York has lost: Museum of the City of New York (2020). *Why the Census Matters. mcny.org/ story/why-census-matters*

'arbitrary and capricious': *Department of Commerce v. New York, 588 U.S. 2561, 2564* (2019)

Florence Kelley biographical information: *socialwelfare.library.vcu.edu/people/kelley-florence*

abusive husband: *florencekelley.northwestern.edu/ florence/arrival*

Inspired by Charles Booth: Residents of Hull House (1895). *Hull-House Maps and Papers.* New York: T. Y. Crowell & Company, p. viii.

2.5 million: New York City Department of City Planning (2011).

the rest of the state combined: *en.wikipedia.org/ wiki/List_of_cities_in_New_York*

'Insistent probing into the lives of the poor': Residents of Hull House (1895), p. 14.

'single most important work': Sklar, K. K. (1991). Hull-House Maps and Papers: social science as women's work in the 1890s. In M. Bulmer, K. Bales & K. K. Sklar (Eds.). *The Social Survey in Historical Perspective, 1880–1940* (pp. 111–47). Cambridge University Press.

'for all Florence Kelley's sins': Aptheker, H. (1966). Du Bois on Florence Kelly. *Social Work* 11(4): 98–100.

whilst Jane Addams: *nobelprize.org/prizes/ peace/1931/addams/facts*

$15.6 billion: *The Washington Post* (2019). *2020 Census: What's new for the 2020 Census?*

A Census on Demand

£482 million: Economic & Social Research Council (n.d.). *Census: past, present and future* [fact sheet]. *bit.ly/3v4YkZZ*

they refined a method: Deville, P. et al. (2014). Dynamic population mapping using mobile phone data. *PNAS* 111(45): 15888–93.

detect and direct aid: *bit.ly/2PCciC5*

An American Exodus

The underlying aggregated and anonymized insights were provided by Teralytics Inc. *teralytics.net*

Light-detecting satellites: NASA Earth Observatory (2018). *Night Lights Show Slow Recovery from Maria.*

3.3 million residents: US Census Bureau (2019). *More Puerto Ricans Move to Mainland United States, Poverty Declines.*

The United Commutes

Jefferson's unheeded recommendation: Stein, M. (2009). *How the States Got Their Shapes.* Washington, DC: Smithsonian Books, pp. 1–9.

an array of commuting hubs: Dash Nelson, G. & Rae, A. (2016). An Economic Geography of the United States: From Commutes to Megaregions. *PLoS One* 11(11): e0166083.

Texas and California: Stein, M. (2009). pp. 33–8, 269.

a concession to Michigan: Ibid., pp. 143–4.

tip of Delaware: Ibid., pp. 52–6, 236–7.

Roads to Recovery

toddler in the village of Meliandou: CNN (2015). *Ebola: Who is patient zero? Disease traced back to 2-year-old in Guinea.*

more than 11,000 people: *cdc.gov/vhf/ebola/history/ 2014-2016-outbreak/index.html*

grouped Africa's road network: Strano, E. et al. (2018). Mapping road network communities for guiding disease surveillance and control strategies. *Scientific Reports* 8: 4744.

Mali: World Health Organization (2014). *Mali confirms its first case of Ebola.*

Senegal: Reuters (2014). *Senegal tracks route of Guinea student in race to stop Ebola.*

Nigeria: Bell, B. et al. (2016) Overview, Control Strategies, and Lessons Learned in the CDC Response to the 2014–2016 Ebola Epidemic. *MMWR* 65(Suppl-3): 9.

To Spain: World Health Organization (2014). *Ebola virus disease – Spain.*

Italy: World Health Organization (2015). *First confirmed Ebola patient in Italy.*

UK: World Health Organization (2014). *Ebola virus disease – United Kingdom.*

To US: Bell et al. (2016), p. 10.

Light Levels

'The Blue Marble': *wikipedia.org/wiki/The_Blue_Marble*

'Black Marble': *nasa.gov/topics/earth/earthmonth/ earthmonth_2013_5.html*

For more information on NASA's nighttime lights product suite, see: NASA Earth Observatory (2017). *Night Light Maps Open Up New Applications.*

in the wake of hurricanes: NASA Earth Observatory (2017). *Pinpointing Where Lights Went Out in Puerto Rico.*

LED bulbs: Bennie, J. et al. (2014). Contrasting trends in light pollution across Europe based on satellite observed night time lights. *Scientific Reports* 4: 3789.

second-largest urban area in Africa: *en.wikipedia. org/wiki/List_of_urban_areas_in_Africa_by_population*

80 million people: United Nations, Population Division (2018). *World Urbanization Prospects: Total Population at Mid-Year by region, subregion and country, 1950–2050 (thousands).*

billions to boost tourism: Oxford Business Group (2018). *Development plans for West Saudi Arabian cities unveiled.*

millions of refugees: UNHCR (2021). *Syria Refugee Crisis Explained.*

switch back on: Adventure.com (2017). *When the lights go out: Inside Iraq's surprising nightlife boom.*

25 million households: *IEEE Spectrum* (2019). A Power Line to Every Home: India Closes In on Universal Electrification.

602 kilowatt hours: *data.worldbank.org/indicator/ EG.USE.ELEC.KH.PC*

'clap their hands and get loud': *The Wall Street Journal* (2015). North Korea Downplays Lack of 'Flashy Lights'.

long-distance migrants increased: *China Labour Bulletin* (2020). Migrant workers and their children.

The Lure of Cities

map of population change: The built-up grid (GHS-BUILT-S2 R2020A) was derived from a Sentinel-2 global image composite for 2018 using Convolutional Neural Networks (GHS-S2Net). *European Commission, Joint Research Centre.* *bit.ly/30WRSVW*

312 urban areas: United Nations, Population Division (2018). *World Urbanization Prospects: Population of Urban Agglomerations with 300,000 Inhabitants or More in 2018, by country, 1950–2035 (thousands).*

United States has 96: Ibid.

'special economic zones': *en.wikipedia.org/wiki/ Special_economic_zones_of_China*

rural and urban settlements of 330,000: Shenzhen Municipal Statistics Bureau (2016). *Shenzhen Statistical Yearbook 2016* [in Chinese]. Beijing: China Statistics Press, p. 4.

thirteen million: Shenzhen Government Online (2020). *About Shenzhen: Profile. bit.ly/3lvUZhT*

Jing-Jin-Ji: *The New York Times* (2015). Chinese Officials to Restructure Beijing to Ease Strains on City Center.

exceeds Beijing in size and population: Schneider, M. & Mertes C. M. (2014). Expansion and growth in Chinese cities, 1978–2010. *Environ. Res. Lett.* 9: 024008.

would surpass Tokyo: World Bank (2015). *East Asia's Changing Urban Landscape: Measuring a Decade of Spatial Growth.* Urban Development Series. Washington, DC: World Bank, p. 75.

Six million people: United Nations, Population Division (2018).

thousands of companies: *South China Morning Post* (2020). How 4 Chinese millennials have found secret of hi-tech success in Chengdu.

one of its first national hi-tech zones: PR Newswire (2020). *Chengdu Hi-tech Zone Made an Increase by 7% in Industrial Added Value in the First Half of the Year.*

more residents than Canada and Australia: *Nature* (2020). Making it in the megacity; United Nations, Population Division (2018). *World Urbanization Prospects: Total Population at Mid-Year by region, subregion and country, 1950–2050 (thousands).*

opened in 1989: *South China Morning Post* (2018). A tale of two cities: Shenzhen vs Hong Kong.

Yantian five years later: *en.wikipedia.org/wiki/ Yantian_International_Container_Terminals*

third busiest container port: *en.wikipedia.org/wiki/ List_of_busiest_container_ports*

half headed for North America: *bit.ly/3vCPZwR*

bridge-tunnel system: *wikipedia.org/wiki/Hong_ Kong-Zhuhai-Macau_Bridge*

another super span: *South China Morning Post* (2012). Link spanning Pearl River Delta from Shenzhen to Zhongshan approved.

Revolutionary Transport

'asphalt terror': Provo (1965). *Provokatie no. 5* [leaflet]. *provo-images.info/Provokaties.html*

10,000 white bicycles: the *Guardian* (2016). Story of cities #30: how this Amsterdam inventor gave bike-sharing to the world.

impounded by the police: Ibid.

to discourage theft: British Library (n.d.) *'Provo.'* *vll-minos.bl.uk/learning/histcitizen/21cc/counterculture/ assaultonculture/provo/provo.html*

Ease of Access

'end of geography': *AAG Newsletter* (2016). The End(s) of Geography?

'death of distance': Cairncross, F. (2002). The death of distance. *RSA Journal* 149(5502), 40–42.

the model behind these maps: Weiss, D. J. et al. (2018). A global map of travel time to cities to assess inequalities in accessibility in 2015. *Nature* 553: 333–6.

'friction surface': Ibid.

Rivers of Connectivity

to know where you are: *wikipedia.org/wiki/Mobile_phone_tracking*

Africa's digital revolution: the *Guardian* (2016). A day in the digital life of Africa.

more common in North Korea: *Los Angeles Times* (2009). Cellphones catching on in North Korea.

incapable of connecting: *The Mirror* (2019). North Korea releases smartphone that only runs government-approved apps and blocks foreign media.

1 million active fixed-line accounts: *itu.int/en/ITU-D/Statistics/Pages/stat/default.aspx*

180 million mobile subscriptions: *The Punch* (2020). Nigeria's active mobile telephone lines now 180 million.

Octopus's Garden

29 October 1969: NPR (2009). *'Lo' And Behold: A Communication Revolution.*

fifty kilobits per second: *computer.howstuffworks.com/arpanet.htm*

twenty-two minutes: If encoded at 256kbps, a song requires 32KB of space per second. 'Come Together' is 258 seconds, so the file would be 8.26 MB. 8.26MB = 66,080 kbits. Divided by 50kbps = 1,322 seconds or 22 minutes. At 128kbps, it would've taken 11 minutes.

just 400 fibre-optic cables: *telegeography.com/submarine-cable-faqs-frequently-asked-questions*

The longest: *wikipedia.org/wiki/SEA-ME-WE_3*

200 terabits: *en.wikipedia.org/wiki/MAREA*

all 280 million Beatles records ever purchased: *wikipedia.org/wiki/List_of_best-selling_music_artists*

more people and devices go online: MarketsandMarkets (2020). *Submarine Cable System Market: Size, Share, System and Industry Analysis and Market Forecast to 2025.*

Facebook is helping to fund: TechCrunch (2020). *Facebook, telcos to build huge subsea cable for Africa and Middle East.*

nearly triple: Facebook Engineering (2020). *Building a transformative subsea cable to better connect Africa.*

Undersea cable varieties: Carter, L., Burnett, D., Drew, S., Marle, G., Hagadorn, L., Bartlett-McNeil, D. & Irvine, N. (2009). *Submarine Cables and the Oceans: Connecting the World.* UNEP-WCMC Biodiversity Series No. 31., pp. 17–20.

HOW WE'RE DOING

'I regarded it as axiomatic': Du Bois, W. E. B. (1940). *Dusk of Dawn: An Essay Toward an Autobiography of a Race Concept.* New York: Harcourt, p. 68.

Truth to Power

For more on the politics and past of mapping, see: Kitchin, R., Dodge, M. & Perkins, C. (2011). *The Map Reader: Theories of Mapping Practice and Cartographic Representation.* London: John Wiley & Sons Ltd.

desired path of a storm: *wikipedia.org/wiki/Hurricane_Dorian–Alabama_controversy*

'to make it more of a fact': Latour, B. (1986). Visualization and Cognition: Thinking With Eyes and Hands. In H. Kuklick & E. Long (Eds.). *Knowledge and Society: Studies in the Sociology of Culture Past and Present* (Vol. 6, pp. 1–40). Jai Press.

His logbooks did: Novaresio, P. (1996). *The Explorers.* New York: Stewart, Tabori & Chang, p. 191.

'discoveries': *bit.ly/2O1Ojft*

gathered in Berlin: Heath, E. (2010). Berlin Conference of 1884–1885. In H. L. Gates & K. A. Appiah (Eds.). *Encyclopedia of Africa* (p. 177). Oxford University Press.

border dispute: *wikipedia.org/wiki/Bakassi*

'we just took a blue pencil': Darwin, L. et al. (1914). The Geographical Results of the Nigerian-Kamerun Boundary Demarcation Commission of 1912–13: Discussion. *The Geographical Journal* 43(6): 648–51.

'the color line': Douglass, F. (1881) The Color Line. *North American Review* 132(295): 567–77.

'possible to draw': Du Bois, W. E. B. (1903). *The Souls of Black Folk.* Chicago: A. C. McClurg & Company, p. 125.

budgets of 150 Black families: Du Bois, W. E. B. (ca. 1900). *[The Georgia Negro] Income and expenditure of 150 Negro families in Atlanta, Ga., U.S.A.* [chart]. From Library of Congress, Prints and Photographs Division. *loc.gov/pictures/resource/ppmsca.33893*

unworthy of study: Morris, A. D. (2015). *The Scholar Denied.* Oakland: University of California Press, p. 7.

redlining: The Richmond Digital Scholarship Lab digitized the redlined areas from a 1937 Home Owners' Loan Corporation map. *bit.ly/3bEUTBu* Temperature data is from Landsat 8 imagery courtesy of the US Geological Survey. Data compiled by and downloaded from ArcGIS.com.

higher health risks: *The New York Times* (2020). How Decades of Racist Housing Policy Left Neighborhoods Sweltering.

'white fellow-citizens': Du Bois, W. E. B. (1899). *The Philadelphia Negro.* Philadelphia: University of Pennsylvania, p. 1.

'we must no longer guess': Du Bois, W. E. B. (1902). *The Negro Artisan.* Atlanta: Atlanta University Press, p. 1.

Sam Hose: Mathews, D. G. (2017). *At the Altar of Lynching: Burning Sam Hose in the American South.* Cambridge: Cambridge University Press.

'careful and reasoned statement': Du Bois, W. E. B. (1940). *Dusk of Dawn: An Essay Toward an Autobiography of a Race Concept.* New York: Harcourt, p. 67.

'Two considerations': Ibid., 67–8.

'The cure': Ingersoll, W. T. (1960). Oral history interview of W. E. B. Du Bois by William Ingersoll. W. E. B. Du Bois Papers (MS 312). Special Collections and University Archives, University of Massachusetts Amherst Libraries, pp. 146–7.

'The details of finishing': Du Bois, W. E. B. (1968). *The Autobiography of W. E. B. Du Bois: A Soliloquy on Viewing My Life from the Last Decade of Its First Century.* New York: International Publishers, p. 221.

'best sociological work': Ibid., p. 204.

'being met with shotguns . . . distribution of the population': Ibid., p. 226.

'touched on political matters': Ibid., p. 227.

destroyed the only copy: US Department of Labor (1974). *Black Studies in the Department of Labor 1897–1907. dol.gov/general/aboutdol/history/blackstudiestext*

'During the last ten years': BlackPast (2008). *(1909) Ida B. Wells, 'Lynching, Our National Crime'. bit.ly/2OpJHj9*

Persons lynched by geographical division: NAACP (1919). *Thirty Years of Lynching In the United States, 1889–1918.* New York: NAACP, p. 39.

lobbying effort: Francis, M. M. (2014). *Civil Rights and the Making of the Modern American State.* Cambridge: Cambridge University Press, pp. 98–126.

drafted by NAACP member Albert E. Pillsbury: *loc.gov/exhibits/naacp/the-new-negro-movement.html*

'for the necessity of the law': Library of Congress. *Congressman L. C. Dyer to John R. Shillady concerning an anti-lynching bill, April 6, 1918* [typed letter]. Courtesy of the NAACP.

to retrieve those missing: Jenkins, J. A. et al. (2010). Between Reconstructions: Congressional Action on Civil Rights, 1891–1940. *Studies in American Political Development* 24: 57–89.

congressmen taunted them: *Congressional Record,* House, 67th Cong., 2nd sess. (26 January 1922): 1785. *bit.ly/38wG8yE*

ultimately passed 231–119: Jenkins et al. (2010).

African-American voices had been heard: Francis (2014).

Southern Democrats filibustered it out of the Senate: Jenkins et al. (2010).

'The Shame of America': NAACP (1922). *The Shame of America* [advertisement]. *The New York Times. historymatters.gmu.edu/d/6786*

nearly two hundred attempts: *The Washington Post* (2018). Why Congress failed nearly 200 times to make lynching a federal crime.

Justice for Victims of Lynching Act: CNN (2019). *Senate passes anti-lynching bill in renewed effort to make it a federal hate crime.*

failed to act: *The New York Times* (2020). Frustration and Fury as Rand Paul Hold Up Anti-Lynching Bill in Senate.

'does not claim to be a Communist': FBI (1942). *William Edward Burehardt Dubois* [sic] (Report No. 100-1764), p. 5. bit.ly/3qze0kA

founder of modern sociology: Morris (2015).

innovative infographics: Battle-Baptiste, W. & Rusert, B. (Eds.). (2018). *W. E. B. Du Bois's Data Portraits: Visualizing Black America.* New York: Princeton Architectural Press.

digitized papers: credo.library.umass.edu/view/collection/mums312

unflinching data journalist: To learn more about how Wells used data to counter false narratives during her time, see: Missouri Historical Society. (2020, 5 August). A Conversation with Michelle Duster: Ida B. Wells and Today's Street Journalism [video]. youtube.com/watch?v=IK7-kIWtkFo

obituary in 2018: The New York Times (2018). Ida B. Wells, Who Took on Racism in the Deep South With Powerful Reporting on Lynchings.

'outstanding and courageous reporting': pulitzer.org/winners/ida-b-wells

Red Record of Lynching map: catalog.archives.gov/id/149268727

Buzzfeed didn't need: Buzzfeed News (2020). Find The Police And Military Planes That Monitored The Protests In Your City With These Maps.

people shot and killed by police in the US: washingtonpost.com/graphics/investigations/police-shootings-database/

a fault along the high-voltage lines: Caracas Chronicles (2019). Nationwide Blackout in Venezuela: FAQ.

extensive bribery scandal: La Nación (2019). Driver's notebooks exposed Argentina's greatest corruption scandal ever: ten years and millions of cash bribes in bags.

daily charts: twitter.com/jburnmurdoch/status/1245466020053164034

protests that toppled governments: National Geographic (2019). What was the Arab Spring and how did it spread?

emoji-based map: twitter.com/hkmaplive

eagerness to shut the app down: the Guardian (2019). Tim Cook defends Apple's removal of Hong Kong mapping app.

exclamation points screamed danger: Quartz (2019). Real-time maps warn Hong Kong protesters of water cannons and riot police.

States of Mind
The report showed: Helliwell, J. F., Layard, R., Sachs, J. & De Neve, J.-E. (Eds.). (2020). World Happiness Report 2020. New York: Sustainable Development Solutions Network

Passport Check
'safe conduct' letter: Holy Bible, New International Version, 1978/2011, Nehemiah 2:1–7.

database of visa requirements: github.com/ilyankou/passport-index-dataset

Algeria intends to introduce eVisas: L'Expression (2020). Le visa électronique bientôt introduit.

international dollars: An international dollar is a hypothetical unit of currency that has the same purchasing power parity that the US dollar had in a given year.

fallen 65 per cent: passportindex.org/world-openness-score.php

Carbon Overhead
same atmospheric burden: Wynes, S. & Nicholas, K. A. (2017). Environ. Res. Lett. 12: 074024.

doubles the warming effect: IPCC (2001). Aviation and the Global Atmosphere: Executive Summary. grida.no/climate/ipcc/aviation/064.htm

flygskam: The Wall Street Journal (2019). 'Flight Shame' Comes to the U.S.—Via Greta Thunberg's Sailboat.

numbers at Swedish airports down: Reuters (2020). Sweden's rail travel jumps with some help from 'flight shaming'.

new highs: Ibid.

tagskryt: The Wall Street Journal (2019).

410kg: calculator.carbonfootprint.com (LHR–IST, economy return ticket)

more CO2 than the average citizen: ourworldindata.org/per-capita-co2

11.2 million commercial flights . . . more than a billion passengers: Federal Aviation Administration (2020). Air Traffic by the Numbers, p. 6.

In Exhaustive Detail
8.9 million people in 2015: Burnett, R. et al. (2018). Global estimates of mortality associated with long-term exposure to outdoor fine particulate matter. PNAS 115(38): 9592–7

790,000 in Europe: Lelieveld, J. et al. (2019). Cardiovascular disease burden from ambient air pollution in Europe reassessed using novel hazard ratio functions. European Heart Journal 40(20): 1590–6.

fumes from cruise liners: Transport & Environment (2019). One Corporation to Pollute Them All: Luxury cruise air emissions in Europe.

exhaust swirling over the UK: centreforcities.org/reader/cities-outlook-2020/air-quality-cities

European Commission sued: the Guardian (2018). UK taken to Europe's highest court over air pollution.

Electric Currents
isn't a coincidence: Thornton, J. A. et al. (2017). Lightning enhancement over major oceanic shipping lanes. Geophys. Res. Lett. 44(17): 9102–11.

Policing the Air
over less affluent areas: Walker, G. et al. (2005). Industrial pollution and social deprivation: Evidence and complexity in evaluating and responding to environmental inequality. Local Environment 10(4): 361–77.

rely on spot checks: Personal communications with Cameo.tw.

nine thousand air-quality sensors: Ibid. For the latest figures, see: wot.epa.gov.tw

fined a bottling factory: Taiwan Ratings (7 October 2019). Taiwan Hon Chuan Enterprise Co. Ltd.'s Air-Pollution Incident Has Minimal Credit Impact. rrs.taiwanratings.com.tw

WHO limits: World Health Organization (2005). WHO Air quality guidelines for particulate matter, ozone, nitrogen dioxide and sulfur dioxide.

Looking for Lead
switched . . . to save money: NPR (2016). Lead-Laced Water In Flint: A Step-By-Step Look At The Makings Of A Crisis.

foul brown water: The Detroit News (2015). Flint resident: Water looks like urine, smells like sewer.

'serious' lead levels: NPR (2016).

designed a model: For details, see: Abernethy, J. et al. (2018). ActiveRemediation: The Search for Lead Pipes in Flint, Michigan. KDD '18: Proceedings of the 24th ACM SIGKDD International Conference on Knowledge Discovery & Data Mining. pp. 5–14.

followed their advice: The Atlantic (2019). How a Feel-Good AI Story Went Wrong in Flint.

clean water to drink: Politico (2020). Flint Has Clean Water Now. Why Won't People Drink It?

hit rate: The Atlantic (2019); personal communications with Webb, J.

up to $5,000 per home: Ibid.

Untenable Conditions
roots of gentrification: Zuk, M. et al. (2018). Gentrification, Displacement and the Role of Public Investment. Journal of Planning Literature 33: 31–44.

eleven thousand housing complaints a week: There were 377,766 service requests for apartment maintenance and 223,835 for lack of heat or hot water. See: NYC (2019). 311 Sets New Record with 44 Million Customer Interactions in 2018.

advanced, ongoing and potential gentrification: Chapple, K. & Thomas, T. (2020). Berkeley, CA: Urban Displacement Project. bit.ly/3cuvJo9

Long Island City: The Bridge (2019). Lessons of Rezoning: When It Doesn't Work Out as Planned.

SoHo: The New York Times (2020). Will SoHo Be the Site of New York City's Next Battle Over Development?

Gowanus: City Limits (2020). 3 thoughts on 'Debate in Gowanus About Whether to Pause or Push Rezoning'.

last affordable neighbourhoods: The New York Times (2019). It's Manhattan's Last Affordable Neighborhood. But for How Long?

'failed to take a hard look': Curbed New York (2019). Inwood rezoning struck down following community challenge.

'parse every sub-issue': Curbed New York (2020). New York Court Quashes Push for Racial Equity in Inwood Rezoning.

'Piano District': Welcome2TheBronx (2019). We are the South Bronx, NOT 'SoBro'!

Jerome Avenue: Curbed New York (2018). What happens to Jerome Avenue after its rezoning?

hesitant to lend: the *Guardian* (2020). 'Not what it used to be': in New York, Flushing's Asian residents brace against gentrification.

up 86 per cent: *The New York Times* (2020). The Decade Dominated by the Ultraluxury Condo.

fourth-highest: Ibid.

population change: NYU Furman Center's CoreData.nyc (2018). *Neighborhood Indicators: BK03 Bedford Stuyvesant* [table]. *furmancenter.org/neighborhoods/view/bedford-stuyvesant*

North Shore: silive.com (2020). *A look at 17 proposed projects that could help revitalize the North Shore with state funding.*

Southern Inhospitality
900,000 households were evicted in 2016: *evictionlab.org/national-estimates*

laws tend to favour landlords: Hatch, M. E. (2017). Statutory Protection for Renters: Classification of State Landlord-Tenant Policy Approaches. *Housing Policy Debate* 27(1): 98–119.

children are particularly vulnerable: Greenberg, D. et al. (2016). Discrimination in Evictions: Empirical Evidence and Legal Challenges. *Harvard Civil Rights-Civil Liberties Law Review* 51: 115–58.

'If incarceration has become typical': Desmond, M. (2012). Eviction and the Reproduction of Urban Poverty. *American Journal of Sociology* 118(1): 88–133.

kept the wolf from more than a million doors: Eviction Lab (2020). *Eviction Moratoria have Prevented Over a Million Eviction Filings in the U.S. during the COVID-19 Pandemic.*

Subsidizing housing: Vox (2020). *Joe Biden's housing plan calls for universal vouchers.*

jobs and schools as well: Desmond, M. (2016). *Evicted: Poverty and Profit in the American City.* New York: Crown, p. 296.

large cities with the highest eviction rates: *evictionlab.org/rankings/#/evictions*

Unequal Loads
working-age: Time-use surveys in most countries considered 'working age' to be ages 15–64. However, Lithuania was 20–64; China was 15–74; and Australia was 15 and older.

unpaid labour can include: Miranda, V. (2011). Cooking, Caring and Volunteering: Unpaid Work Around the World. *OECD Social.*

Globally, women do: McKinsey Global Institute (2015). *The Power of Parity: How advancing women's equality can add $12 trillion to global growth*, p. 2

only activity that skews male: Miranda (2011), p. 25.

months of additional work: UN Women (2020). *COVID-19 and its economic toll on women: The story behind the numbers.*

'Despite the clear gendered implications': Ibid.

Bursts of Cowardice
ACLED: Raleigh, C. et al. (2010). Introducing ACLED-Armed Conflict Location and Event Data. *Journal of Peace Research* 47(5): 651–60.

nearly 700 million: World Bank (2019). *Population, female – India* [chart].

Reported instances: All events described come from event summaries in a dataset specific to political violence targeting women & demonstrations featuring women. For more on this dataset, see: Kishi, R., Pavlik, M. & Matfess, H. (2019). *'Terribly and Terrifyingly Normal': Political Violence Targeting Women.* Austin, TX: Armed Conflict Location & Event Data Project.

A Visible Crisis
trace their history: Mohajan, H. K. (2018). History of Rakhine State and the Origin of the Rohingya Muslims. *IKAT: The Indonesian Journal of Southeast Asian Studies* 2(1): 19–46.

'textbook ethnic cleansing': UN News (2017). *UN human rights chief points to 'textbook example of ethnic cleansing' in Myanmar.*

footage shows: BBC News (2017). *Rohingya crisis: Drone footage shows thousands fleeing.*

Kutupalong Refugee Camp: *wikipedia.org/wiki/Kutupalong_refugee_camp*

expected 75,000: World Food Program USA Blog (2020). *Rohingya Crisis: A Firsthand Look Into The World's Largest Refugee Camp.*

population density: Cousins, S. (2018). Rohingya threatened by infectious diseases. *The Lancet. Infectious Diseases* 18(8): 609–10.

twice rejected offers: the *Guardian* (2019). Rohingya refugees turn down second Myanmar repatriation effort.

UN report warned: UN Human Rights Office (29 April 2020). *bit.ly/30hY77w*

fenced the perimeter: Reliefweb (2020). *Joint Letter: Re: Restrictions on Communication, Fencing, and COVID-19 in Cox's Bazar District Rohingya Refugee Camps. bit.ly/3cBTAlY*

georeferenced drone photographs: ESRI (2020). *Relief Workers Rely on Drone Imagery to Help Bangladesh Refugee Camp.*

lost their shelters: UN News (2019). *As monsoon rains pound Rohingya refugee camps, UN food relief agency steps up aid.*

A fire: *The New York Times* (2021). Fire Tears Through Rohingya Camp, Leaving Thousands Homeless Once More.

running out of room: *Global Village Space* (2020). Rohingya in Bangladesh plead for cemeteries.

Bombshell Reports
Mr. Kissinger/The President: The National Security Archive (2004). *The Kissinger Telcons, Document 2: Kissinger and President Richard M. Nixon, 9 December 1970, 8:45 p.m.* [transcript], p. 1. *nsarchive2.gwu.edu/NSAEBB/NSAEBB123*

Nixon secretly ordered: *The New York Times* (1976). Nixon Again Deplores Leak on Bombing Cambodia.

Operation Menu: *en.wikipedia.org/wiki/Operation_Menu*

Operation Freedom Deal: *en.wikipedia.org/wiki/Operation_Freedom_Deal*

one in four cluster bomblets: Martin, M. F. et al. (2019). *War Legacy Issues in Southeast Asia: Unexploded Ordnance (UXO)* (CRS Report No. R45749), p. 6.

killed/injured: Landmine & Cluster Munitions Monitor (2018). *Cambodia. bit.ly/2QbVvGl*

Clinton declassified . . . humanitarian gesture: *Foreign Policy* (2012). Mapping the U.S. bombing of Cambodia.

about twenty per cent: Martin et al. (2019), p. 11.

most bombed country: *halotrust.org/where-we-work/south-asia/laos/*

'mine-free' within the next decade: *The Phnom Penh Post* (2020). Landmine fatalities drop.

bomb any target they wanted: Kiernan, B. (2004) *How Pol Pot Came to Power: Colonialism, Nationalism, and Communism in Cambodia, 1930–1975.* New Haven, CT: Yale University Press, p. 307.

than on Japan: Lipsman, S. & Weiss, S. (Eds.). (1985). The false peace. In *The Vietnam Experience* (Vol. 13, p. 53). Boston Publishing Company.

North Vietnamese headquarters: Owen, T. (n.d.) *Sideshow? A Spatio-Historical Analysis of the US Bombardment of Cambodia, 1965–1973.*

compels North Vietnamese forces to retreat: Ibid.

nearly a hundred thousand tons: National Museum of the United States Air Force (2015). *Operation Niagara: A Waterfall of Bombs at Khe Sanh.*

24,000 fighter-bomber and 2,700 B-52 bomber sorties: Defense POW/MIA Accounting Agency (n.d.). *Khe Sanh. bit.ly/3qX0XcX*

scrap metal collectors: Martin et al. (2019), p. 11.

digging a pond: VnExpress International (2020). *900-kg wartime bomb found in famous Vietnam battlefield.*

Landslides and flooding: *Viet Nam News* (2020). Four bombs safely removed from landslide sites in Quang Tri Province.

over 3,400 deaths: *VietNamNet* (2020). International donors assist Quang Tri's bomb, mine clearance efforts.

the first Vietnamese province: Ibid.

caves on Co Roc and from an area northwest: Shore II, M. S. (1969). *The Battle for Khe Sanh.* Washington, DC: US Marine Corps, p. 58.

NVA attacks Hill 861: For a detailed account of this battle, watch: Flitton, D. (Writer/Director). (1999, May 7). Siege at Khe Sanh (Episode 7) [TV series episode]. In Mcwhinnie, D. (Executive Producer), *Battlefield Vietnam.* Lamancha Productions. Available: *youtube.com/watch?v=sb1YDpO2f9I*

NVA tanks overrun: Ibid.

Bombing thwarts: Ibid.

108 220-kilogram bombs: Owen, T. & Kiernan, B. (2007). Bombs Over Cambodia: New Light on US Air War. *The Asia-Pacific Journal* 5(5): 2420.

The terrain in these three maps comes from CIA maps: *shadedreliefarchive.com/Indochina_CIA.html*

End Times

'to preserve our civilization': Boyer, P. S. (1985). *By the Bomb's Early Light.* New York: Pantheon, p. 70.

enlisted a colleague's wife: *Physics World* (2020). Doomsday Clock ticks closer to disaster.

looked good on the page: *The Atlantic* (2015). Designing the Doomsday Clock.

Rabinowitch . . . science and security board: *Physics World* (2020).

such relief in surviving: A new era. (1991). *Bulletin of the Atomic Scientists* 47(10): 3.

'the preaching of doom': Boyer (1985), p. 70.

Global arsenal: We compiled data for this chart from *ourworldindata.org/nuclear-weapons* (1945–2014) and from the *Bulletin of the Atomic Scientists'* Nuclear Notebook (2015–17).

Turning Points: To learn more about the minute hand's movements, see: *thebulletin.org/doomsday-clock/timeline*

'catastrophic effects': *The Denver Post* (2007). Global warming advances Doomsday Clock.

WHAT WE FACE

'Any person, who': Smithsonian Institution (1859). *Annual Report of the Board of Regents of the Smithsonian Institution Showing the Operations, Expenditures, and Condition of the Institution for the Year 1858.* Washington, DC: James B. Steedman, pp. 31–2.

The Search for Certainty

portrait of the Earth: *nasa.gov/image-feature/satellite-captures-four-tropical-cyclones-from-space*

nine named storms: *The New York Times* (2020). Hurricane Forecast: 'One of the Most Active Seasons on Record'.

as many as twenty-five: Ibid.

the most ever recorded: *The New York Times* (2020). The 2020 Hurricane Season in Rewind.

weather radar in the 1960s: *en.wikipedia.org/wiki/Weather_radar*

'meteor': the *Guardian* (2011). Weatherwatch: Meteorology blame it on Aristotle.

'When we have fully learned': Fleming, J. R. (1990). *Meteorology in America, 1800–1870.* Baltimore: The Johns Hopkins University Press, p. 78.

a map of the US: Ibid., pp. 143–5 as well as Hoover, L. R. (1933). *Professor Henry Posts Daily Weather Map in Smithsonian Institution Building, 1858* [painting]. From Smithsonian Institution Archives, ID 84-2074.

'not only of interest to visitors': Smithsonian Institution (1859), p. 32.

'an object of much interest': Ibid.

every morning at 10 a.m.: Ibid.

'Smithsonian observers': Fleming (1990), p. 88.

'records of upwards of half a million': Smithsonian Institution (1858). *Annual Report of the Board of Regents of the Smithsonian Institution Showing the Operations, Expenditures, and Condition of the Institution for the Year 1857.* Washington, DC: William A. Harris, pp. 27–8.

'When I sow in spring': *William Bacon's Letter to Joseph Henry (January 3–4, 1852)* [edited transcript]. Joseph Henry Papers (Volume 8), Smithsonian Institution Archives. *siarchives.si.edu/collections/siris_sic_13123*

'that a cold spell': Smithsonian Institution (1861). *Annual Report of the Board of Regents of the Smithsonian Institution Showing the Operations, Expenditures, and Condition of the Institution for the Year 1860.* Washington, DC: George W. Bowman, p. 102.

drawings of snow crystals: Smithsonian Institution (1863). *Annual Report of the Board of Regents of the Smithsonian Institution Showing the Operations, Expenditures, and Condition of the Institution for the Year 1862.* Washington, DC: George W. Bowman, p. 102.

telegraphic experiments . . . Civil War: Miller, E. R. (1931). New Light on the Beginnings of the Weather Bureau from the Papers of Increase A. Lapham. *Monthly Weather Review* 59: 66.

observers and budget: This chart is adapted from figures 4.1 and 4.3 in Fleming (1990).

traded barometers for bayonets . . . a fire in Henry's office: Fleming (1990), pp. 146–7.

'peculiarities of the climate': Smithsonian Institution. (1873). *Annual Report of the Board of Regents of the Smithsonian Institution Showing the Operations, Expenditures, and Condition of the Institution for the Year 1871.* Washington, DC: Government Printing Office, p. 23.

'Weather Synopses and Probabilities': Glahn, B. (2012). *The United States Weather Service: The First 100 Years.* Rockville, MD: Pilot Imaging, p. 5. *bit.ly/2OY61R6*

wrecking some 3,000 ships at a cost of $7 million: Fleming (1990), p. 153.

'The map brings out': Ibid., map available: *bit.ly/3rTX2yN*

'what practical value': Miller (1931), p. 67.

Paine . . . who had studied: Ibid., p. 68.

relieved to see: Fleming (1990), p. 161.

'probabilities' and 'indications': Glahn (2012), pp. 5–6.

twenty-four hours in advance: Ibid., p. 12.

'tornado' was verboten: Larson, E. (2000). *Isaac's Storm.* New York: Vintage Books, p. 9.

refused to issue a storm warning: Ibid., pp. 9, 142.

eight thousand people were dead: *Forbes* (2017). As Terrible as Harvey Is, The Galveston Hurricane Of 1900 Was Much, Much Worse.

'There is the eye': Mrk Cntrmn (2016, 12 November). *KHOU's Dan Rather news highlights during Hurricane Carla 1961* [video]. *youtube.com/watch?v=MW9njTWaSFI*

no one had seen one: *The Atlantic* (2012). Dan Rather Showed the First Radar Image of a Hurricane on TV.

'Anyone with eyes': Rather, D & Herskowitz, M. (1977). *The Camera Never Blinks.* New York: William Morrow, p. 49.

then the largest weather-related evacuation in US history: *The Atlantic* (2012).

twice as much damage: Calculated in 2020 US dollars from *en.wikipedia.org/wiki/Hurricane_Carla* and *en.wikipedia.org/wiki/1900_Galveston_hurricane*

only forty-six: National Weather Service (2011). *Hurricane Carla – 50th Anniversary.*

two degrees hotter: *climateactiontracker.org/global/cat-thermometer*

'Doubtless there would be failures': Miller (1931), p. 67.

Heat Gradient

reliable baseline period: To learn why 1961–90 is used as the baseline period, see: *crudata.uea.ac.uk/cru/data/temperature/#faq5*

ten hottest years: NOAA National Centers for Environmental Information (2020). *State of the Climate: Global Climate Report for Annual 2019.* *ncdc.noaa.gov/sotc/global/201913*

Too Hot to Hajj

participated in 2019: General Authority for Statistics (2019). *Hajj Statistics 1440,* pp. 10, 23. *stats.gov.sa/en/28*

spike in Saudi Arabia: *worldometers.info/coronavirus/country/saudi-arabia*

strict limits: *The New York Times* (2020). Saudi Arabia Drastically Limits Hajj Pilgrimage to Prevent Viral Spread.

Since the 1990s . . . as bad or worse: Kang, S. et al. (2019). Future Heat Stress During Muslim Pilgrimage (Hajj) Projected to Exceed 'Extreme Danger' Levels. *Geophys. Res. Lett.* 46(16): 10094–100.

Site of 2015 crush: *The New York Times* (2015). How the Hajj Stampede Unfolded.

Days 1–5: *saudiembassy.net/hajj*

Burn Scars

incinerated Paradise: *en.wikipedia.org/wiki/Camp_Fire_(2018)*

ignited tropical forests from Amazonia: *National Geographic* (2019). As the Amazon burns, cattle ranchers are blamed. But it's complicated.

to Indonesia; Singapore: Reuters (2019). *Singapore smog worst in three years as forest fires rage.*

skylines in Seattle: *The Washington Post* (2018). Wildfire smoke is choking Seattle, obscuring the view and blocking out the sun.

Siberia: NBC News (2020). *Climate concerns as Siberia experiences record-breaking heat.*

Verkhoyansk, Russia: *The Washington Post* (2020). *Hottest Arctic temperature record likely set in Siberian town.*

didn't expect for another eighty years: CBS News (2020). *Arctic records its hottest temperature ever.*

Sakha Republic: *go.nasa.gov/3OZMToA*

Smoke plumes extended to Alaska: KVAL (2020). *Siberian wildfire smoke reaches Alaska, Pacific Northwest.*

than Belgium emits: Deutsche Welle (2020). *Record heat wave in Siberia: What happens when climate change goes extreme?*

'zombie fires': *The Washington Post* (2020). 'Zombie fires' are burning in the Arctic after surviving the winter.

as small as a parking space: Global Forest Watch (2016). *Fighting fires with satellites: VIIRS fire data now available on Global Forest Watch.*

plundered rather than protected: *The New York Times* (2019). *Under Brazil's Far-Right Leader, Amazon Protections Slashed and Forests Fall.*

21,000 more hotspots: *bit.ly/3bZQhG3* (Filter by biome: Amazon)

'lies': BBC (2019). *Amazon deforestation: Brazil's Bolsonaro dismisses data as 'lies'.*

Guinea's dry season: NASA Earth Observatory (2006). *Fires in Guinea.*

Angola's runs from May to October: NASA Earth Observatory (2007). *Fires in Angola.*

melt permafrost . . . cycle of warming: NBC News (2020). *Climate concerns as Siberia experiences record-breaking heat.*

killed at least a billion animals: the *Guardian* (2020). Almost 3 billion animals affected by Australian bushfires, report shows.

nearly a third of the world's koala population: the *Guardian* (2019). Australia's environment minister says up to 30% of koalas killed in NSW mid-north coast fires.

Cartographers, please forgive our use of hexagons on an equirectangular projection!

One Stormy Sea
excess heat trapped by greenhouse gas emissions: Wallace-Wells, D. (2019). *The Uninhabitable Earth.* New York: Tim Duggan Books, p. 95.

holds less oxygen: Ibid., p. 97.

kills heat-sensitive species: Schmidt, C. W. (2008). In Hot Water: Global Warming Takes a Toll on Coral Reefs. *Environmental Health Perspectives* 116(7): A292–9.

pumps more moisture: Wallace-Wells (2019), p. 80.

disrupts currents: Hu, S. et al. (2020). Deep-reaching acceleration of global mean ocean circulation over the past two decades. *Science Advances* 6(6): eaax7727.

'dead zones': *Independent* (2019). 'Dead zones' expanding rapidly in oceans as climate emergency causes unprecedented oxygen loss.

half of Australia's Great Barrier Reef: Wallace-Wells (2019), p. 96.

swelled in size, force: *The New York Times* (2020). Climate Change Is Making Hurricanes Stronger, Researchers Find.

saturation: *The New York Times* (2019). Climate Change Fills Storms With More Rain, Analysis Shows.

lingering longer: Li, L. & Chakraborty, P. (2020). Slower decay of landfalling hurricanes in a warming world. *Nature* 587: 230–34.

$125 billion in damage: Blake, E. S. & Zelinsky, D. A. (2018). *National Hurricane Center Tropical Cyclone Report: Hurricane Harvey*, p. 9.

regions of the ocean: *en.wikipedia.org/wiki/Tropical_cyclone_basins*

number of tropical cyclones: *en.wikipedia.org/wiki/Tropical_cyclones_by_year*

43 cyclones per year: Ibid., calculated for 1980–2019 only.

costliest on record: *en.wikipedia.org/wiki/Hurricane_Harvey*

deadliest named storm: *en.wikipedia.org/wiki/Cyclone_Nargis*

Ice Flows
For more on the ice flow data: *its-live.jpl.nasa.gov*

advancing until 2018: NASA Earth Observatory (2019). *Retreat Begins at Taku Glacier.*

gone in just 200 years: Zeiman, F. et al. (2016). Modeling the evolution of the Juneau Icefield between 1971 and 2100 using the Parallel Ice Sheet Model (PISM). *Journal of Glaciology* 62(231): 199–214.

first 45 kilometres of the Taku Valley: Ibid.

snow line was too high: Pelto, M. (2019). Exceptionally High 2018 Equilibrium Line Altitude on Taku Glacier, Alaska. *Remote Sensing* 11(20): 2378.

would rise seven metres: Aschwanden, A. et al. (2019). Contribution of the Greenland Ice Sheet to sea level over the next millennium. *Science Advances* 19: eaav9396.

slides even faster: Phillips, T. et al. (2013). Evaluation of cryo-hydrologic warming as an explanation for increased ice velocities in the wet snow zone, Sermeq Avannarleq, West Greenland. *JGR Earth Science* 118(3): 1241–56.

Greenland mass variation: *climate.nasa.gov/vital-signs/ice-sheets*

Treading Water
67 nuclear weapons: *atomicheritage.org/location/marshall-islands*

typhoons . . . dengue fever: *The New Yorker* (2020). The Cost of Fleeing Climate Change.

a third already live in the US: Ibid.

'It's a fight to the death': BBC News (2019). *Climate change: COP25 island nation in 'fight to death'.*

projected rate: Gesch, D. et al. (2020). Inundation Exposure Assessment for Majuro Atoll, Republic of the Marshall Islands Using A High-Accuracy Digital Elevation Model. *Remote Sensing* 12(1): 154.

doesn't happen uniformly: NASA (2020). *Sea Level 101: What Determines the Level of the Sea?*

Caught at Sea
yields began to decrease: *The New York Times* (2019). The World Is Losing Fish to Eat as Oceans Warm, Study Finds.

island nations . . . will be gutted: Phys.org (2020). *Study: Ocean fish farming in tropics and sub-tropics most impacted by climate change.*

unique movement signatures: Kroodsma, D. et al. (2018). Tracking the global footprint of fisheries. *Science* 359(6378): 904–8.

learned to spot: Boerder, K. et al. (2018). Global hot spots of transshipment of fish catch at sea. *Science Advances* 25: eaat7159.

some 37 billion data points: Global Fishing Watch (n.d.). *Our digital ocean: Transforming fishing through transparency and technology* [fact sheet]. *bit.ly/2QgBwqh*

to bypass regulations: Boerder et al. (2018).

Chinese refrigerator ship: SkyTruth (2017). *Reefer Fined $5.9 Million for Endangered Catch in Galapagos Recently Rendezvoused with Chinese Longliners.*

After a rendezvous: Global Fishing Watch and SkyTruth (2017). *The Global View of Transshipment: Revised Preliminary Findings*, p. 14.

Montevideo, Murmansk, home ports in China: Ibid.

trafficking and other abuses: McDonald, G. G. et al. (2021). Satellites can reveal global extent of forced labor in the world's fishing fleet. *PNAS* 118(3): e2016238117.

Fasten Your Seatbelts
hurled passengers from their seats: *en.wikipedia.org/wiki/United_Airlines_Flight_826*

nine serious injuries: Federal Aviation Administration (2020). *Attention Passengers: Sit Down and Buckle Up* [fact sheet]. *bit.ly/3qWMYUn*

a billion passengers: Bureau of Transportation Statistics (2020). *2018 Traffic Data for U.S Airlines and Foreign Airlines U.S. Flights.*

rough air ahead: Storer, L. N. et al. (2017). Global Response of Clear-Air Turbulence to Climate Change. *Geophys. Res. Lett.* 44(19): 9976–84.

Simulations show: Ibid.

All-Seeing Eyes
six-metre waves: Copernicus EMS (2018). *Copernicus EMS Supports Monitoring of Deadly Earthquake and Tsunami in Indonesia.*

Photos from the scene: *The New York Times* (2018). Witness: Scenes From the Indonesian Tsunami.

overview of the damage: *bit.ly/30VeB5P*

neighbourhoods erased: Reuters (2018). *Destruction in Palu.*

how far the earth had shifted: Copernicus EMS (2019). *Copernicus EMS Risk and Recovery Mapping: Ground deformation analyses, Sulawesi, Indonesia.*

prevent further casualties: Ibid.

more than 5,000: *emergency.copernicus.eu/mapping/ems/rapid-mapping-portfolio*

potential roosts for bats: *bit.ly/3cNLPtw*

undersea landslides: *EOS* (2020). Social Media Helps Reveal Cause of 2018 Indonesian Tsunami.

turned earth into ooze: *The New York Times* (2018). A Tsunami Didn't Destroy These 1,747 Homes. It was the Ground Itself, Flowing.

What the Satellite Sees: Dorati, C., Kucera, J., Marí i Rivero, I. & Wania, A. (2018). Annex 1: Damage Assessment. In *Product User Manual for Copernicus EMS Rapid Mapping, JRC Technical Report JRC111889* (pp. 23–5).

Move Fast, Break Maps

forty thousand contributors: *wiki.openstreetmap.org/wiki/Stats*

83% of the global street network in 2016: Barington-Leigh, C. & Millard-Ball, A. (2017). The world's user-generated road map is more than 80% complete. *PloS One.* 12(8): e0180698.

rely upon the free service: Anderson, J. et al. (2019). Corporate Editors in the Evolving Landscape of OpenStreetMap. *ISPRS International Journal of Geographic Information* 8: 232.

become an internet provider: *connectivity.fb.com*

not always helpful: *twitter.com/floedermann/status/1155960862747680770*

Salt It Where the Sun Don't Shine

sixteen centimetres: *weather.gov/mrx/tysclimate*

sixth of Chicago's average: *weather.gov/lot/ord_rfd_monthly_yearly_normals*

may get a ton: *Scientific American* (2019). Love Snow? Here's How It's Changing.

$2.3 billion: *bit.ly/30XbzOv*

a way to treat roads: Rodriguez, T. K. et al. (2019). Allocating limited deicing resources in winter snow events. *Journal of Vehicle Routing Algorithms* 2: 75–88.

saline runoff: *Smithsonian* (2014). What Happens to All the Salt We Dump On the Roads?

excessive corrosion: The Earth Institute, Columbia University (2018). *How Road Salt Harms the Environment.*

ten hours of sunlight: SunCalc. *bit.ly/3eilBS7*

The New Ages

10.9 billion people by century's end: United Nations, Population Division (2019). *World Population Prospects 2019: Highlights,* p. 1.

ratio will flip for the first time: Pew Research Center (2019). *World's population is projected to nearly stop growing by the end of the century.*

350,000 workers by 2024: Nippon.com (2019). *Japan's Historic Immigration Reform: A Work in Progress.*

sub-Saharan population could triple by 2100: Pew Research Center (2019).

By 2100, India . . . five of which are in Africa: Ibid.

EPILOGUE

'That you cannot navigate': Wright, J. K. (1942). Map Makers are Human: Comments on the Subjective in Maps. *Geographical Review* 32(4): 527–44.

data was seen as vital: The Conversation (2020). *Next slide please: data visualisation expert on what's wrong with the UK government's coronavirus charts.*

existed for years: González, M. C. et al. (2008). Understanding individual human mobility patterns. *Nature* 453: 779–82.

online dating profiles: BBC (2015). *China 'social credit': Beijing sets up huge system.*

approving the use of tracking technologies: the *Guardian* (2020). Watchdog approves use of UK phone data to help fight coronavirus.

effectiveness of localized lockdowns: Gibbs, H. et al. (2021). Human movement can inform the spatial scale of interventions against COVID-19 transmission. *MedRxiv* 10.26.20219550

share highly personal mobility data: Korea Centers for Disease Control and Prevention, Cheongju, Korea (2020). Contact Transmission of COVID-19 in South Korea: Novel Investigation Techniques for Tracing Contacts. *Osong Public Health Research Perspectives* 11(1): 60–63.

garnered support in Korea: Kye, B. & Hwang, S. J. (2020). Social trust in the midst of pandemic crisis: Implications from COVID-19 of South Korea. *Research in social stratification and mobility* 68: 100523.

The UK had 27,454: Our World in Data. *bit.ly/3dQ7kvO*

'Mounting evidence': World Health Organization (2020). *Joint Statement on Data Protection and Privacy in the COVID-19 Response.*

enough to reveal my daily schedule: Perez, B. et al. (2018). You are your Metadata: Identification and Obfuscation of Social Media Users using Metadata Information. *Proceedings of the Twelfth International AAAI Conference on Web and Social Media,* 241–50.

accounts of where infected patients had been: *news.seoul.go.kr/welfare/archives/513105* (Retrieved 5 January 2020).

'attacks on the liberty of the individual': Plague Checked by Destruction of Rats. Kitasato on the Limitation of Outbreaks at Kobé and Osaka. (1900). *The British Medical Journal* 2(2078): 1258.

Cases clustered: Nakaya, T. et al. (2019). Space-time mapping of historical plague epidemics in modern Osaka, Japan. *Abstracts of the International Cartographic Association* 1: 267. *doi.org/10.5194/ica-abs-1-267-2019* ; Suzuki, A. (2006). Cotton, Rats and Plague in Japan.

infected fleas . . . ships from India: Suzuki (2006).

many feared for their safety: The Conversation (2020). *Tracing homophobia in South Korea's coronavirus surveillance program.*

employer of the first recorded case: *The Korea Herald* (2020). COVID-19 patient went clubbing in Itaewon.

victim of hate crimes: BBC News (2019). *Gay in South Korea: 'She said I don't need a son like you'.*

manage an outbreak: Park, S. et al. (2020). Information Technology–Based Tracing Strategy in Response to COVID-19 in South Korea—Privacy Controversies. *JAMA* 323(21): 2129–30.

87 million Facebook users: *The New York Times* (2018). Facebook Data Collected by Quiz App Included Private Messages.

'I see': NBC News (2018, 10 April). *Senator Asks How Facebook Remains Free, Mark Zuckerberg Smirks: 'We Run Ads'* [video]. *youtube.com/watch?v=n2H8wx1aBiQ*

GDPR: TechCrunch (2018). *WTF is GDPR?*

joint hottest year on record: the *Guardian* (2021). Climate crisis: 2020 was joint hottest year ever recorded.

FLATTENING THE EARTH

For a good primer on different map projections, see: Battersby, S. (2017). Map Projections. *The Geographic Information Science & Technology Body of Knowledge* (2nd Quarter 2017 Edition).

Spilhaus: For more on his projections, see: *jasondavies.com/maps/spilhaus* and *bit.ly/3bqEG2N*

qibla maps: Tobler, W. (2002). Qibla, and related, Map Projections. *Cartography & Geographical Information Science* 29(1): 17–23.

'One-World Island': *bfi.org/about-fuller/big-ideas/spaceshipearth*

GRATITUDE

Many brilliant people took time to meet with us, share data and discuss ideas for maps and graphics. Our thanks to: Paul Naylor and Charlie Glynn for walking us through Britain's favourite trails; Adam Crymble for sharing his knowledge of vagrant lives; and to Anne Kelly Knowles and Levi Westerveld for broadening our horizons about what a map can be. Thanks to David Reich for demystifying the genome; James Russell at the Nantucket Historical Association for helping us to identify significant whaling voyages; and to Ben Schmidt for alerting us to the depths of the ICOADS database.

A big thank you to Kubi Ackerman and the Museum of the City of New York for inviting us to map the city's population. Thank you Alessandro Sorichetta, Andy Tatem and the WorldPop team for the French population data and to friend and Francophile, Nicholas Quiring, for his fine suggestions on that map. Teralytics Inc. shared population flows from Puerto Rico; Emanuele Strano provided the clustering of Africa's roads; and we are indebted to long-term collaborator and friend Oliver O'Brien for supplying data on the worlds of bike sharing and surnames.

We were delighted to include the Taiwan air pollution data supplied by Chi-Chieh Peng and the team at CAMEO as well as the efforts of Eric Schwartz, Jacob Abernethy and Jared Webb to rid Flint and other cities of polluted water. Thanks also to Yale Fox at Rentlogic for revealing the challenges that New York's renters can face when finding a home and to Dustin Croul for helping us concatenate a year of protests.

For our visualizations of the climate crisis, Ed Hawkins pointed us to the data we needed on global heating; Elfatih A. B. Eltahir clarified his findings on the future of the hajj; Dean B. Gesch graciously supplied his data on sea level rise (even releasing it openly for anyone to use); and Paul Williams and Luke Storer patiently took us through the complexities of their data on turbulence. Thanks also to Michael Foumelis and Marcello De Michele for supplying the earthquake displacement data for Sulawesi and to Budhu Bhaduri and Olufemi Omitaomu for their data on de-icing Knoxville.

Profound thanks to Kathleen Stewart and Junchuan Fan for the data behind our map of app-user tracking in Washington, D.C. Thanks too to Beatrice Perez for deciphering a tweet, Tomoki Nakaya for providing the map of Osaka and to Laura Gerrish, who spent a weekend tracing an iceberg's journey for us.

In the earliest days of this project, the map collections of the British Library, Los Angeles Public Library and the Clark Library at the University of Michigan inspired the book's design. Special thanks to Tim Utter for gathering so many gems for us. At the other end of the production schedule were the efforts of our meticulous map editors. *Atlas of the Invisible* would be an atlas of mistakes without them. Truly, we can't thank them enough.

FROM JAMES: I have the joy of working with a brilliant team of interns, PhD students, researchers and academics at UCL. So thanks to Nicol Nógrádi and Finbar Aherne for their summer spent crunching data and to Alyson Lloyd, Jason Tang, Balamurugan Soundararaj, James Todd, Terje Trasberg, Justin van Dijk, Mirco Musolesi for direct help with data or just being an unwitting sounding board for ideas.

My heartfelt thanks to family and friends for their continued support and enthusiasm. Finally, this book could not have been created without Isla by my side. I owe my greatest gratitude to her.

FROM OLIVER: Four years is a long time to make a book. It's an even longer time to watch someone struggle to make a book. Thank you to all the friends who revived me after long days in the studio; to my mother, who instilled a love of maps and history; to my brother, Justin, who has encouraged and inspired me from day one; and to my wife, Sophie, for her limitless love, support and reassurance – and for sharing a year of sleep and steps with us.

Finally, our utmost appreciation for our agent Luigi Bonomi and the teams at Particular Books and W. W. Norton. Helen Conford and Cecilia Stein believed in us from the start; Chloe Currens helped us crack the book's structure; Jim Stoddart offered sound design advice; and Yang Kim paired us with Nathan Burton, who distilled all our ideas into the perfect cover. All writers should be so lucky to have Richard Atkinson and Tom Mayer commenting in their Google Docs. Their enthusiasm, thoughtful edits and periodic pep talks propelled us onward and reminded us that everything's better with a bit more wonder.

The AUTHORS

James Cheshire is a Professor of Geographic Information and Cartography at University College London. In 2017, the Royal Geographic Society honoured him with the Cuthbert Peek Award 'for advancing geographical knowledge through the use of mappable Big Data'. **Oliver Uberti** is a former senior design editor for *National Geographic*, who continues to help scientists translate their research into memorable visuals. He has designed figures, endpapers and book covers for a range of high-profile academics, including geneticist David Reich and his bestseller *Who We Are and How We Got Here*.

James and Oliver have been making maps together for ten years. Their bestselling debut, *London: The Information Capital*, won the British Cartographic Society award for cartographic excellence. They won it again with their next book, *Where the Animals Go*, which Jane Goodall hailed for its 'help in our fight to save wildlife and wild habitats'. For their work on these atlases, James and Oliver were awarded the Corlis Benefideo Award for Imaginative Cartography by the North American Cartographic Information Society. Their maps have hung in exhibitions at the Swiss Museum of Design, the Museum of the City of New York and the Nantucket Whaling Museum and been featured in *National Geographic*, *Wired*, the *Financial Times* and the *Guardian*. The two collaborate across the curvature of the Earth from their respective outposts in London and Los Angeles. Perhaps one day their dogs, Howard and Misti, will meet.

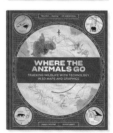